ENCYCLOPEDIA OF ISLAMIC DOCTRINE

VOLUME 7
FORGOTTEN ASPECTS OF ISLAMIC WORSHIP
PART TWO

SHAYKH MUHAMMAD HISHAM KABBANI

AS-SUNNA FOUNDATION OF AMERICA

Library of Congress Cataloging in Publication Data

Kabbani, Shaykh Muhammad Hisham.
Encyclopedia of Islamic Doctrine Vol. 7: Forgotten Aspects of Islamic Worship: Part Two
[Arabic title: *al-Musuat al-islami aqida ahl al-sunnah wa al-jamaat*]
p.   cm.
   Indices.
Islam—doctrines. 2. Heretics, Muslim. 3. Wahhabiyah.
I. Kabbani, Shaykh Muhammad Hisham. II. Title.

ISBN: 1-871031-88-5

Published by
As-Sunna Foundation of America Publications
607A W. Dana St.
Mountain View, CA 94041
e-mail: asfa@sunnah.org
www: http://sunnah.org

Distributed by
KAZI Publications
3023 W. Belmont Avenue
Chicago, IL 60618
Tel: 773-267-7001; Fax: 773-267-7002
e-mail: kazibooks@kazi.org
www: http://www.kazi.org

CONTENTS

1. Questions and Answers of Mainstream Islam on Various Issues

1.1. Introduction

Questions addressed in this section include among others:

Is it permissible for Muslims to pray with their shoes on?

Is wiping over socks valid in *wudu*?

What is the Islamic position on keeping the beard and removing facial hair?

What is the tradition (*sunna*) of carrying a stick?

Is it acceptable to kiss the hand of a scholar or elder?

Is prayer other than in congregation (*jamaa*) unacceptable?

Is it necessary to pray the noon prescribed prayer (*salat al-zuhr*) after finishing the Friday congregational prescribed prayer (*salat al-juma*)? What are the conditions for the validity of Friday congregational prescribed prayer (*salat al-juma*)?

Is seclusion in a mosque during the last ten days of Ramadan (*itikaf*) only to be performed in one of the three mosques (Makka, Madina, and Jerusalem) and not any other?

What is the Islamic view on allegiance (*baya*) to Imams?

According to mainstream Islam, who is eligible to interpret and explain hadith and deduce religious edicts (*fatawa*)?

What is the understanding of "following qualified opinion" (*taqlid*) of scholars in Islam?

Can garments hang below the ankles, even trousers?

Must one enunciate the intention to perform the prescribed prayer before beginning the prescribed prayer (salat)?

May one raise the hands after takbirat al-ihram?

May one enunciate the basmala and amin in Surah al-Fatiha?

Must one place one's foot next to his neighbor's foot in the prescribed prayer (salat)?

May one recite Surah al-Fatiha without pausing after every verse?

May one sit in tawarruk in the last cycle (rakat) of dawn prescribed prayer (fajr) and Friday congregational prayer (juma)?

May one count tasbih with both hands?

May one supplicate after prescribed prayer (salat)?

May one make collective supplication?

May one raise the hands in supplication and wipe the face afterwards?

Certain issues have come to the attention of Muslims because of recent "Salafi" rulings that contradict the mainstream Islamic view. However, only the "Salafi" view has been presented whether in books or on the internet. Nasir al-Din Albani's book of prayer according to the "Salafi" school, entitled Kitab al-salawat al-nabi (The Prophet's Prayer) and his fatawa presented on the internet[1] contains many serious errors and incorrect rulings concerning issues of jurisprudence (fiqh). The following is the mainstream Islamic reply to these and other issues juxtaposed with the aberrant fiqh of the "Salafis."

1.2. REGARDING PRESCRIBED PRAYER (SALAT) AND ABLUTION (WUDU)

Q. Is it permissible for Muslims to pray with their shoes on?

1.2.1. MAINSTREAM ISLAMIC VIEW ON PRAYING WITH SHOES ON

The following are the established positions of the scholars

---

1 The text of Albani's responses is quoted as displayed on the internet website hyperlink http://www.uh.edu/campus/msa ("Articles"section as of August, 1997).

of mainstream Islam on the question of praying while wearing shoes.

1 Al-Jaziri, *al-Fiqh ala al-madhahib al-arbaa:*

> Entering a mosque (*masjid*) or place of prayer wearing shoes with impurities on them is permitted in case of need (*yajuz li al-haja*). However, it is imperative to take precautions so as not to defile the mosque with what may fall from the shoes. This is the ruling of the Maliki and Shafii schools. The Hanafis say, "Everything that entails bringing something impure into the masjid is disliked to the point of being forbidden (*yukrahu tahriman*)." The Hanbalis say, "If bringing something filthy into the mosque leads to the falling of an impurity inside (or onto) the mosque, then it is forbidden (*haram*) to bring it inside, otherwise it is not forbidden."[2]

Said ibn Yazid relates: I asked Anas ibn Malik, "Did Allah's Messenger pray while wearing sandals?" He answered, "Yes."[3] Imam Nawawi said:

> There is in this hadith the permission to pray wearing sandals and leather socks provided one has not ascertained that there is an impurity on them. As to whether, when the sole of the socks (or sandals) are soiled with some impurity and the wearer rubs them on the ground, his prayer as he wears them is valid, there are two sayings of Shafii's, Allah be well pleased with him. The sounder of the two is that it is invalid.[4]

Ibn Hajar said:

> Ibn Battal said, "Praying while wearing sandals presupposes that there is no impurity on them. This said, it is one of the "permitted things" (*min al-rukhas*), as Ibn Daqiq al-Id said, not one of the praiseworthy one's (*la min al-mustahabbat*), for to pray while wearing one's shoes does not enter into the

2 Abd al-Rahman al-Jaziri, *al-Fiqh ala al-madhahib al-arbaa*, Book of Prayer, Heading: *Naqsh al-masjid wa idkhal shayin najisin fih* [Engraving the Place of Prayer and Bringing Something Impure Into It].

3 *Sahih Bukhari*: Book of *salat*, Chapter entitled: "Prayer While Wearing Sandals" and *Sahih Muslim*: Book of Mosques and Places of Prayers, Chapter entitled: "The Permissibility of Praying While Wearing Sandals."

4 Nawawi, *Sharh sahih Muslim*, *Kitab* 5, *Bab* 14, Hadith 60/555.

desired intent of *salat*, and although shoes are among the garments that beautify ["Wear your beautiful apparel at every time and place of prayer" (7:31)], nonetheless the fact that they are in contact with the ground where impurities abound may well make them fall short of that rank. And should attending to self-beautification conflict with seeing to the removal of impurities, the latter takes precedence because repelling corruption comes before pursuing benefits." Ibn Battal said, "Except if a proof-text be produced placing the removal of impurities after self-beautification in order of priority." Ibn Hajar comments, "Abu Dawud and Hakim relate from the narration of Shaddad ibn Aws from the Prophet (ﷺ), "Be different from the Jews, for they do not pray in their sandals nor in their leather socks," therefore the praiseworthiness of praying while wearing shoes is only for the purpose of the aforementioned difference."[5]

2 The Companion Abd Allah ibn Umar disliked to pray while wearing his sandals.[6]

3 Al-Shurunbali said:

Of the acts disliked in a ritual prayer according to the Hanafi school is the performance of *salat* while "wearing clothes for daily use which are not always free from dirt." Shoes enter into this category.[7]

4 Abu Said al-Khudri, and Bakr ibn Abd Allah relate:

While Allah's Messenger was leading his Companions in prayer he took off his sandals and laid them on his left side; so when the people saw this they removed their sandals. When he finished his prayer he asked, "What made you remove your sandals?" They replied, "We saw you remove your sandals, so we removed ours." He said, "Gabriel came to me and informed me that there was filth on them. When any

5 Ibn Hajar, *Fath al-bari bi sharh sahih al-Bukhari*, Book of *salat*, *Bab* 24, hadith 386.

6 This is related in the *Musannaf Ibn Abi Shayba* (1:109b) as stated by Muhammad Rawwas Qalaji in his *Mawsuat fiqh Abd Allah ibn Umar* [Encyclopedia of the jurisprudence of Abd Allah ibn Umar] (Beirut: Dar al-nafais, 1986) p. 486 #3.

7 Al-Shurunbalali, *Nur al-idah wa najat al-qulub* (The light of clarification and the salvation of hearts), trans. and expanded as *Salvation of the Soul and Islamic Devotions* by Muhammad Abu al-Qasim (London: Kegan Paul International, 1981) p. 119 #53.

of you comes to the mosque, he should look: if he finds filth on his sandals, he should wipe it off and then pray in them."[8]

Baha al-Din al-Maqdisi al-Hanbali (d. 624) said:

The face of the evidence in the hadith of Abu Dawud is that the Prophet (ﷺ) had not been aware of the impurity mentioned until told about it, and then he resumed his prayer where he left it off. If the prayer had been invalidated (by the interruption) he would have repeated it from the beginning . . . The same holds when a person forgets (to check his sandals for filth): if he realizes there is filth while he is praying, and he is able to eliminate it without much effort, he eliminates it and resumes his prayer where he left it off as the Prophet (ﷺ) did. Otherwise he starts the prayer over.[9]

Imam Kawthari pointed out that the sandals worn in the time of the Prophet (ﷺ) were soft and supple enough so as to permit the bending of the toes while in prostration to meet the conditions of valid prostration, according to the Prophet's hadith, "I have been ordered to prostrate on seven bones."[10]

1.2.1.1. ALBANI'S INCORRECT ENCOURAGEMENT TO PRAY WEARING SHOES
Prayer Wearing Shoes and the Command to Do So

"He used to stand (in prayer) bare-footed sometimes and wearing shoes sometimes."

He allowed this for his *umma*, saying: When one of you prays, he should wear his shoes or take them off and put them between his feet, and not harm others with them.

He encouraged prayer wearing them sometimes, saying: Be different from the Jews, for they do not pray in their shoes nor in their *khuff*s (leather socks).

---

8 In the *Sunan* of Abu Dawud (Book of *salat*, Chapter entitled: "On Praying in Sandals").

9 Al-Maqdisi, *al-Udda sharh al-umda* (The preparation: A commentary on (Muwaffaq al-Din al-Maqdisi's) *al-umda*, Book of *salat*, Chapter entitled: "The conditions necessary for *salat*."

10 In Bukhari and Muslim.

Occasionally he would remove them from his feet while in prayer and then continue his prayer, as Abu Saeed al-Khudri has said:

The Messenger of Allaah (*sallallaahu alaihi wa sallam*) prayed with us one day. Whilst he was engaged in the prayer he took off his shoes and placed them on his left. When the people saw this, they took off their shoes. When he finished his prayer he said, "Why did you take your shoes off?" They said, "We saw you taking your shoes off, so we took our shoes off." He said, "Verily Jibreel came to me and informed me that there was dirt (or he said "something harmful;" in another narration: filth) on my shoes, so I took them off. Therefore, when one of you goes to the mosque, he should look at his shoes: if he sees in them dirt - or he said: something harmful-(in another narration: filth) he should wipe them and pray in them."

When he removed them, he would place them on his left and he would also say, "When one of you prays, he should not place his shoes on his right nor on his left, where they will be on someone elses right, except if there is no one on his left, but he should place them between his feet."

1.2.1.2. ALBANI IS NOT A RECOGNIZED AUTHORITY IN JURISPRUDENCE

How well Ibn Uyayna spoke when he said, "The hadith may misguide except one who has *fiqh*."[11] Imam al-Lucknawi said, "We do not accept the word of the copiers of hadith that are devoid of *fiqh* over that of the authorities in *fiqh*."[12] The actual significance of these hadiths lies in the *permission*, not the praiseworthiness, of praying while wearing one's shoes, which is far from clear in the excerpts quoted by Albani. It must be known to everyone who wishes to follow the principles of mainstream Islam in this and every matter, that Nasir al-Din al-Albani is neither an authority on *fiqh* nor an authority in any of the mainstream Islamic schools of law. In this matter, as in many others, especially regarding the pillar of *salat*, he departs from the correct view of all four schools, misinterprets the evidence he quotes, and ends up confusing people with strange

---

11 Ibn Abi Zayd, *al-Jami fi al-sunan* (1982 ed.) p. 118.
12 Abd al-Hayy al-Lucknawi, *Umdat al-riaya fi hall sharh al-wiqaya* (p.440-44).

advice. For instance, in this case he first suggests, in the chapter title, that the Prophet (ﷺ) commanded people to pray wearing shoes unconditionally. Second, he says "he allowed this for his *umma*." Third, "he encouraged prayer wearing them sometimes," and last, he says that the Prophet (ﷺ) "occasionally would remove them from his feet while in prayer."

These are partial, misleading, and wrong inferences that could lead to serious consequences for those who follow them. To begin with, it is never advisable for Muslims to follow or propagate the opinions of scholars who have singled themselves out in their opinions.

The establishment of the legal status of human actions in Islam is based on the authoritative interpretation of the Quran and hadith, according to the established understanding and practice of the community of scholars, foremost among them the Companions of the Prophet (ﷺ). The books of *fiqh* are replete with the expressions: "The majority of scholars say . . ."; "The scholars unanimously say . . ."; "Some scholars say . . ."; "The greater number of the scholars say . . ."; "Those of this school say, while those of that school say . . ." This careful, comprehensive method is supported in both the Quran and the hadith, which both address the issue of consensus (*ijma*). Indeed, *ijma* is the third source for the derivation of the Sharia (Islamic system of law). The opinion of a single scholar that departs from *ijma*, even if it should claim a basis in Quran and hadith, constitutes dissent and deviation (*shudhudh*).[13]

1.2.2. WIPING OVER SOCKS
Q. Is wiping over socks valid for *wudu*?
1.2.2.1. MAINSTREAM ISLAMIC VIEW OF WIPING OVER LEATHER SOCKS (*KHUFFAYN*) AND SLIPPERS (*JAWRABAYN*)[14]

It is permissible to wipe over the *khuff* (soft leather boot) instead of performing *wudu* directly on the feet, provided that the *khuff* meet a particular set of conditions, and the person using the *khuff* has not done something to forfeit his use of them. As for the *khuff*, they must:

---

13 As in the opinion of Imam Ahmad which we have quoted in the section on *ijma*.
14 Soft leather boots. Modern socks do not qualify.

> Be pure
> Be impermeable to water
> Cover the entire area where *wudu* is made for the
>   feet (i.e. cover up the ankle-bones)
> Be strong enough to walk in long enough to carry
>   out basic needs while travelling
> Not have holes except for the foot or for laces, and
> They must not be put on until the person has
>   completed *wudu*.

As for the person wearing them, travellers can wipe over the *khuff* without removing them for up to three days and nights. Residents may do so for one day and the following night. This period of time starts not from when they are originally put on, but from the time the person breaks *wudu*. A stationary person who then undertakes a journey has three days and three nights beginning the moment he first lost *wudu* less the time he was still stationary.

Other than the Hanbali school, the view is that the *khuff* must be impermeable to water, cover the ankle bones, and be strong enough to walk a certain distance in without becoming worn. The Hanafis also have a dispensation *(rukhsa)* for wiping over the thick *jawrabayn,* or soft non-leather shoe (whether made of wool *(suf)*, cotton *(qutn)*, linen *(kattan)*, or fur *(shar)*, or felt *(wabr)*), provided they are not transparent, they are thick enough to walk in for three miles *(parsang)* without wearing through to the skin, and provided they hold up by themselves.[15] Tirmidhi narrates that Imam Abu Hanifa, in his last illness, wiped over his *jawrabayn* and then said, "Today I did something that I never used to do: I wiped over my *jawrabayn* without wearing my sandals."[16]

The main position of the *Hanbali* school is the same as the *Hanafi* school, with emphasis on but two points: 1) the *jawarib* must be thick, and 2) they must be sufficiently resistant to wear and tear while walking in them. This is stated plainly by Ibn Qudama:

> Imam Ahmad said, "Wiping over the soft non-leather shoe is impermissible unless it is thick-textured *(jawraban safiqan)* and stands alone on one's

---

15 This is stated by Muhammad and Abu Yusuf.

16 See al-Kasani's *Badai al-sanai* (1:10) and al-Haskafi's *al-Durr al-mukhtar* with Ibn Abidin's commentary (1:348).

> leg without collapsing, just like the *khuff*, and the
> people used to wipe on the *jawrabayn* only because, in
> their usage, it provided the same function as the
> khuff and stood up on the leg like the *khuff*, allowing
> one to come and go with it.

Shawkani said, "The *khuff* is a leather shoe that covers the ankle-bones. The *jurmuq* (spat) is larger than it and is worn over it, while the *jawrab* is larger than the *jurmuq*."[17] This definition, along with Imam Ahmad's specifications, gives an image of the *jawrab* as being different from even the largest woolen socks available today, and invalidates the view of those who claim that *jawrab* merely refers to "socks."[18]

It should be stressed that in none of the reports adduced to support this position is the fabric of the *jawarib* specified, so it is not certain exactly what fabric the Companions wiped when they wiped the *jawarib*.

These are the reports:

1 a) Al-Mughira ibn Shuba said, "The Prophet (ﷺ) made *wudu* and wiped over his *jawrabayn* and sandals *(nalayn)*."[19] Tirmidhi said:

> It is *hasan sahih*, and this is the position of more
> than one of the people of knowledge, and it is adopt-
> ed by Sufyan al-Thawri, Ibn al-Mubarak, al-Shafii,
> Ahmad, and Ishaq, who all said one may wipe over
> the *jawrabayn* even if not wearing sandals, provided
> they are thick.

Tirmidhi then narrates the report about Abu Hanifa already mentioned. Ibn Majah also narrated it from Abu Musa al-Ashari and added that al-Mualla said, "I do not know that he narrated this except he mentioned both the *jawrabayn* and the sandals together."

1 b) Tirmidhi's inclusion of al-*Shafii* is contradicted by

---

17 Shawkani, *Nayl al-awtar* (1:178).

18 Sufyan al-Thawri's position is identical with that of Imam Ahmad: see Ibn al-Mundhir, *al-Awsat* (1:264); al-Jassas, *Ahkam al-Quran* (2:350); Ibn Qudama, *al-Mughni* (1:295); Nawawi, *al-Majmu* (1:540); Ibn Hazm, *al-Muhalla* (2:86); Baghawi, *Sharh al-sunna* (1:458); and *Musannaf Abd al-Razzaq* (1:218).

19 Both Ibn Majah (*Sunan*, book of *al-Tahara wa sunanuha*) and Tirmidhi (*Sunan*, book of *Tahara*) narrated it through Abu Qays al-Awdi (d. 120).

Shawkani, who specifies that Shafii stated, "Wiping over the *jawrabayn* is impermissible except if wearing sandals and one can walk about in them."[20]

2 Al-Nasai narrates the same report as above from al-Mughira through Abu Qays and then says, "We do not know anyone who followed Abu Qays in this narration. What is sound and correct from al-Mughira is that the Prophet (صلى الله عليه وسلم) wiped over his *khuff*s [only]."[21]

3 Ahmad[22] and Abu Dawud narrate the same report from al-Mughira through Abu Qays and the latter says:

> Abd al-Rahman ibn Mahdi used not to narrate this hadith because what is recognized from al-Mughira is that the Prophet (صلى الله عليه وسلم) wiped over his *khuff*s [only]. The wiping of the Prophet (صلى الله عليه وسلم) over the *jawrabayn* is also narrated from Abu Musa al-Ashari, but the chain of that narration is neither linked back to the Prophet (صلى الله عليه وسلم) nor strong. Those who wiped over the jawrabayn are: Ali ibn Abi Talib, Ibn Masud, al-Bara ibn Azib, Anas ibn Malik, Abu Umama, Sahl ibn Sad, Amr ibn Hurayth, and it has also been narrated from Umar ibn al-Khattab and Ibn Abbas.[23]

Shawkani, concerning the list of the Companions cited by Abu Dawud[24] as permitting wiping over the *jawrabayn*, says that Ibn Sayyid al-Nas added Abd Allah ibn Umar, Sad ibn Abi Waqqas, Abu Masud al-Badri, and Uqba ibn Umar.[24]

1.2.2.1.1. The "Salafi" Misinterpretation of Wiping Over Socks

A handful of scholars, among them Ibn Taymiyya, and more recently, Mawdudi,[25] Sayyid Sabiq,[26] and Nasir al-Din Albani in his *fatawa*, have regarded ordinary socks as valid for wiping in *wudu* in the same way as *khuff*s. This opinion is aberrant (*shadhdh*).

---

20 Shawkani, *Nayl al-awtar* (1:180).
21 Al-Nasai, *Sunan*, book of *Tahara*.
22 Ahmad, *Musnad*.
23 Abu Dawud, *Sunan*, book of *Tahara*.
24 Shawkani, *Nayl al-awtar* (1:180), Ibn Sayyid al-Nas, *Sharh al-Tirmidhi*.
25 Mawdudi, *Rasail-o-Masail*.
26 Sayyid Sabiq, *Fiqh al-sunna*.

1.2.2.1.2. The False Translation of *khuffs* as "Socks" in *Fiqh al-sunna*

The English translation of Sayyid Sabiq's *Fiqh al-sunna* is particularly misleading with regard to this question, as it systematically and incorrectly translates *khuff* as "sock." Instead, among the Arabs the word *khuff* denoted something tough enough to wear by itself when travelling, and into which laces could be woven. This is far from what anyone imagines socks to be. Then, when it comes to translating *jawrab*, the translator of *Fiqh al-sunna* uses "slippers." This results in absurd expressions like "thick slipper." Thus, in addition to the strange positions taken by Sayyid Sabiq, there is the added obstacle of an irresponsible and gravely defective translation. The following is the text of the translation, with this author's commentary in square parentheses:

> WIPING OVER SOCKS (*KHUFFAYN*)
> [correct translation: Wiping over soft leather boots]
> Wiping over the socks [correct translation: soft leather boots] is part of the sunnah. Nawawi states, "All those who qualify for *ijma* (consensus) agree that it is allowed to wipe over the socks [correct translation: soft leather boots] - during travelling or at home, if needed or not - even a woman who stays at home or a handicapped person who cannot walk can do so. The Shiah and Khawarij reject it, but their rejection is not valid.
>
> Says Ibn Hajar in *Fath al-bari*, "All of the preservers (of hadith) are of the opinion that wiping over the socks [correct translation: soft leather boots] has come through a continuous transmission. Some have collected all of its narrations (from among the companions), and its number exceeds eighty. This includes hadith from the ten people who were promised paradise."
>
> The strongest hadith on this point has been related by Ahmad, Bukhari, Muslim, Abu Dawud and Tirmidhi on the authority of Hammam an-Nakhai who said, "Jarir ibn Abdullah urinated, performed ablution and wiped over his socks" [correct transla-

tion: soft leather boots]. It was said to him, "You do that and you have urinated?" He said, "Yes, I saw the Messenger of Allah, upon whom be peace, urinate and then do likewise." Said Ibrahim, "They were amazed at that hadith, because Jarir had embraced Islam ten years after the revelation of *Surah al-Maidah*, one of whose verses (5:6) requires that the feet be washed.

This hadith helps us understand the verse by confining it to one who is not wearing socks [correct translation: soft leather boots]. This constitutes a particular case, and the person who wears socks [correct translation: soft leather boots] can just wipe over them.

WIPING OVER SLIPPERS (*JAWRABAYN*)
[correct translation: soft non-leather shoes]

It is allowed to wipe over slippers [correct translation: soft non-leather shoes], as this has been related from many companions.

Says Abu Dawud, "Wiping over slippers [correct translation: soft non-leather shoes] (has been done by) Ali ibn Abu Talib, Ibn Masud, al-Bara ibn Azib, Anas ibn Malik, Abu Umamah, Sahl ibn Sad and Amr ibn Harith. It has also been related from Umar ibn al-Khattab and Ibn Abbas." Ammar, Bilal ibn Abdullah ibn Abu Awfa and Ibn Umar also have hadiths on this subject.

In Ibn al-Qayyim's *Tahdhib as-sunan*, he relates from Ibn al-Mundhir, "Ahmad made a statement about the permissibility of wiping over slippers [correct translation: soft non-leather shoes] because of his fairness and justice. Nevertheless, the basis of this permissibility is the practice of the companions and manifest analogy. There is no real difference between socks [correct translation: soft leather boots] and slippers [correct translation: soft non-leather shoes]. It is correct that they take the same ruling. Most scholars say that one can wipe over either one." Those who permit it include Sufyan ath-Thawri, Ibn al-Mubarak, Ata, al-Hasan and Said ibn al-Musayyab.

Commenting on this subject, Abu Yusuf and Muhammad said, "It is allowed to wipe over them if they are thick and completely hide what they cover."

Abu Hanifah did not approve of wiping over thick slippers [correct translation: soft non-leather shoes], but he changed his mind three or seven days before his death. He wiped over his slippers during his illness and said to his visitors, "I did what I used to tell people not to do." [Abu Hanifa's statement was, "Today I did something that I never used to do: I wiped over my socks without wearing my sandals."27]

(End of the translated text of *Fiqh al-sunna*.)

Reply of Mainstream Islamic Scholars

Shams al-Haqq Azimabadi, a scholar of mainstream Islamic thought said:

The permissibility of wiping over *khuff*s is well-established. There are some reports of wiping on *jawarib*, but it should be realized that their component material could be of leather [this is incorrect: if they were made of leather they would be *khuff*s], cotton, wool, etc. How, then, do you entitle yourself to regard wiping on cotton socks as permissible when none of the hadiths mention the material of those socks on which the Prophet (ﷺ) or the Companions wiped? What is established beyond doubt is only wiping on leather; anything else is speculative. We cannot establish a legal ruling of permissibility on this issue through speculative evidence, because the wiping is a concession to begin with. The default is that the feet should be washed, and the concession of wiping can only be taken when it can be verified that the conditions for wiping are satisfied. Analogy in matters of prescribed worship is ill-advised, at best."28

Although a person has the right to follow a scholar whom he trusts, it is very inadvisable to do so in cases where that scholar has departed from the mainstream by permitting something the majority of scholars have deemed impermissible. A leader of prayers in particular should try his utmost to make sure his prayer is valid according to all schools of thought, in order to satisfy all the members of his congregation. It is therefore a cause for concern that some people insist on wiping on their thin, cotton (or other) socks and then leading the prayer. Those members of the congregation who see this and do not believe it is

27 Tirmidhi narrated it in his *Sunan*.

28 Shams al-Haqq Azimabadi, *Awn al-mabud bi sharh sunan Abi Dawud* (Allah's Assistance: Commentary on Abu Dawud's *Sunan*).

valid will either pray individually, thereby losing the reward of congregational prayer, or repeat their prayer individually afterwards, which may cause them inconvenience (for example, if their time away from work is limited).

1.2.2.2. ALBANI'S DEVIATION ON THE ISSUE OF WIPING OVER SOCKS

Albani's ruling on wiping on socks shows a disturbing disregard for the actual stipulations of the *sunna*. He claims:

Q. What is the commandment regarding wiping over the *khuff*s (moccasins [sic], leather socks)?"

> [Albani's answer:] "Wiping over the *khuff*s is a *mutawaatir* practice; there are many, many *ahaadeeth* about it. In fact, the matter is even easier for the people, since there are *ahaadeeth* which mention that the Messenger used to wipe over his socks also. Wiping over socks, even if they are of thin material, is supported by a large majority of Muslim *ulamaa*, including Umar bin al-Khattaab, as Imaam Nawawi has mentioned in his book *Al-Majmoo Sharh al-Muhadhdhab*."

Albani thus claims that the Prophet (ﷺ) and Umar wiped over what we call "socks" just as one does over the *khuff*s. This is false, since their *jawarib* and our socks are different. Further, he used this statement to support his *fatwa* that wiping over thin socks is lawful, even suggesting that Nawawi in *al-Majmu* confirms it. In reality, the material of the so-called "socks" that the Prophet (ﷺ) and the Companions used is not established. Imam Nawawi never allowed wiping on socks of thin material, and his position is stated clearly in *Minhaj al-talibin*, book of *Tahara*, where he says, "A woven fabric *(mansuj)* that is not impermeable to water is unacceptable for wiping."

1.2.2.4. MAUDUDI'S UNPRECEDENTED VIEW ON THE ISSUE OF WIPING OVER SOCKS

Maulana Abul Ala Mawdudi, the Indian "Salafi" scholar,

similarly came up with an unprecedented *fatwa*. His argument is as follows:

> The majority of the followers of the *sunnah* are agreed that wiping over leather socks is permissible, but as for the conditions prescribed by the jurists regarding the description of the woolen [*sic.*] and cotton socks, I have been able to find no basis thereof. The *sunnah* is explicit that the Holy Prophet (ﷺ) did sometimes wipe over his socks and shoes, but we do not find any specifications or description of the socks anywhere. I am, therefore, satisfied that the conditions imposed by the jurists have no basis whatsoever, and if a person wipes over the socks without any regard for them, his *wudu* will be complete and he will not be violating any injunction of the Shariah. The concession of wiping over the socks is just like the concession of *Tayammum*, which has been granted in special circumstances when keeping the feet covered up may be absolutely necessary and washing them every time harmful or involving unnecessary hardship. The concession is, in fact, a special favor of Allah Almighty and may be availed of as such. One may, therefore, wipe over any description of socks that one may be wearing, with complete satisfaction of the heart, even over a bandage that one may have put on the feet to keep them safe from cold or dust, or to cover a wound."29

Mawdudi's view has caused outrage among scholars all over the world. It is unfortunate that it is inserted into a manual that is presented as Hanafi fiqh, for there is nothing Hanafi in this *fatwa*. His statement that the stipulations of the jurists are baseless is itself baseless. His comparison of "the concession of wiping over the socks" with "the concession of *tayammum*" is an innovation. Further, he somehow claims that he discovered something nobody knew before him. It would have been more proper to say, "I disagree with them." It is a *fatwa* that, like the irresponsible translation of *Fiqh al-sunna* regarding this issue, is more dangerous than helpful to English-speaking Muslims.

29 See Mawdudi, *Rasail-o-Masail* Vol. II, p. 37, as quoted in *Everyday Fiqh* Vol. I pages 73-74 by Muhammad Yusuf Islahi, translated into English by Abdul Aziz Kamal, Islamic Publications (Pvt.) Limited: Lahore, Pakistan, c. 1975 - 1993.

As for the book *Everyday Fiqh*, it claims to "represent the Hanafi school in the main, with footnotes on the views of other schools." Even if the book is, overall, an accurate manual on Hanafi fiqh, it sometimes quotes a verdict from outside the Hanafi school, presents the reasoning behind this view, but neglects to mention evidence from the Hanafis. Wiping socks is a case in point. Such a book should therefore be used with great caution and checked against more reliable sources.

In conclusion, the safest view on what footwear may be worn during *wudu* is that of the author of *Awn al-mabud*, Shams al-Haqq Azimabadi, whereby the established evidence supports leather shoes or leather socks. In fact, leather footwear is an exclusive condition for wiping in the Maliki school. The hadith on the *jawarib* cannot be used as evidence for establishing wiping socks, because there are fundamental dissimilarities between the traditional *jawarib* and modern socks. The former were hand-made, large, and often replaced the entire shoe in traveling. The three stipulations for *jawarib* namely, that the material of the footwear should be thick, water-proof, and resistant to wear and tear so as not to become transparent when walking over a certain distance, should be met scrupulously by Allah's servants, if they wish to safeguard their prayer and their *wudu*. The Prophet (ﷺ) said, "Leave what causes you to doubt and keep what does not cause you to doubt."[30]

1.3. ETIQUETTE OF KEEPING A BEARD AND REMOVING FACIAL HAIR

Q. What is the Islamic position on keeping the beard and removing facial hair?

1.3.1. MAINSTREAM ISLAMIC VIEW

The proof for the etiquette of trimming the beard is in the known practice of the Companions including, but not restricted to, Ibn Umar. To invoke an analogy to the Prophet's order to lift up the *izar* is out of place, as that is a command that has a *hukm* of its own; namely, that it is detestable to drag one's lower garment on the ground, and that it is desirable that the

---

30 Tirmidhi narrated it from Ali and he graded it *hasan sahih*.

ankle-bones remain uncovered. The Prophet's original command to leave the beard is understood in the context of differing from non-Muslims, not leaving it absolutely, as is confirmed by the practice of Ibn Umar, who trimmed whatever grew in excess of a fistful.

The beard of the male Muslim is one of the outward symbols of Islam and, as al-Badr al-Ayni pointed out, it is important that it not be made to look unkempt and disheveled. The Prophet (ﷺ) said, "Allah is Beautiful and He loves beauty." The *tabii* Ata ibn Abi Rabah said, "There is no harm in trimming a little from the length and sides of his beard, if it grows large and long." Al-Nakhi, another *tabii*, related that the Companions used to trim their beards on the sides. It is preposterous and reprehensible to suggest that such trimming is against the *sunna,* as both they, and the authorities among the *tabiin* who reported from them, were certainly more knowledgeable in the *sunna* than we are. As the scholars said, "The *sahaba* were all legally upright *(udul),* by consensus *(ijma)* of Muslim scholars, and it is inconceivable that they would institutionalize and set a precedent that was in direct defiance of a religious obligation."

The best discussion in English on the tradition *(sunna)* of keeping the beard is by Nuh Keller:

> Ibn Umar relates from the Prophet (ﷺ) that he said, "Do otherwise than those who ascribe partners to Allah *(al-mushrikin)*; leave beards be, and trim mustaches." And Ibn Umar, when he went on *hajj* or *umra*, grasped his beard with his hand, and removed what was in excess of it.[31]
>
> In the Hanafi school of law, there is no harm *(la bas)* in trimming the edges of the beard, though a handful is *sunna*, for when a narrator (Ibn Umar, in this case), has done something in ostensive contravention to what he has narrated (the words "leave beards be"), Hanafi bases of jurisprudence say this shows that the narrator knows that the Prophet (ﷺ) (Allah bless him and give him peace) has indicated that the original ruling has been superseded *(man-*

---

31 *Sahih al-Bukhari*, 9 vols. Cairo 1313/1895. Reprint (9 vols. in 3). Beirut: Dar al-Jil, n.d., 7.206: 5892 and *Sahih Muslim*, 5 vols. Cairo 1376/1956. Reprint. Beirut: Dar al-Fikr, 1403/1983, 1.222: 259.

sukh) by a subsequent one–permitting the beard to be trimmed, in this case. But trimming it when it is already less than a handful is not permissible in the Hanafi school.[32]

Muhammad ibn Hasan al-Shaybani reports in Kitab al-athar, from Imam Abu Hanifa, that "the sunna concerning it [the beard] is the handful, and consists in a man grasping his beard with his hand, and whatever exceeds that, he cuts".[33]

A Hanafi shaykh whom my wife and I study with, has told us (without mentioning a reference) that there is disagreement as to where this "handful" should begin from, some holding that one puts the index finger of it just below the lower lip, while according to others, one puts it below the bottom of the chin. The former will obviously result in a much shorter "handful."

The Shafii scholar Imam Nawawi in his commentary on Sahih Muslim says of the above hadith:

As for trimming the mustache, it is also a sunna. It is praiseworthy to begin from the right side . . As for how much should be trimmed, the soundest position is that one trims it until the edge of the lip appears, not trimming it down to the roots. As for the versions of the hadith containing the words crop mustaches, (*ihfu al-shawarib*) they mean "crop that which grows over the lips," and Allah knows best.

As for leave beards be, it means "make them ample" (Ar. *tawfir*, to make much, abundant, copious) and is also the meaning of make beards plenteous (*awfu al-liha*) in other versions of the hadith. It had been the Persians custom to cut their beards, so the Sacred Law forbade that."[34]

Imam Baghawi records that "Malik has said, "Shaving the mustache is an innovation (*bida*) that has appeared among people."[35]

Ibn Daqiq al-Eid says, "I do not know anyone who has understood from the command to leave beards be

32 Ibn Abidin, *Radd al-muhtar   ala al-durr al-mukhtar*, 5 vols. Bulaq 1272/1855. Reprint. Beirut: Dar Ihya al-Turath al-Arabi, 1407/1987, 2.113.

33 *Ibid*, 5.261.

34 *Sahih Muslim bi Sharh al-Nawawi*, 18 vols. Cairo 1349/1930. Reprint (18 vols. in 9). Beirut: Dar al-Fikr, 1401/1981, 3.149.

35 Imam Baghawi, *Sharh al-sunna*, 16 vols. Damascus: al-Maktab al-Islami, 1400/1980, 12.108.

that it is permissible to do them up so that they seem copious, as some people do."[36]

In his commentary on *Sahih al-Bukhari*, the great Hanafi hadith Imam Badr al-Din al-Ayni says:

If one objects: "What does leave beards be mean, when to leave be (*al-ifa*) literally means to make plenteous, and there are people, who, if they were to leave their beard, following the outward sense of leave beards be, their beard would become outrageous in length and width, and look disgusting, so that the person would become a topic of conversation, or a proverb"–The reply is that it is established from the Prophet (ﷺ) that this hadith is conditioned by a specific context [i.e. the demand to do the contrary to what the Persians and non-Arabs did, established by the first words of the hadith], and that the amount and definition of the beard that is unlawful to leave uncut have been differed upon by the early Muslims. . .

The meaning, in my opinion, is "as long as it does not exceed what is customary among [religious] people." Ata [ibn Abi Rabah, Mufti of Makka, d. 114/732], has said, "There is no harm in trimming a little from the length and sides of his beard, if it grows large and long, in order to avoid notoriety, or if one risks being made fun of."[37]

Imam Baghawi says, "Leaving the beard be means making it ample (tawfiruha) . . . It is related from Ibn Umar that he used to grasp his beard with his whole hand, then remove what was in excess of that. This was also related from Abu Hurayra. Ibrahim [al-Nakhai, d. 108/726] said: "They [the Sahaba] used to trim their beards on the sides."[38]

For trimming the beard, one may adduce as evidence the hadith of Umar ibn Harun, from Usama ibn Zayd, from Amr ibn Shuayb, from his father, from his grandfather, that the Prophet (ﷺ) "used to trim from his beard, from its sides and its length."[39] The last narrator in the hadiths chain of transmission, Umar ibn Harun, is agreed-upon among most hadith Imams

---

36 Ibn Hajar al-Asqalani: *Fath al-bari bi sharh Sahih al-Bukhari*, 14 vols. Cairo: al-Maktaba al-Salafiyya, 1390/1970, 10.351.

37 *Umdat al-qari sharh Sahih al-Bukhari*, 20 vols. Cairo: Mustafa Babi al-Halabi, 1392/1972, 18.76.

38 Imam Baghawi, *Sharh al-sunna*, 12.1089.

39 *Sunan al-Tirmidhi* 5 vols. Cairo n.d. Reprint. Beirut: Dar Ihya al-Turath al-Arabi, n.d., 5.94: 2762.

as being "fatally weak" (*matruk*) despite (or perhaps because of) which, Tirmidhi mentions after citing the hadith that his own shaykh, Bukhari, had a good opinion of the narrator. The hadith perhaps remains weak, but Bukhari's opinion carries its weight. My shaykh in Shafii *fiqh*, Abd al-Wakil Durubi used to cite it, and I have not met a single Shafii scholar (*faqih*) who did not trim his beard to considerably less than the-handful-below-the-chin length.

The following points can be inferred from all of the above. . . :

The hadith about "Leaving the beard be" are unconditional, that is, can be read to indicate that it is obligatory not to cut the beard at all.

This ruling seems to be conditioned by a number of considerations from the actual practice of the Sahaba, who were trained by the Prophet (ﷺ) and intimately familiar with his appearance, such as:

That Ibn Umar, one of the most learned Sahaba and keenest in following the sunna, used to cut his beard when he went on *hajj* or *umra*, that is, presumably in anticipation of entering the *ihram* or "state of pilgrim sanctity" in which it is unlawful for a Muslim to cut or otherwise remove any hairs of his beard, a situation in which a learned person could be expected to trim the maximum allowable, since he would be unable to so (while in *ihram*) for some time to come. This shows that the unconditionality of the hadith was, in Ibn Umar's view, conditioned by trimming the beard, in all probability by instruction or example of the Prophet (ﷺ), since the *sahaba* were all legally upright (*udul*) by consensus (*ijma*) of Muslim scholars, and it is inconceivable that they would institutionalize and set a precedent that was in direct defiance of a religious obligation.

Imam Baghawi reports that trimming the beard was also the practice of Abu Hurayra, another of the foremost scholars of the Sahaba, and Baghawi reports from Ibrahim al-Nakhai, the shaykh of the early Muslim community in Iraq, that the *sahaba* used to trim their beards on the sides.

If the earliest Muslims had all had beards down to their waists or to their knees from never cutting them, this would have been conveyed to us by hadiths, but it has not.

The wisdom of letting beards be, as in the above hadith of Bukhari and Muslim, is doing otherwise than the non-Muslims. Other hadith, related in the *Musannaf* of Ibn Abi Shayba and other sources, explicitly state that the Persians used to shave their faces and grow their mustaches long. Distinguishing ourselves from them could be accomplished with considerably less than a long beard.

General Islamic values entail beauty in behavior, manners, and dress. When a man once asked if liking fine clothes and sandals was a form of arrogance, the Prophet (ﷺ) said: "Verily, Allah is Beautiful and loves beauty" (*Sahih Muslim*, 1.93:91).

The general Islamic demand for beauty entails refinement and moderation, at minimum meaning not to deliberately seek notoriety through one's appearance. The Prophet (ﷺ) of Islam has said: "Whoever dresses in a garment of notoriety in this world, Allah will dress him in a garment of humiliation on Judgment Day" (*Musnad* al-Imam Ahmad, 6 vols. Cairo 1313/1895. Reprint. Beirut: Dar Sadir, n.d., 2.139), a well authenticated (*hasan*) hadith. One's standards for this are not non-Muslims, however, as the Prophet (ﷺ) has said: "Whoever imitates a people is one of them" (*Sunan Abi Dawud*, 4 vols. Cairo n.d. Reprint (4 vols. in 2). Istanbul: al-Maktaba al-Islamiyya, n.d. 4.44: 4031). Rather, the standard is that of other religious Muslims.

In consideration of these general values ((4) and (5)), Imam al-Ayni above investigates the length that obliges one to cut the beard, though he reports that the earliest authorities did not agree on this.

To summarize, to have a beard is obligatory for the Muslim man. The wording of the above *sahih* hadith indicates it should be abundant, though this is conditioned by the *urf* or common acknowledgement for it among religious, practicing Muslims. The early Muslims trimmed their beards, and there is not an unequivocal text (*nass*) that establishes a fixed legal limit to length and size. While the *sunna* is considered by many *ulama* to be "the handful," my own sheikhs trimmed their beards considerably closer than this, and they were *ulama*. It is my conviction and the premise of my approach to Islamic law that Allah will not punish the ordinary Muslim for something differed about between traditional *ulama*.

These considerations are particularly relevant to the circumstance that Islam has now spread to virtually every race on earth, and that genetically, not every man can grow a beard like Ibn Umar's. In my view, the differing capacities make preferable the more general *fiqh* criteria of (1) having a beard, (2) "abundance" according to one's capacity, so it doesn't look like the shaving of the non-Muslims, (3) and well-keptness that accords with the general Islamic standards of beauty (among people who are practicing Muslims) and avoidance of notoriety–rather than a certain mandatory length. And Allah knows best.[40]

1.3.2. ALBANI'S RESTRICTION OF TRIMMING THE BEARD AND REMOVING FACIAL HAIR

Albani writes:

It is not permissible for the Muslim to remove any hair from the beard except what the Lawgiver has allowed. It is reported from one of the companions who narrated the hadeeth, "Leave the beard and trim the moustaches," Abdullaah bin Umar, that he used to remove from his beard what was below a fistful. Apart from that, trimming the beard is against the *sunnah*, whether or not the man's beard is pleasing to him, and whether or not it is pleasing to others, for all of Allaah's creation is handsome, as in the saheeh hadeeth, where the Prophet saw a man with a long waist-shirt and ordered him to have his *izaar* halfway up his shins; the man gave the excuse that he had a defect in his ankles, so the Prophet said: "All of Allaah's creation is handsome." (Saheeh-Ahmad and others. This phrase is actually of Quranic origin cf. Sajdah 32:7).

Really we must memorise this hadeeth well in order to answer the misconceptions in issues like this. One who says that "my wife has a lot of hair and I do not want to go near her" should remember this

---

40 End of quote from Nuh Keller.

hadeeth, and in fact remember the saying of Allaah: "So set your face truly to the faith, Allaah's handiwork according to the pattern on which He has made mankind, (let there be) no change in the creation of Allaah." (Roum 30:30).

Also the hadeeth "Allaah has cursed the woman who tattoos and the one who asks for it, the woman who plucks the eyebrows and the one who asks for it and the woman who makes gaps in her teeth, who change the creation of Allaah for the sake of beauty."(Bukhari, narrated by Abdullah bin Masood)

These few quotes are enough as proof to show that it is not allowed to change the creation of Allaah in any way . . . (etc.)

1.3.3. MAINSTREAM ISLAMIC REPLY TO ALBANI'S RESTRICTIONS

It would seem also that the *fatwa* given above erroneously suggests that women leave all facial hair alone as well. The reply claims, in the section on women, that "These few quotes are enough as proof to show that it is not allowed to change the creation of Allaah in any way." In an effort to correct this false notion, the following is a more accurate translation of the hadith about women removing their facial hair, accompanied by the words of Nawawi and Ibn Hajar:

> The Prophet (☙) said, "May Allah curse women who wear false hair or arrange it for others, who tattoo or have themselves tattooed, who pluck facial hair or eyebrows or have them plucked, and women who separate their front teeth for beauty, altering what Allah has created."[41]
>
> Ibn Hajar al-Asqalani said, in commenting on this hadith:
>
> Nawawi said, "An exception from the prohibition of plucking away facial hair is when a woman has a beard, mustache, or hair growing between her lower lip and chin, in which cases it is not unlawful for her to remove it, but rather is commendable (*mustahabb*)," the permissibility being on condition that her husband knows of it and gives his permission, though

---

41 Dhahabi narrated it in *al-Kabair* and he said: "It is agreed upon [by Bukhari and Muslim]."

it is prohibited if he does not, because of the deception it entails.[42]

The question is sometimes asked, "In what circumstances is it allowable for a male Muslim to shave his beard off or not to grow one at all? Is military service a valid excuse?" "Necessities make prohibited things permitted (*al-darurat tubihu al-mahzurat*)." The question is to define necessity in this case. Protection of one's life, safety, livelihood, and religion all qualify as a necessity, and in some countries military service is unavoidable except at unbearably high personal cost. Indeed, in some countries, the beard was made either illegal by law under threat of major punishment or a cause for harrassment and persecution by the authorities.

1.4. REGARDING THE TRADITION (*SUNNA*) OF CARRYING A WALKING STICK

Q. What is the *sunna* of carrying a stick? Is it a *sunna* of the *khutba* only? Is it exclusively for the Messenger of Allah?

1.4.1. MAINSTREAM ISLAMIC VIEW ON THE TRADITION (*SUNNA*) OF CARRYING A WALKING STICK

Carrying a walking stick, staff, or cane for the adult male Muslim is, by general agreement of the *ulama*, a *sunna* of the Prophet (ﷺ) and, in the Shafii and Maliki schools, one of the desirable articles of the etiquette of the Friday sermon (*khutbat al-juma*). Imam Shafii carried a stick at all times in his life, even when he was not old, ailing, or travelling.[43] As for the statement, *al-tawakku ala al-asa min sunnat al-anbiya*, al-Qari said, "*Kalamun sahih wa laysa lahu aslun sarih* (it is a true statement but without an explicit basis)." He continued, saying that its implicit basis is the mention of Moses' staff in the Quran, and the mention of the Prophet's staff in several instances in the hadith.[44]

The Prophet (ﷺ) held a walking stick while delivering the *khutba*: On the authority of al-Hakam ibn Hazn al-Kulafi with a good chain, he said:

---

42 Ibn Hajar, *Fath al-bari* (10:378).
43 As Nawawi relates in the introduction to his *al-Majmu*.
44 Ajluni mentioned this in *Kashf al-khafa*.

We stayed with the Prophet (ﷺ) a few days during which we witnessed the Friday (*juma* prescribed prayer). During the latter the Prophet (ﷺ) stood leaning on a walking stick (*asa*) or a bow (*qaws*), praised Allah and glorified him with a few excellent and blessed words, then he said, O people, you will not do, nor will you bear to do all that you have been ordered; nevertheless do as much as you can and be glad.[45]

On the authority of al-Barra ibn Azib:

We were sitting in the mosque on the day of Adha and the Prophet (ﷺ) came to us and greeted the people and said, "The first act of devotion (*nusuk*) on this Day of yours is prayer." After which he went forward and prayed two *rakat*, gave *salam*, and then faced the people and was given a bow or a walking stick upon which he leaned (for his *khutba*). Then he praised Allah and glorified Him . . .[46]

On the authority of Khalid ibn Jabal al-Adwani with a good chain, he saw the Prophet (ﷺ) in the Eastern part of the tribe of Thaqif (in Taif) standing and leaning on a bow or stick, at the time when he came requesting their support. Khalid said, "And I heard him recite: *was-samai wat-tariq* (*Surah* 86)."[47]

The Prophet (ﷺ) was "given a bow or a walking stick" before the *khutba*, and he leaned on one when he addressed the people of Taif, as no self-respecting Arab was ever seen addressing people in a public forum without a walking stick in his hand, as it adds gravity to his appearance.[48] This is one of the customs of the Arabs which, like the turban, the Prophet (ﷺ) retained and made part of his *sunna*.

The Prophet (ﷺ) deliberately carried a walking stick during the rites of pilgrimage. On the authority of Ibn Abbas:

The Prophet (ﷺ) circumambulated the Holy House on the Farewell Pilgrimage riding a camel. He

---

45 Abu Dawud in his *Sunan* (Book of *salat*) and Ahmad in his *Musnad* (4:212) narrate.

46 Also in the *Musnad* (4:282, 304). Abu Dawud (book of *salat*) through the same authority only mentions the bow.

47 Also in the *Musnad* (4:335).

48 As the Mutazili writer al-Jahiz explained in his "Book of the Staff."

touched the Corner (the Black Stone) with a bent-headed walking stick (*mihjan*)."[49]

Muslim reports it also through Jabir, who adds that he did so in order to be seen by the people and to be asked questions, and through Abu al-Tufayl, who says, "I saw Allah's Messenger (ﷺ) circumambulating the House, and touching the corner with a walking stick that he had with him, and then kissing the walking stick." This example was followed to the letter by Ibn Abbas who, on the authority of Mujahid, would hit the Black Stone with his walking stick and then kiss the walking stick.[50]

The Prophet (ﷺ) was described on numerous occasions either holding a walking stick, or stressing its symbolism or value. In the following examples, he referred to the walking stick carried by a Muslim as one of the signs of the approach of the Last Day. He made the walking stick a gift of gratitude from himself and a sign between himself and one of the Companions on the Day of Resurrection. He also alluded to the walking stick as the symbol of the finality of his prophethood:

Ahmad narrates, on the authority of Abu Said al-Khudri with a good chain, that the Prophet (ﷺ) said:

> By the One in Whose hand is my soul, the Hour shall not rise until one of you, after leaving his family, shall hear his own sandal or whip or stick telling him what happened to his family after he left them.[51]

Ahmad relates, through al-Zuhri on the authority of Abdullah ibn Unays, that after the latter went upon the Prophet's order and killed Khalid ibn Sufyan ibn Nabih, who was gathering a group to attack the Prophet (ﷺ), he came back and the following took place: Abd Allah said: The Prophet (ﷺ) walked with me then entered his house and gave me a staff saying, "Keep this, O Abdullah ibn Unays." I went out with it among the people and they asked what was this walking stick. I replied that the Prophet (ﷺ) had given it to me and ordered me to keep it. They said, "Go back and ask the Prophet (ﷺ) about it." I went back and said, "O Prophet (ﷺ), why did you

---

49 Bukhari and Muslim, Book of *hajj*.
50 Ahmad related it in his *Musnad* with a good chain (1:338).
51 *Ibid.* (3:89).

give me this staff?" He said, "As a sign (*ayat*) between you and me on the Day of Resurrection. Very few will be the one's who have a staff on that Day."[52]

The narrator continues:"Abdullah ibn Unays added the staff to his sword and was never found without it until the day he died, at which time he ordered that it be brought to him. It was put with him when he was shrouded and they were buried together".[53]

This hadith shows the value the Arabs put on the staff in general, a value that the Prophet (🕮) did not reject in his behavior.

Note that the Prophet (🕮) gave specific instructions concerning found walking sticks, which shows the profusion of their usage in early Muslim society. The Prophet (🕮) warned everyone against taking someone else's walking stick, although it is permissible to keep an unclaimed walking stick if found. Ahmad and Tirmidhi relate, both on the authority of Abdullah ibn al-Saibs great-grandfather, that the Prophet (🕮) said, "Let none of you take his brother's possession whether in seriousness or in jest, and if one of you finds his brother's walking stick, let him return it to its owner."[54] Regarding permission to keep an unclaimed walking stick, Abu Dawud relates, on the authority of Jabir ibn Abd Allah, that the Prophet (🕮) allowed them to keep for their own use the walking stick, the whip, and the rope, or the like if they find one.[55]

Bukhari relates, on the authority of Ubayd Allah ibn Abd Allah ibn Utba, that when Musaylima the Liar came to Madina, the Prophet (🕮), using a walking stick (*qadib*)–or a palm-tree stalk (*qitatu jarid*)—went to see him. In Ibn Abbas' account he spoke to him. Musaylima said to him, "If you wish, we would not interfere between you and the matter of leadership, on the condition that it be ours after you." The Prophet (🕮) said, "If you asked me for this walking stick, I would not give it to you."

---

52 *Ibid.* (3:496).

53 Ibn Hisham also cites it in his *Sira* (3/4:620 of the Saqqa edition) from Ibn Ishaq's narration. Haytami in *Majma al-zawaid* mentions that Abu Yala also narrated it. He said: "The name of one of the narrators is missing (Abd Allah ibn Unays's son), but the rest of those in its chain are trustworthy."

54 Ahmad, 4:221; Tirmidhi, Book of *Qadar* in his *Sunan*.

55 Abu Dawud, *Sunan*, book of *luqata* ("Objects one finds").

1.4.2. ALBANI'S DENIAL OF THE *SUNNA* OF CARRYING A WALKING STICK

It is none of these: to carry a stick is not the *sunnah*, neither generally nor during the *khutba*. The hadeeth, "To carry a stick is an example of the prophets" is fabricated, as I have explained in *Silsilah al-Ahaadeeth ad-Daeefah*. The Prophet used to have a stick which he would use as a *sutrah* while travelling or for the Eid prayer when there was no *sutrah* at the place of prayer. Hence, if a person needs a stick, as Allaah addresses Moosaa in the Quraan: . . . and what is that in your right hand, O Moosaa! He said. It is my rod, on it I lean, with it I beat down fodder for my flock, and in it I find other uses.(Taa Haa 20:17-18) or due to old age, then it is undoubtedly correct to carry a stick. However, as for an ordinary person, it is in no way from the *sunnah* to needlessly carry a stick, especially in an age where many people do without walking, let alone needing to carry a stick, due to conveyance in cars, buses etc, from the means provided by Allaah.

1.4.3. FURTHER EXAMPLES OF THE PROPHET'S USE OF A WALKING STICK

Ibn Majah, Abu Dawud, Nasai, and Ahmad relate on the authority of Awf ibn Malik al-Ashjai that the Prophet (ﷺ) came out ("into the mosque" in Abu Dawud and Ahmad) and saw that a man had hanged a bunch of grapes ("dates of inferior quality" in Abu Dawud and Ahmad).[56] The Prophet (ﷺ) had a walking stick with his hand and he began to poke and jab at the grapes saying, "If he had wished, the giver of this charity could have given better than this. Truly, the giver of this charity shall eat worthless dates on the Day of Resurrection."

Ahmad relates, on the authority of Abu Umamah: The Prophet (ﷺ) came out and met us and he was leaning upon a walking stick (*asa*). We stood up for him and he said, "Do not stand up in the manner of the non-Arabs who adulate each other."[57] Note that the prohibition of standing up was in relation to the intention of worldly praise. Nawawi shows that it is

---

56 Ibn Majah, Abu Dawud, and Nasai in their *Sunan* (Books of *zakat*) and Ahmad in his *Musnad* (6:23, 28).

57 Ahmad, *Musnad* (5:253).

good to stand out of respect for an elder or a scholar.[58] Aisha said:

> Whenever Fatima entered a room where the Prophet (ﷺ) was sitting the latter would get up and greet her, take her hand, kiss her, and make her sit in his place; and whenever he would enter a room where she was sitting she would get up and greet him, take his hand, kiss him, and make him sit in her place.[59]

Bukhari narrates, on the authority of Abu Abd ar-Rahman as-Sulami from Ali, that the Prophet (ﷺ) and some Companions were sitting in the cemetery of Baqi after a funeral (*janaza*), and the Prophet (ﷺ) began to scrape the ground with his staff (*mikhsara* or *ud*). Then he raised his head and said, "None of you is created except his place is foreordained in paradise or in hell."[60]

Bukhari also relates, on the authority of Abu Musa, that the latter was in the company of the Prophet (ﷺ) in one of the gardens of Madina and in the hand of the Prophet (ﷺ) there was a walking stick (*ud*), and the Prophet (ﷺ) was striking upon the water and the mud with it. A man came and asked permission to enter the garden. The Prophet (ﷺ) said, "Open the gate for him, and give him the glad tidings that he shall enter paradise." Abu Musa said, "I went, and behold! It was Abu Bakr. So I opened the gate for him and informed him of the glad tidings of entering paradise."

1.4.4. THE COMPANIONS ALSO CARRIED WALKING STICKS

Malik relates, on the authority of al-Saib ibn Yazid with a very strong chain, that he said:

> Umar had ordered Ubayy ibn Kab and Tamim al-

---

58 Nawawi, *al-Rukhsa bi al-qiyam.*

59 It is a sound narration related in Abu Dawud's *Sunan* (Book of *Adab*), Tirmidhi's *Sunan* (Book of *Manaqib*), and Nasai's *Sunan*. Al-Hakim said in the *Mustadrak*: "It is a sound *(sahih)* narration according to the criteria of Bukhari and Muslim." al-Zaylai in *Nasb al-raya* (4:258) said: "Tirmidhi said: *hadith hasan* – a fair narration – and in some of the manuscripts: *hasan sahih*." Ibn al-Muqrina rrates it in *al-Rukhsa* (p. 91 #26).

60 Bukhari, *Sahih* (Book of Commentary of the Quran and in the Book of *Adab*). It is also related in Muslim, Abu Dawud (Book of *sunna*), and Ahmad in his *Musnad* (1:132).

> Dari to pray eleven *rakat* with the people, and the imam would read hundreds of verses, until we were leaning on our staffs because of the long duration of our standing, and we did not leave until the first glimpse of dawn.[61]

Abu Dawud narrates from Hilal ibn Yasaf, with a chain that contains an unknown narrator, that the latter said:

> We went to Wabisa, and I said to my companion, "Let us observe his dignified appearance." He had a low-top *qalansuwa* (hat) with ear-coverings and a dust-colored woolen burnus (hooded cloak), and he was leaning on a staff while praying. After we greeted him we spoke to him and he said, "Umm Qays bint Mihsan told me that the Prophet (ﷺ) used to lean on a pillar in his mosque after he aged and put on weight."[62]

The hadith that the Prophet (ﷺ) owned a walking stick that he called *al-mamshuq*, as narrated by Tabarani on the authority of Ibn Abbas, contains in its chain Ali ibn Urwa, who is "fatally weak" (*matruk*) according to the Imams of hadith. Yet Ibn al-Athir[63] and Ibn Qunfudh both relate it.[64]

The above is enough evidence that the walking stick is a customary *sunna* of the Prophet (ﷺ) and the Companions, and that no one has authority to deny now what all *ulama* have accepted before. One might wonder why there is dissent in this area, as in so many other major and minor points that the rest of Muslim scholars have settled once and for all. The following conclusion might shed some light on this strange question.

1.4.5. CONCLUSION: MAINSTREAM ISLAMIC PRACTICE OF CARRYING A WALKING STICK

The third part of the Mutazili Imam al-Jahiz Mahbub al-Kinani's (d. 255) book is entirely devoted to the subject of the staff in and before Islam.[65] The author begins his introduction

---

61 Malik, *Muwatta*.

62 Abu Dawud, in the chapter entitled "Leaning on a staff during prayer" in his *Sunan* (Book of *salat*).

63 Ibn al-Athir, *al-Nihaya* (2:382).

64 Ibn Qunfudh, *Wasilat al-islam* (p. 122).

65 *Al-Bayan wa al-Tabyin*. The third part is entitled *Kitab al-asa* (The book of the staff).

by mentioning the Shuubiyya, a movement within the third-century Islamic community that attacked Arab customs and the Arabs status as cultural paradigms for Muslims. In the name of "equalization" (taswiya), he says, they criticized, among other things, the continued use of the staff (mikhsara) by Arab speakers (khutaba) and in public life. Al-Jahiz retorts:

> Do not give the slightest credit to those who dis-approve using a walking stick, whether to lean upon, or to point at something, or to walk on the ground, or to speak, or on any occasion.[66]

He shows, with the use of poetry and proverbs, that the staff was used and honored in virtually every facet of daily life among the Arabs, including fighting and traveling; and that after Islam, carrying the staff came to symbolize being a Muslim. He says:

> Many have used this line of poetry to describe Muslim speakers, "When they pound the minbar [i.e. ascend it with staff in hand] they can trace, with the end of their staff, even the defect in one's eye"[67] . . . and it is said of someone who secedes from the Community, "So-and-so has split the staff of Muslims" (fulanun shaqqa asa al-muslimin), and it is also called "the staff of religion" (asa al-din).[68]
>
> The Prophet, carrying a cane or walking stick (﷽), used to address people, and it is enough of a proof for its great utility and exalted position. The caliphs perpetuated its use, and so did the great Muslim speakers.[69]

Al-Jahiz concludes his book by pointing out that the staff and the turban symbolize Islam, and by stressing the tremendous value Allah puts on outward signs; he writes:

> Allah Almighty said, "Their signs are on their faces from the trace of prostration" (48:29), and "We have made you nations and tribes so that you may

---

66 Al-Bayan wa al-tabyin, 1313 H, p. 49.
67 Ibid. p. 50.
68 Ibid. p. 59.
69 Ibid. p. 69.

come to know each other, and the worthiest among you
are the most Godfearing" (49:13). Among the Arabs,
wearing a turban and carrying a staff are among the
"signs." It may be that the speaker of a *khutba* does
not wear a covering (*milhafa*) nor a robe (*jubba*) nor
an ankle-length shirt (*qamis*) nor a mantle (*rida*), but
what he cannot do without is the turban (*imama*) and
the stick (*mikhsara*).[70]

This is the position of the Shafii school of law in the matter,
as Imam Ghazali said, "It is desirable to wear the turban for
salat al-juma, especially for the Imam."[71] Imam Nawawi, "It is
the *sunna* for the Imam during the *khutba* . . . to lean on a
sword, a stick, or something similar."[72]

1.5. KISSING THE HAND OF A RELIGIOUS SCHOLAR

Q. Is it acceptable to kiss the hand of a religious
scholar (*alim*) or elder?

1.5.1. MAINSTREAM ISLAM ENCOURAGES KISSING THE HAND OF A RELIGIOUS SCHOLAR

Allah ordered the Prophet (ﷺ), "*Lower your wing for the
believers*" (15:88). From this some have inferred the order to
show courtesy to Muslims. He said, "*Who magnifies the sacred
symbols of Allah, then it is better for him with his Lord*" (22:30),
and, "*Who magnifies the symbols of Allah then it is truly from
the piety of hearts*" (22:32). The scholars are, after the prophets,
the greatest symbols of Allah on earth and the receptacles of
the religion. To insult a Muslim is one of the major sins (*kabair*)
and to insult the scholars is even worse since, as Imam al-
Shafii said the scholars are the foremost saints. That is why the
Prophet (ﷺ) warned strenuously against threatening the
rights of the scholar in Islam, when he said in an authentic
hadith, "Whoever does not know the rights of our scholars is
not one of my Community," This hadith is authenticated by
Albani.[73]

The least one may say about kissing the scholars hand in
Islam is what Imam Ahmad said: "*La basa bihi* (there is no

---

70 *Ibid.* p. 76.
71 Imam Ghazali, in the book of *Juma* of his *Ihya*.
72 Nawawi, in the book of *Juma* of his *Minhaj al-talibin*.
73 Albani. *Sahih al-targhib* 1:44.

harm in it)." It is futile to add to this verdict. However, the author's position, that of Tamim ibn Salama, Sufyan al-Thawri, and the school of Imam Shafii, including Bayhaqi and Nawawi, is that this act is *sunna* and *mustahabb*. It shows the necessary or magnification (*tazim*), and reverence (*tawqir*), of a person of religion and knowledge in Islam. As shown by the narrations, it is closer to the practice of the Companions with the Prophet (ﷺ), the knowledgeable one's among themselves, and the true Salaf.

The ruling of the authorities that kissing the scholars hand is *mustahabb* is categorically proven by the fact that when Imam Muslim met Imam Bukhari, he sought to kiss not merely his hands, but his feet. This was not gratuitous behavior on the part of Imam Muslim, but an excellent and meritorious display of humbleness and respect. Imam Muslim purposefully imitated Abu Ubayda when he met Umar ibn al-Khattab in Jerusalem, who themselves imitated those of the "Ten Promised Paradise" by the Prophet (ﷺ). This last is enough proof in itself that it is *sunna*.

It is authentically recorded that others of mainstream Islam did this also like the *tabiis* Khaythama ibn Abd al-Rahman al-Jufi (d. 85) and Talha ibn Musarrif (d.112) kissing each others hand; the same Talha kissing the hand of Malik ibn Mighwal (d. 159); and Sufyan ibn Uyayna and Fudayl ibn Iyad kissing the hand and foot of Husayn ibn Ali al-Jufi (d. 203).

1.5.2. ALBANI'S INCORRECT DISCOURAGEMENT OF KISSING THE HAND OF A RELIGIOUS SCHOLAR

Kissing the hand of an religious scholar (*alim*) has a basis in the *sunna*; however, this basis is one of allowable action, not one of a recommended example. Nowadays in many Islaamic lands, many of the shaykhs do not know the example of the Prophet of shaking hands with his Companions: as Abu Dhar said, "Whenever the Messenger of Allaah met us, he would shake hands with us." These shaykhs only know how to extend their hands to be kissed; as for extending the hand to shake, they have no idea! This sort of kissing in place of shaking hands is not allowed. The Prophet encouraged his *umma*, "Any two Muslims who meet and shake hands before parting, their sins fall as leaves fall from a tree in autumn."

1.5.3. FURTHER ELABORATION OF THE MAINSTREAM VIEW AND REFUTATION OF ALBANI

This question is not one of Muslim brothers meeting and shaking hands, but about the etiquette of the ordinary Muslim meeting the older *alim*, or scholar of Religion. Similarly, the hadith of the Prophet's meeting the Companions and shaking their hands is not as relevant as the hadiths of the Companions approaching the Prophet (ﷺ) and kissing his hand. This is an important difference that is altogether overlooked, whether inadvertently or deliberately, in the above answer. Nor did it escape notice that Albani's reply declares that the same thing is allowed and yet not allowed at the same time.

As for Albani"s claims that "Nowadays in many Islaamic lands, many of the shaykhs do not know the example of the Prophet (ﷺ) of shaking hands with his Companions" and "These shaykhs only know how to extend their hands to be kissed; as for extending the hand to shake, they have no idea," they are *iftira*, or slanderous fabrication. Hasan Ali al-Saqqaf amply demonstrated a number of similar insults aimed by Albani toward the *ulama*.[74]

Narrations of the Prophet (ﷺ) relevant to kissing the hands of the *ulama*:

Usama ibn Sharik narrates, "I went to see the Prophet (ﷺ) while his Companions were with him, and they seemed as still as if birds had alighted on top of their heads. I gave him my salam and I sat down. [Then Bedouins came and asked questions which the Prophet (ﷺ) answered.] . . . The Prophet (ﷺ) then stood up and the people stood up. They began to kiss his hand, whereupon I took his hand and placed it on my face. I found it more fragrant than musk and cooler than sweet water."[75]

---

74 Hasan Ali al-Saqqaf, *Qamus shataim al-Albani.*

75 Ibn al-Muqri in *al-Rukhsa* (p. 58 #2) narrates it with a chain which Ibn al-Hajar graded as "strong" *(sanaduhu qawiy)* in *Fath al-bari* (1989 ed. 11:67) and he listed it among the "good" *(jayyid)* narrations of Ibn al-Muqri on the topic. Imam Bayhaqi included it as part of the proofs for the fact that giving honor to the Prophet is part of faith in Chapter 15 of his *Shuab al-iman* entitled: The Fifteenth Branch of Faith, Namely a Chapter on Rendering Honor to the Prophet, Declaring His High Rank, and Revering Him *(al-khamis ashar min shuab al-iman wa huwa babun fi tazim al-nabi sallallahu alayhi wa sallama wa ijlalihi wa tawqirih).* Ibn al-Irabi narrated it with a stronger chain yet in his book *al-Qubal.* Not to be confused with Abu Bakr ibn al-Arabi al-Maliki or Shaykh Muhyiddin Ibn Arabi, this is the one identified by Dhahabi in his *Tadhkirat al-huffaz* (3:852) as "The Imam, the hadith master *(hafiz)*, the *zahid*, the

Jabir said, "Umar ibn al-Khattab got up and kissed the hand of Allah's Messenger."[76]

Tabari narrates it *mursal* (missing the Companion-link) through al-Suddi. He comments on verse 5:101, *"Do not ask of things which once shown to you would hurt you,"* saying:

> Umar ibn al-Khattab got up and kissed the foot of Allah's Messenger and said, "O Messenger of Allah, we are pleased with Allah as our Lord, with Islam as our religion, and with Muhammad as our Prophet (ﷺ), and with the Quran as our Book. Forgive, and Allah will forgive you *(fafu afallahu anka)*." And he did not cease until the Prophet (ﷺ) softened.[77]

The hadith is established as authentic by the following narrations in Bukhari:[78]

> Al-Zuhri said: Anas bin Malik told me: The Prophet (ﷺ) came out after the sun passed the midpoint of the sky and offered the *Zuhr* prayer (in congregation). After finishing it with *Taslim*, he stood on the pulpit and mentioned the Hour and mentioned there would happen great events before it. Then he said, "Whoever wants to ask me any question, may do so, for by Allah, you will not ask me about anything but I will inform you of it as long as I am at this place of mine." The people were weeping profusely (because of the Prophet's anger). Allah's Messenger kept saying, "Ask Me! " Then a man got up and asked, Where will my entrance be, O Allah's Messenger?" The Prophet (ﷺ) said, "The fire." Then Abd Allah ibn Hudhafa got up and asked, "Who is my father, O Allah's Messenger?" The Prophet (ﷺ) replied, "Your father is Hudhafa." The Prophet (ﷺ) then kept on

shaykh of the *Haram*, Abu Said Ahmad ibn Muhammad ibn Ziyad ibn Bishr ibn Dirham al-Basri al-Sufi, the author of many books, and he was trustworthy and well-established in his narrations *(thiqa thabt)*, a knower of Allah *(arif)*, scrupulous with his Lord *(rabbani)*, and famed for his great rank." It is partially narrated, without the mention of the kiss, by Abu Dawud (#3855), Tirmidhi (2038 – *hasan sahih*), Ibn Majah (3436), al-Hakim (4:399), and Ahmad (4:278).

76 Ibn al-Muqri narrates it in *al-Rukhsa* (p. 71 #11) and although its chain contains Ubayd Allah ibn Said who is weak, Ibn Hajar included it among Ibn al-Muqri's good narrations *(min jayyidiha)* on the subject *(Fath al-bari* 11:66).

77 Tabari, *Tafsir.*

78 Bukhari, *Sahih* (Vol. 1 p. 76).

saying (angrily), "Ask me! Ask me!" Umar then fell to his knees and said, "We have accepted Allah as our Lord, Islam as our religion and Muhammad as our Messenger." Allah's Messenger became quiet when Umar said that. Then Allah's Messenger said, "Woe! By Him in Whose Hand my life is, paradise and hell were displayed before me just now, across this wall while I was praying, and I never saw such good and evil as I have seen today."

Muslim's version adds, "There was no harder day on the Companions than that day."[79]

Ibn Hajar, in his commentary on the collated accounts of this hadith, says:

> There is in this hadith [evidence for]: the Companions' acute observation of the Prophet's states and the intensity of their fear when he became angry, lest it result in a matter that would become generalized and extend to all of them; Umar's confidence in the Prophet's love (*idlal*); the permissibility of kissing the foot of a man; the permissibility of anger in exhortation; the students kneeling in front of the one who benefits him; the followers kneeling before the one followed if asking him for a certain necessity; the lawfulness of seeking refuge from dissension when something occurs which might initiate it; the use of pairing subjects in *dua* as in his words, Forgive, and Allah will forgive you (*fafu afallahu anka*).[80]

Umm Aban, daughter of al-Wazi ibn Zari narrated that her grandfather Zari al-Abdi, who was a member of the deputation of Abd al-Qays, said, "When we came to Madina, we raced to be first to dismount and kiss the hand and foot of Allah's Messenger . . ."[81]

---

79 Muslim, *Kitab al-fadail*. Bukhari narrates it in the third chapter of *Kitab al-itisam bi al-kitab wa al-sunna*, entitled: "What is disliked in asking too many questions, and those who take on what does not concern them, and Allah's saying: *"Do not ask about things which once shown to you would hurt you"* (5:101)." (English: Volume 9, Book 92, Number 397). The *Sahih* contains other versions of this hadith such as in *Kitab al-ilm*, chapter 28: "On anger during exhortation" and chapter 29: "On kneeling before the Imam or *muhaddith*." (English: Volume 1, Book 3, Number 90-93), and in *Kitab mawaqit al-salat*, chapter 11: "The time of noon prescribd prayer (*zuhr*) is after the sun passes the zenith." (Volume 1, Book 10, Number 515).

80 Ibn Hajar. *Fath al-bari* 1989 ed. 13:335.

81 Abu Dawud narrates it in his *Sunan*, book of *Adab*.

Bukhari relates a similar hadith from her: We were walking and someone said: "There is the Messenger of Allah," so we took his hands and feet and kissed them.[82]

Albani's isolated claim that Umm Aban is an unknown (*majhula*)[83] is put to rest by the hadith master Haythami's remark that, "Its narrators are trustworthy, as for Umm Aban, Abu Dawud narrated from her and he kept silent concerning her narration."[84] The vast majority of the Imams of hadith consider silence, on any of their parts, acceptance, not *tajhil*. Worth noting is also the fact that Ibn al-Arabi and al-Baghawi narrated the hadith in *Mujam al-sahaba*, and they, like the rest of the hadith masters who cited this hadith, raised no doubt concerning Umm Aban. Moreover, the declaration of a narration as weak on the basis of a narrator can only be done through the mention of that narrator in one of the books of the *Duafa*, and not through any other way. These rules show why all these scholars considered, either explicitly or tacitly, that the hadith was authentic.

From Safwan ibn Asal al-Muradi: "One of two Jews said to his companion, 'Take us to this Prophet so we can ask him about Moses' ten signs'. . . [The Prophet (ﷺ) replied in full and then] they kissed his hands and feet and said, "We witness that you are a Prophet (ﷺ) '". . ."[85]

Burayda said, "When we were with Allah's Messenger on an expedition when a bedouin came and asked for a miracle. The Prophet (ﷺ) pointed at a tree and said to the bedouin, 'Tell that tree: "Allah's Messenger (ﷺ) summons you."' The bedouin did, whereupon the tree swayed and brought itself out, and came to the presence of the Prophet (ﷺ) saying, "O Messenger of Allah (ﷺ)!" The bedouin said, "Now let it return to its place!" When Allah's Messenger ordered it, the tree went back. The bedouin

---

82 Bukhari. *Adab al-mufrad*. Ibn al-Muqri narrates it in his *Kitab al-rukhsa* (p. 80 #20), al-Tayalisi in his *Musnad*, al-Bazzar in his *Musnad* (3:278), Bayhaqi in the *Sunan* (7:102), and Ibn Hajar in *Fath al-bari* (1989 ed. 11:67 *Istidhan* ch. 28 #6265) said: "Among the good narrations in Ibn al-Muqri's book is the hadith of al-Zari al-Abdi." It was declared a fair *(hasan)* hadith by Ibn Abd al-Barr, and al-Mundhiri confirmed it in *Mukhtasar al-sunan* (8:86).

83 Albani. *Daif al-adab al-mufrad* (p. 89 #154).

84 Haythami. *Majma al-zawaid* (9:390).

85 Narrated by Ibn Abi Shayba (Book of *Adab*, Chapter entitled A Man Kissing Another Man's Hand When He greets Him), Tirmidhi (Book of *Adab*) who declared it *hasan sahih*, al-Nasai, Ibn Majah (Book of *Adab*), and al-Hakim who declared it *sahih*.

said, let me prostrate to you!' The Messenger answered, 'If I commanded anyone to do that, I would command the wife to prostrate to her husband.' The bedouin said, 'Then give me permission to kiss your hands and feet.' The Prophet (☙) gave him permission."86

Ibn Umar was sent with a detachment by the Prophet (☙). The people wheeled round in flight. He said, "I was one of those who wheeled round in flight. When we stopped, we asked, 'What should we do? We have run away from the battlefield and deserve Allah's wrath.' Then we said, 'Let us enter Madina, stay there, and go there while no one sees us.' So we came and thought, 'If we present ourselves to the Prophet (☙), and if there is amnesty for us we shall stay; if there is something else, we shall leave.' So we sat down waiting for the Prophet (☙) before the dawn prescribed prayer. When he came out, we stood up to him and said, 'We are the one's who have fled.' He turned to us and said, 'No, you are the one's who return to fight after wheeling away'. We then approached and kissed his hand, and he said, 'I am the main body of the Muslims (*ana fiatu al-muslimin*).'"87

Albani alone declares this hadith weak, on the sole grounds that all of its chains contain Yazid ibn Abi Ziad, who is weak.88

86 Qadi Iyad narrated it in *al-Shifa* (1:299) and al-Bazzar in his *Musnad* (3:49). The editor of Suyuti's *Manahil al-safa* (p. 124 #575) said: See *Kashf al-astar* (3:132). Ghazali cites the account of the kiss in the *Ihya* and al-Hakim in the *Mustadrak* as well as Ibn Muqri. Both al-Hakim and al-Iraqi declared its chain authentic *(sahih)*, as stated by al-Zabidi in his *Ithaf* (6:280) while Dhahabi declared it weak. However, Ibn Hajar included the hadith of Burayda among Ibn al-Muqri's good narrations *(min jayyidiha)* on the subject of kissing the hand, and Qadi Iyad also mentions a similar narration from Ibn Umar which Suyuti said was narrated by Darimi, Bayhaqi, and al-Bazzar with a sound chain. Qadi Iyad said the hadith of the tree's uprooting and coming to the Prophet is also narrated by Jabir, Ibn Masud, Yala ibn Murra, Usama ibn Zayd, Anas ibn Malik, Ali ibn Abi Talib, Ibn Abbas, and others who all agreed on the same account and so did the *Tabiin* who related it.

87 Narrated by Bukhari in his *Adab al-mufrad*, see *Bab taqbil al-yad* (Chapter on Kissing the Hand) and *Bab taqbil ar-rijl* (Chapter on Kissing the Foot), also in Abu Dawud's *Sunan* (Book of *Jihad*, chapter on desertion in the face of the enemy)–al-Iraqi said: "with a fair *(hasan)* chain," see Zabidi's *Ithaf* (6:280)–also in Tirmidhi's *Sunan*, (book of *Jihad*, chapter on flight in the face of the enemy) but without mention of the kissing and he said: *hasan gharib*, also Ibn Majah's *Sunan* (Book of *Adab* #3704), Bayhaqi through al-*Shafii* in his *Sunan* (9:76-77) and in *Dalail al-nubuwwa*, Ibn Abi Shayba in his *Musannaf* (8:749-750 *Adab*), al-Khattabi through al-Humaydi in *Gharib al-hadith* (1:331), Abu Yala in his *Musnad* (8:42), Ibn Sad in his *Tabaqat* (4:1/107) and Ahmad in the *Musnad* (2:58, 2:70) and also without mention of kissing (2:86, 2:100, 2:111). Ibn Hajar in *Fath al-bari* (1989 ed. 11:67) cited it in his list of the narrations providing evidence for kissing the hand and he did not weaken it.

88 Albani, *Daif al-adab al-mufrad*.

Yet, none of the masters cited above declared the hadith weak as other factors preclude it. Further, the hadith is cited in full as evidence on the rulings concerning desertion or flight in the face of the enemy.[89] Suyuti also cites the hadith in his discussion of the verses:[90]

> *When you meet disbelievers in hostile array, never turn your backs on them. If any do turn their back on them on such a day–unless it be in a stratagem of war, or to retreat to a troop of one's own–he draws on himself the wrath of Allah, and his abode is the Gehenna, an evil end* (8:15-16).

In conclusion, it is as Tirmidhi and Iraqi said, and as all confirmed tacitly, that the hadith is *hasan*.

A narration states that Kab ibn Malik al-Ansari came and kissed the hand and knees of the Prophet (ﷺ) after he was forgiven and exonerated of the charge of hypocrisy that had followed his sitting out the Prophet's expedition to Tabuk.[91]

Bayhaqi, Ghazali and Ibn al-Muqri cite it from Kab with a weak chain according to al-Iraqi: "When Allah sent down my acquittal, I went to the Messenger of Allah (ﷺ) and kissed his hand and knee." (*lamma nuzilat tawbati ataytu al-nabi sallallahu alayhi wa sallam fa qabbaltu yadahu wa rukbatahu*). Al-Haythami also states, among others, that Tabarani narrates it with a chain that contains a weak narrator.[92] Nevertheless, Ibn Hajar cites it from Ibn Mardawayh without weakening it, in his commentary on the long hadith of Kab in Bukhari, which provides the context of the incident:[93]

> . . . The period of fifty nights was completed from the time when Allah's Messenger prohibited the people from talking to us. When I had offered the dawn (fajr) prescribed prayer on the fiftieth morning on the roof of one of our houses and while I was sitting in the

89 Al-Qurtubi in his *Jami li ahkam al-quran* (Dar al-hadith ed. 7:365-366) and Ibn Kathir in his *Tafsir* (2:294 / 3:567) – which would be impermissible if it were indeed weak.

90 Suyuti, *al-Durr al-manthur* (3:174).

91 Bayhaqi in *Dalail al-nubuwwa*, Ghazali in the *Ihya*, and Ibn al-Muqri in *al-Rukhsa*.

92 Al-Haythami, *Majma al-zawaid* (8:42). (cf. Al-*Kabir* 19:42).

93 Ibn Hajar, *Fath al-bari* 1989 ed. 8:155 book of *Maghazi* ch. 80.

condition that Allah described (in the Quran), my very soul seemed straightened to me and even the earth seemed narrow to me for all its spaciousness. There I heard the voice of one who had ascended the mountain of Sala calling with his loudest voice, "O Kab ibn Malik! Good news!" I fell down in prostration before Allah, realizing that relief had come. Allah's Messenger had announced the acceptance of our repentance by Allah when he had offered the dawn (fajr) prescribed prayer. The people then went out to congratulate us. Some bearers of good tidings went out to my two fellows, a horseman came to me in haste, and a man of Banu Aslam came running and ascended the mountain and his voice was swifter than the horse. When he (i.e. the man) whose voice I had heard, came to me conveying the good tidings, I took off my garments and dressed him with them; and by Allah, I owned no other garments than them on that day. Then I borrowed two garments and wore them and went to Allah's Messenger.

The people greeted me in droves, congratulating me on Allah's acceptance of my repentance, saying, "We congratulate you on Allah's Acceptance of your repentance." When I entered the mosque I saw Allah's Messenger sitting with the people around him. Talha ibn Ubayd Allah swiftly came to me, shook hands with me and congratulated me. By Allah, none of the Emigrants got up for me except him (i.e. Talha), and I will never forget Talha for this. When I greeted Allah's Messenger he said, his face bright with joy, "Be happy with the best day of your life since your mother delivered you." I said to the Prophet (ﷺ), "Is this forgiveness from you or from Allah?" He said, "No, it is from Allah." Whenever Allah's Messenger became happy, his face would shine as if it were a piece of the moon, and we all knew that characteristic of him. When I sat before him, I said, "O Allah's Messenger! Because of the acceptance of my repentance I will give up all my wealth as alms for the sake of Allah and His Messenger." Allah's Messenger said, "Keep some of your wealth, as it will be better for you." I said, "Then I will keep my share from Khaybar," and I added, "O Allah's Messenger! Allah has saved me to tell the truth; so it is a part of my repentance to tell the truth as long as I am alive. By Allah, I do not know anyone of the Muslims whom Allah has helped to tell the truth more than me. Since I have mentioned that truth to Allah's Messenger until today, I have never intended to tell a lie. I hope that Allah will also save me (from telling lies) the rest of my life." So Allah revealed to His Messenger the verses:

Allah has turned in mercy to the Prophet, and to the Muhajirin and the Ansar who followed him in the hour of hardship. After the hearts of a party of them had almost swerved aside, then turned He unto them in mercy. Lo! He is Full of Pity, Merciful for them.

And to the three also (did He turn in mercy) who were left behind, when the earth, vast as it is, was straitened for them, and their own souls were straitened for them till they bethought them that there is no refuge from Allah save toward Him. Then turned He unto them in mercy that they (too) might turn (repentant unto Him). Lo! Allah! He is the Relenting, the Merciful. O ye who believe! Be careful of your duty to Allah, and be with the truthful (9:117-119).

By Allah, Allah has never bestowed upon me, apart from His guiding me to Islam, a greater blessing than the fact that I did not lie to Allah's Messenger, which would have caused me to perish as those who have lied perished, for Allah described those who lied with the worst description He ever attributed to anybody else. Allah said, *"They (the hypocrites) will swear by Allah to you when you return to them* (up to His saying) *certainly Allah is not pleased with the rebellious people"* (9:95-96). Kab added, "We, the three persons, differed altogether from those whose excuses Allah's Messenger accepted when they swore to him. He took their pledge of allegiance and asked Allah to forgive them, but Allah's Messenger left our case pending till Allah gave His Judgment about it, regarding which Allah said: *"And to the three whose case was delayed"* (9:118).

What Allah said (in this verse) does not indicate our failure to take part in the Ghazwa, but it refers to the deferment of making a decision by the Prophet (ﷺ) about our case in contrast to the case of those who had taken an oath before him and he excused them by accepting their excuses.

Al-Zabidi, Ghazali's commentator, says that Kab was one of the Helpers (*ansar*) who had stayed behind in the campaign of Tabuk. Altogether there were eighty-odd individuals, according to the hadith of Kab in Bukhari. However, the repentance is from the charge of hypocrisy (*nifaq*), not from staying behind during a campaign, and this is made explicit by Kab himself in the last words of Bukhari's narration. The incident is alluded to in the verse: *"And to the three whose case was delayed until the earth seemed straightened for them for all its spaciousness, and their very lives seemed straitened for them, until they realized that there was no recourse from Allah except to Him, then He relented towards them so that they repented. He is Oft-Returning, Most Merciful"* (9:118).

Ubada ibn al-Samit said: The Prophet (ﷺ) said, "He is not one of us who does not respect our elders, does not show mercy to our little one's or does not recognize the rights of our scholars."94

> Kathir ibn Qays said, "I was sitting with Abu al-Darda in the mosque of Damascus. A man came to him and said, 'Abu al-Darda, I have come to you from the city of Allah's Messenger for a narration I have heard that you relate from the Prophet (ﷺ). I have come for no other purpose.'
>
> He said, 'I heard Allah's Messenger say: "If anyone travels on a road in search of knowledge, Allah will cause him to travel on one of the roads of paradise, the angels will lower their wings from good pleasure with one who seeks knowledge, and the inhabitants of the heavens and the earth and the fish in the depth of the water will ask forgiveness for the learned man. The superiority of the learned man over the ordinary believer is like that of the moon on the

---

94 An authentic hadith narrated by Ahmad in his *Musnad* (5:323), al-Hakim in *al-Mustadrak* (1:122)–al-Dhahabi agreed with him on the authentication of the hadith, – and Tabarani in *al-Mujam al-kabir*. Al-Haythami in *Majma al-zawaid* (1:127, 8:14) said its chain was fair (*hasan*). So did al-Mundhiri in *al-Targhib wa al-tarhib* (1:125). Shaykh Albani the leader of the "Salafis" said one time that it was sound (*sahih*), and one time that it was fair (*hasan*), respectively in *Sahih al-targhib* (1:44) and *Sahih al-Jami al-saghir* (5:103)! al-Ajurri (d. 360) cited it in *Akhlaq ahl al-Quran*, 2nd ed., ed. Muh. Amr ibn Abd al-Latif (Beirut: Dar al-kutub al-ilmiyya, 1407/1987) p. 136-137. Al-Hakim said: "He is not one of us" means: He is not on our path nor does he follow our guidance. Tirmidhi in the *Sunan* (3:216) said: Some of the scholars said it means: He is not of our *sunna*, and: He does not follow our etiquette (*adab*).

night when it is full over the rest of the stars. The learned are the inheritors of the prophets,[95] and the prophets have neither dinar nor dirham, leaving only knowledge, and he who takes it takes an abundant portion.'"[96]

1.5.4. NARRATIONS OF THE COMPANIONS AND THEIR EXPLICIT PRACTICE OF KISSING THE HAND

Tamim ibn Salama relates with a chain of trustworthy narrators that Abu Ubayda ibn al-Jarrah kissed Umar's hand when the latter came to Damascus, after which they both began to weep. Tamim said, "Therefore they considered that kissing the hand is *sunna*." In another version, "Kissing the hand is *sunna*." And in another, "Kissing is *sunna*."[97]

The meaning of Tamim's comment is that these two are of the ten who were given the glad tidings of paradise, and they would not have done it if it were not the *sunna*.

Muhammad ibn Ahmad al-Minhaji al-Suyuti (d. 880) cites it, but his version states that Abu Ubayda ibn al-Jarrah extended his hand to shake the hand of Umar, and Umar extended his hand, but Abu Ubayda descended to kiss it, wishing to magnify him among the people.[98] At this Umar descended to the foot of Abu Ubayda and kissed it.

Al-Shubi narrates, as does Hammad ibn Salama from

---

95 The hadith, "The learned are the inheritors of the Prophets" is narrated from Abu al-Darda by Tirmidhi, Ahmad (5:196), Abu Dawud, Ibn Majah, Ibn Hibban in his *Sahih*, Bayhaqi in the *Shuab al-iman*, Darimi in the *Muqaddima* of his *Sunan*, and Bukhari in the Book of Knowledge in his *Sahih* in *muallaq* form (i.e. without chain). Al-Raghib al-Asfahani (d. 425) said in his dictionary *Mufradat alfaz al-quran* under the entry *w-r-th*: "Suyuti said: Shaykh Muhyiddin al-Nawawi was asked about it and he said it was weak *(daif)* – that is: in its chain – even if it is true *(sahih)* – that is: in its meaning. Al-Mizzi said: This hadith has been narrated through chains that attain the rank of *hasan*. It is as al-Mizzi said, and I have seen fifty chains for it, which I collected in a monograph. Here end Suyuti's words."

96 Abu Dawud narrated it in his *Sunan* as the first hadith of the book of *Ilm*, also Ibn Majah and Darimi in the *muqaddima* of their *Sunan*, all of them with a weak chain which, however, is strengthened by the fact that Bukhari in his *Sahih*, Tirmidhi in his *Sunan*, Ahmad in his *Musnad*, Bayhaqi in his *Sunan* all narrate various parts of this hadith.

97 Ibn Abi Shayba narrates it in his *Musannaf* (8:750 *Adab*), Bayhaqi in his *Sunan* (7:101 *Nikah*), both from Sufyan al-Thawri who narrated it in his *Jami*. Ibn al-Arabi mentions it in the *Siyar* (1:15). Abu Nuaym also mentions it but through another chain. Ahmad cites it in *Kitab al-wara* (p. 113 #510). Bayhaqi narrates it in his *Kitab al-adab* (p. 181 #296). Ghazali in his *Ihya* also cited it. Ibn Taymiyya cites it as evidence in the *Mukhtasar al-fatawa al-misriyya* (p. 563-564).

98 Suyuti, *Ithaf al-akhissa bi fadail al-masjid al-aqsa* (p.231).

Ammar ibn Abi Ammar, that Zayd ibn Thabit intended to go on a trip. At that time, the young Abd Allah ibn Abbas stood humbly at his side and, taking hold of his mounts reins, adopted the attitude of a humble servant in the presence of his master. Zayd said to him, "Don't, O cousin of the Prophet." Abd Allah replied, "Thus we were commanded to treat our *ulama* and elders." Zayd said to him in turn, "Let me see your hand." Abdullah stretched out his hand. Zayd, taking it, kissed it and said, "Thus we were commanded to treat the members of the household of the Prophet (ﷺ)." Al-Abhari and Ghazali mention it, and the latter adds that Umar once helped Zayd Ibn Thabit to mount his camel by holding his foot, and said to the onlookers, "Do the same." Al-Zabidi, Ghazali's commentator said, "i.e. with your *ulama.*"[99]

Bukhari narrates from Abd al-Rahman ibn Razin that one of the Companions, Salama ibn al-Akwa, raised his hands before a group of people and said: "With these very hands I pledged allegiance to the Messenger of Allah," upon hearing which all who were present got up and went to kiss his hand and he did not object.[100]

Abu Malik al-Ashjai said that he once asked another Companion of the Tree, Ibn Abi Awfa, "Give me the hand that swore allegiance to Allah's Messenger, that I may kiss it."[101]

Bukhari also relates with a sound chain that Suhayb, the freedman of al-Abbas, saw Sayyidna Ali kiss the hand and feet of the Prophet's uncle al-Abbas and say to him, "O Uncle! Be pleased with me."[102]

Albani declared this hadith weak, claiming that Suhayb is "not known" (*ghayr maruf*) as a narrator.[103] However, Ibn

---

99 Narrated by al-Khatib in *al-Faqih wa al-mutafaqqih* (2:99), Bayhaqi in *al-Madkhal* (p. 137), and Ibn Sad in his *Tabaqat* (2:360) from Abu Nuaym with a sound (*sahih*) chain according to Ibn Hajar in *al-Isaba* (1:561 "Zayd ibn Thabit"). Also by Tabarani and Ibn al-Muqri in his *Rukhsa* (p. 95 #30), Tabari in his *Tarikh* (11:57, *al-Fath*), and Ibn Asakir in his *Tarikh* in the biography of Zayd.

100 Bukhari, *Adab al-Mufrad*. Ibn al-Muqri narrates it in his *Rukhsa* (p. 72 #12). Narrated with a good chain by Ahmad in his *Musnad* (4:54-55). Ibn Hajar in *Fath al-bari* (11:57) declared its chain good (*jayyid*), and Haythami in *Majma al-zawaid* (8:42) declared its narrators all trustworthy, while Albani declared Bukhari's hadith fair (*hasan*) in his *Sahih al-adab al-mufrad* (p. 372 #747)!

101 Ibn al-Muqri related it with a sound chain.

102 Bukhari, *al-Adab al-mufrad*. al-Muqri also narrates it through Sulayman ibn Ayyub and through a third chain from his shaykh al-Tahawi in *al-Rukhsa fi taqbil al-yad* (p. 73 #13, p. 76 #15).

103 Albani, *Daif al-adab al-mufrad* (p. 89 #155).

Hibban accepted him as trustworthy and al-Dhahabi did not contradict him. Even if this were not the case, Suhayb could not be "not known" as a narrator because the trustworthy narrated from him, such as Abu Salih Dhakwan, al-Mujmir Nuaym ibn Abd Allah, Shuba, Amr ibn Murra, al-Tahawi, and others. Sakhawi said, Daraqutni said, "One from whom two trustworthy narrators (thiqatan) take hadith, his state of "unknowness" (jahalatuhu) is lifted, and his credibility is established."[104] The same was declared by al-Dhuhli, who said "if two or more narrate from him,"[105] and Ibn Abd al-Barr, who said "three or two."[106]

Furthermore, the position of the majority of the hadith authorities is that, if a narrator is not explicitly declared daif in the books of weak narrators, the narrator is considered trustworthy. This was the method followed by the hafiz Haythami, Ibn Daqiq al-Id, al-Mundhiri, al-Zaylai, Majd al-Din Ibn Taymiyya (the grandfather), al-Dhahabi, Ibn Abd al-Hadi, Ibn Qayyim, Ibn Kathir, al-Zarkashi, Shawkani, Ibn Hajar al-Asqalani, and Sakhawi. It is also the method followed by contemporary scholars, including: Shaykh Ahmad Shakir, Shaykh Zafar Ahmad al-Tahanawi, Shaykh Habib al-Rahman al-Azami of India, Shaykh Muhammad Abd al-Rashid al-Numani of Karachi, Shaykh Muhammad Taqi al-Uthmani of Karachi, Shaykh Ismail al-Ansari of Riyadh, and Shaykh Abd Allah ibn al-Siddiq al-Ghumari.[107] Thus Albani cannot declare the entire narration weak on the sole basis of Suhayb's incorrect grading. According to the above criteria, Suhayb is instead a reliable narrator, the chain is sound, and the hadith is authentic.

Bukhari,[108] Ahmad,[109] and Ibn Abi Umar al-Adani[110] also narrate, through Sufyan ibn Uyayna, that Thabit al-Bunani the tabii would come to Anas and kiss his hand because it had touched the Prophet's hand.[111]

---

104 Sakhawi, Fath al-mughith (p. 137).

105 Al-Khatib in al-Kifaya (p. 88).

106 Ibn Abd al-Barr's commentary on Malik's Muwatta. Ibn Abd al-Barr, al-Istidhkar in the chapter entitled Tark al-wudu mimma massathu al-nar.

107 As shown by the late Shaykh Abd al-Fattah Abu Ghudda – rahimahullah – in his marginalia on Abd al-Hayy Lucknawi's al-Raf wa al-takmil fi al-jarh wa al-tadil (p. 232-248).

108 Bukhari, Adab al-mufrad.

109 Ahmad, Musnad (3:111).

110 Ibn Abi Umar al-Adani, Musnad (#19).

111 Ibn al-Muqri cites it in al-Rukhsa (p. 79 #19). The ruling by Albani that this narration is weak (cf. his Daif al-adab al-mufrad p. 88 #153) is rejected, since the

Jamila, Anas ibn Malik's freedwoman and the mother of his child, relates that Anas would say whenever Thabit visited him, "O *jariya*, bring me some perfume for my hand, because whenever Thabit comes he does not accept not to kiss my hand and he says, It is a hand that touched the hand of Allah's Messenger."[112]

This hadith constitutes an important basis for the merit of companionship with those who kept companionship with the Prophet (ﷺ). The practice of obtaining blessing through this means undoubtedly continues in our time. As the Prophet (ﷺ) said, "*Tuba li man raani wa li man raa man raani wa li man raa man raa man raani* (blessed is the one who saw me, and the one who saw the one who saw me, and the one who saw the one who saw the one who saw me."[113] That this blessing still applies in our time is proven by a similar narration: "Blessed once is the one who saw me and believed in me, and blessed seven times is the one who did not see me and believed in me (*tuba li man raani wa amana bi marratan wa tuba li man lam yarani wa amana bi saba marrat*)."[114]

That Anas scented his hand for greeting others is confirmed by Bukhari's narration from Thabit al-Bunani that, "Whenever Anas rose in the morning he would daub his hand with perfume for shaking hands with his brothers."[115]

Mubarak ibn Aqil Abu Sakhr said: I heard Thabit al-Bunani say, "Whenever I visited Anas ibn Malik I would take his hand and kiss it and say, My father for these two hands which touched Allah's Messenger! Then I would kiss his eyes and say, 'My father for these two eyes which saw Allah's Messenger!'"[116]

The Prophet (ﷺ) spoke of Thabit's example when he said, "Among those of my Community who love me most intensely

account is confirmed by the following three sound narrations and therefore it is *sahih li ghayrih*.

112 Narrated with a sound *(sahih)* chain by Ibn al-Muqri in *al-Rukhsa* (p. 68 #7), al-Musili in his *Musnad*, and Abu Nuaym in *Hilyat al-awliya* (2:327) under Thabit al-Bunani's biography.

113 Albani included it among the sound narrations of his *Silsila sahiha* (#1254)!

114 Narrated with a sound chain by Ibn Hibban in his *Sahih*, Ahmad in his *Musnad* (3:71, 5:248, 5:264), al-Hakim in his *Mustadrak*, Tabarani in *al-Kabir* (8:311), Haythami in *Majma al-zawaid* (10:20, 10:67) and others.

115 Bukhari, *al-Adab al-mufrad* with a sound chain. Albani included it in his *Sahih al-adab al-mufrad* (p. 388 #774) and said: *sahih al-isnad!*

116 Al-Haythami in *Majma al-zawaid* (9:325) said: "Its narrators are those of the *sahih* narrations [i.e. retained by Bukhari and Muslim], except Abu Bakr al-

are certain people who will come after me and who would give away their family and property in exchange for seeing me."[117]

Hammad ibn Salama narrated from Thabit al-Bunani that Anas gave an apple to Abu al-Aliya, one of the Tabiin narrators of sound hadith, who began to turn it in his hands and kiss it and place it against his face, saying, "An apple that touched the hand that touched the Prophet's hand."[118]

1.5.5. PRACTICE OF WOMEN KISSING THE PROPHET'S HAND AND FEET FOR BLESSINGS AND TREATING THE WOUNDS OF THE COMPANIONS OUT OF NECESSITY

There are examples in the hadith of the women touching and kissing the hand of the Prophet (ﷺ).

1 Anas ibn Malik related that the slave-women of Madina would **take the hands of the Prophet (ﷺ) and lead him to wherever they pleased.**[119]

Ibn Hajar Asqalani further comments based on hadith from Imam Ahmad and Ibn Majah (both via Ali ibn Zayd, via Anas) that **the Prophet (ﷺ) would not pull his hand away from them until they led him to wherever they wanted.**[120]

2 Anas reported that when the Prophet (ﷺ) slept, **Umm Salaym would take his sweat and hair** and collect it into a glass bottle and mix it with perfume. The Prophet (ﷺ) asked her what she was doing and she responded, "**We hope for its blessing for our children.**" The Prophet (ﷺ) replied, "**Correct (asabti).**"[121] In Bukhari it is mentioned that Anas asked that at the time of his death some of Umm Salaym's perfume that she had mixed with the Prophet's sweat be applied to his body after it was washed and this was granted to him.[122]

3 Anas narrated that his maternal aunt, Umm Haram bint Milhan, would serve food to the Prophet (ﷺ) and clean his hair

---

Muqaddami, and he is trustworthy *(thiqa)*." That is: the chain is sound. Ibn al-Muqri narrates it partially in *al-Rukhsa fi taqbil al-yad* (p. 78 #18).

117 Muslim narrated it in his *Sahih*, book of "Paradise and its bliss and people."

118 Narrated with a sound chain by Ibn al-Irabi in his book *al-Qubal* as well as Ibn Asakir in his *Tarikh* (8:331 *Mukhtasar*).

119 *Sahih Bukhari, Kitab al-Adab*, Chapter *al-Kibr* part 13, p. 102.

120 *Fath al-bari*, part 13, p. 102..

121 *Sahih Muslim, Kitab al-fadail*, Chapter, "The Goodness of the Sweat of the Prophet and the Seeking of Blessings Through It," part 7, p. 82.

122 *Sahih Bukhari, Kitab al-istidhan*, Chapter, "Who Visits a People and Sleeps There," part 13, p. 312.

when he entered the place where she stayed.[123]

4 A woman complained about her husband to the Prophet (ﷺ) so he called for them. They met, and afterwards **she kissed the Prophet's feet.**[124]

5 Salma reported that whenever the Prophet (ﷺ) had an ulcer or boil, **he would order her to apply henna to it**.[125]

6 Abdallah ibn Muhammad ibn Abdallah Ibn Zayd by a woman among them reported that the Prophet (ﷺ) saw her eating with her left hand (she was left handed) so **he tapped her hand** and the food fell from it. He said, "Do not eat with your left hand while Allah has given you a right hand," or "while Allah Almighty has made your right hand free." She said, "My left hand became my right and I did not eat with it afterwards."[126]

7 Rubayya bint Muawwidh reported that the women would go to battle with the Prophet (ﷺ). **They would give water to the men, take care of their wounds, and return the wounded and dead to Madina.**[127]

8 Abu Musa narrated that after breaking his state of consecration (*ihram*) for the pilgrimage, he went to a woman from his community **who combed his hair** or **washed his head**.[128]

Ibn Hajar Asqalani said it appeared to him that she was his sister-in-law.[129]

1.5.6. *FATAWA* AND PRACTICES OF THE *TABIIN* AND MAJOR RELIGIOUS SCHOLARS (*ULAMA*) ON KISSING THE HAND OF A JUST LEADER OF MUSLIMS

Khaythama (d. 85), Talha ibn Musarrif (d. 112), Malik ibn Mighwal (d. 159): Malik heard from Talha, "Khaythama [ibn

123 *Sahih Bukhari, Kitab al-jihad*, Chapter, "The Calling to Jihad and the Martyrdom of Men and Women," part 6 p. 350.

124 Narrated by Bayhaqi in *Dalail al-nubuwwa* from Ibn Umar and Abu Yala and Abu Naim from Jabir ibn Abdallah.

125 In Tirmidhi, section on *tibb*, (medicine).

126 In Imam Ahmad's *Musnad al-madaniyyin* and *Musnad al-ansar*. Ibn Hajar Haythami said Ahmad's men are trustworthy. *Majma al-zawaid*, prt 5, p. 26.

127 *Sahih Bukhari, Kitab al-jihad*, Chapter "Women Treating the Injured in Battle," part 6, p. 420.

128 *Sahih Bukhari, Kitab al-hajj*, Chapter "From the People of the Time of the Prophet," part 4, p. 161. *Sahih Muslim, Kitab al-hajj*, Chapter, "*Fi faskh al-tahlil min al-ihram*," part 4, p. 44.

129 *Fath al-bari*, part 4, p. 161.

Abd al-Rahman al-Jufi] kissed my hand" and Malik added, "And Talha kissed my hand."[130]

Tamim ibn Salama (d. 100), "It is *sunna.*"[131]

Al-Hasan al-Basri (d. 110), "It is *taa*" (an act of obedience to Allah).[132]

Sufyan al-Thawri (d. 161), "It is *sunna*"[133] (*la basa bih*).[134]

Malik (d. 179), *ankarahu.* He condemned it in a worldly context. However, he deemed it *jaiz*, or permissible for the pious scholar.[135]

Musa ibn Dawud al-Dubbi (d. 217) said, "I was with Sufyan ibn Uyayna (d. 198) when Husayn ibn Ali al-Jufi (d. 203) came, and Sufyan stood up and kissed his hand."[136]

Sufyan ibn Uyayna and Fudayl ibn Iyad (d. 187) kissed the hand and foot of Husayn ibn Ali al-Jufi respectively.[137]

Sulayman ibn Harb (d. 224), "It is the minor prostration" (*al-sajda al-sughra*)–i.e. it is disliked.[138]

Ahmad (d. 241), "There is no harm in it (*la basa bih*)."[139]

10 Imam Muslim (d. 261) when he met Imam Bukhari (d. 256) said to him: "Let me kiss your feet, O professor of the two professors (*dani hatta uqabbila rijlayka ya ustadh al-ustadhayn)*".[140]

Ibn Battal (d. 449), "*Mustahabb* (desirable)."[141]

Ghazali (d. 505), ""There is no harm in it (*la basa bih)*.."[142]

Nawawi (d. 676), "*Mustahabb* (desirable)."[143]

---

130 Ibn Abi Shayba in the *Musannaf* (8:750) and Ibn al-Irabi in *al-Qubal* narrate it from Sufyan ibn Uyayna with a sound chain.

131 See his narration above.

132 Ibn Muflih, *al-Adab* 2:271.

133 Ibn al-Muqri *al-Rukhsa* p. 70 #10 through Abu Hatim al-Razi.

134 Ahmad, *al-Wara* #512.

135 Related by Ibn Battal and al-Abhari as well as Ibn Hajar.

136 Narrated with sound chains by Ibn Sad in his *Tabaqat* (6:397 "Husayn al-Jufi") and Ibn al-Irabi in *al-Qubal*. Also al-Mizzi in *al-Tahdhib* (6:452) and al-Dhahabi in the *Siyar* (9:398).

137 Ibn Muflih relates it in *al-Adab al-shariyya* (2:272) from Ibn al-Jawzi in his *Manaqib ashab al-hadith*.

138 Ahmad, *al-Wara* #513.

139 Ahmad, *Kitab al-wara* (p. 113 #509-510), and Ibn Muflih, *al-Adab* (2:270).

140 It is narrated by al-Khatib in his *Tarikh* (13:102), al-Hakim in *al-Tarikh* and *Marifat ulum al-hadith*, Bayhaqi in *al-Madkhal*, Ibn Hajar in *Hadi al-Sari* (p. 488) and his *Nukat* (2:717-719), as well as al-Subki in the chapter of Bukhari in *Tabaqat al-Shafiiyya*, and Ibn al-Muqri (d. 381) in the introduction to his *al-Rukhsa fi taqbil al-yad* (Riyad ed. 1987).

141 Related by Ibn Hajar in *Fath al-bari* (1989 ed. 11:67).

142 Ghazali, *Ihya Ulum ad-din (Kitab al-adab)*.

143 Nawawi, *Fatawa* and Ibn Hajar's *Fath al-bari* 11:67.

Al-Zaylai al-Hanafi (d. 742) said:[144]

> In [Muhammad ibn Hasan al-Shaybani's] *al-Jami al-saghir*, "It is disliked that the man kiss the mouth of another man, or his hand, or any other part of him, or that he hug him." Tahawi said that this is the saying of Abu Hanifa and Muhammad while Abu Yusuf said, "*La basa bi al-taqbil wa al-muanaq*a (there is no harm in kissing and hugging)." They said that the divergence is only insofar as they are unclothed other than with a lower garment: otherwise then there is no harm in it by consensus. That is what the Shaykh chose in his *Mukhtasar*, while Imam Abu Mansur al-Maturidi eliminated the discrepancy by saying that what is disliked is what is done for the purpose of pleasure (*shahwa*), while what is done out of piety (*birr*) and courtesy (*ikram*) then it is allowed (*jaiz*). The sun of Imams, al-Sarakhsi (d. 490) and some of the late authorities allowed the kissing of the scholar's hand and that of the Godwary person (*al-mutawarri*) for the purpose of deriving blessing (*ala sabil al-tabarruk*) . . . and Sufyan al-Thawri said, "Kissing the scholars or the just sultan's hand is a *sunna*."

Hafiz al-Dhahabi (d. 748) writes, in the compendium of his shaykhs:[145]

The Companions saw the Prophet (ﷺ) with their very eyes when he was alive, enjoyed his presence directly, kissed his very hand, almost fought with each other over the remnants of his ablution water, shared his purified hair on the day of the greater pilgrimage, and even if he spat it would virtually not fall except in someone's hand so that he could pass it over his face . . . Don't you see what Thabit al-Bunani did when he kissed the hand of Anas ibn Malik and placed it on his face saying, "This is the hand that touched the hand of Allah's Messenger?" Muslims are not moved to these matters except by their excessive love for the Prophet (ﷺ), as they are ordered to

---

144 Al-Zaylai al-Hanafi, *Tabyin al-haqaiq : sharh Kanz al-daqaiq* (6:25) [a commentary on Nasafi (d. 709)].

145 Al-Dhahabi, *Mujam al-shuyukh* (1:73) in the entry devoted to his *shaykh* Ahmad ibn Abd al-Munim al-Qazwini (#58).

love Allah and the Prophet (ﷺ) more than they love their own lives, their children, all human beings, their property, and paradise and its maidens. There are even some believers that love Abu Bakr and Umar more than themselves . . . Don't you see that the Companions, in the excess of their love for the Prophet (ﷺ), asked him, "Should we not prostrate to you?" And he replied no, and if he had allowed them, they would have prostrated to him as a mark of utter veneration and respect, not as a mark of worship, just as the Prophet Joseph's brothers prostrated to Joseph (ﷺ)" (12:100).[146]

Dhahabi also states, with reference to *ziyara*:[147]

> Al-Hasan ibn al-Hasan ibn Ali relates that he saw a man standing in front of the house that contains the grave of the Prophet (ﷺ), invoking Allah's blessings upon him, whereupon he said to the man, "Don't do that, for Allah's Messenger said, 'Do not make (the visit to) my grave an anniversary festival, and do not turn your houses into graves. Invoke blessings upon me wherever you are, for your invocation reaches me.'" This narration is *mursal* (missing one or more links to the Prophet (ﷺ), and what al-Hasan adduced in his *fatwa* is completely worthless as a proof, because one who stands at the holy *hujra* (room of the Prophet (ﷺ) in all humility and submission, invoking blessings upon his Prophet (ﷺ), O how blessed that one is! For he has made his visitation excellent, and beautified it with humbleness and love, and he has performed more worship than the one who invoked blessings on the Prophet (ﷺ) from his own land or in his prayer. The reason is that the one who performs *ziyara* has both the reward of visiting him and that of invoking blessings upon him; while those who invoke blessings upon him from all over the world only have the reward of invoking blessings upon him; and upon whoever invokes blessings once, Allah sends ten blessings. But the person who visits the Prophet (ﷺ) and does not observe decorum in his visitation, or prostrates to the grave, or does something outside the Law, such a person has done both good and bad. He must be taught gently. Allah is forgiving and merciful.

146 End of Dhahabi's words in *Mujam al-shuyukh al-kabir*.
147 Dhahabi, in *Siyar alam al-nubala* (4:483-485).

By Allah! The Muslim is not moved to distraction and lamentation and kissing the walls and weeping much, except because he is a lover of Allah and of His Prophet (ﷺ). His love is the standard and the distinguishing mark between the people of paradise and the people of hellfire. The visit to his grave is among the best of the acts that draw near to Allah, and as for travelling to visit the graves of prophets and saints, even if we should concede that there is no authorization for it due to the general sense of the Prophet's saying, "Mounts are not saddled except to go to three mosques," nevertheless saddling the mounts to go visit the Prophet (ﷺ) is intrinsic to saddling them to go visit his mosque—which is sanctioned by the Law without contest—for there is no access to his chambers (*hujra*) except after entering his mosque. Therefore let his visitor begin by greeting the mosque, then turn to greet the master of the mosque. May Allah grant us this, and also to you. Amin!"

Ibn Abidin al-Hanafi (d. 1252) said:

There is no harm in kissing the scholar's hand and that of the Godwary man for the purpose of deriving blessing, and it has been said that it is *sunna*. Kissing the scholars and the Godwary person's head is better . . . Kissing the hand of one's friend upon meeting him is disliked by consensus. As for kissing the ground in front of the *ulama* or dignitaries it is forbidden (*haram*), and both the doer and the one who approves it commit a sin, because it resembles idolworship.[148]

Ibrahim ibn Muhammad al-Bajuri al-Shafii (d. 1276) said, "Kissing the righteous man's hand, the scholars, and the ascetic, is *sunna*, while kissing the hand of the rich or influential man is disliked. It is narrated: "Whoever abases himself for a rich man because of his wealth, two thirds of his religion have left him."[149]

---

148 Ibn Abidin al-Hanafi in *Hashiyat radd al-muhtar ala al-durr al-mukhtar* (5:244-246).
149 Ibrahim ibn Muhammad al-Bajuri al-Shafii, in his supercommentary on al-Ghazzi's (d. 917) commentary on Abu Shuja (Ahmad ibn al-Husayn al-Asfahani) entitled *Hashiyat al-bajuri ala sharh ibn al-qasim al-ghazzi ala matn abi shuja* (2:116).

1.6. ABOUT THE CULTURAL PRACTICE OF KISSING FEET OUT OF RESPECT

There is a huge distinction between kissing someone's feet and prostrating. The principle of prostration is to put the forehead on the ground with the Islamic belief that one are doing this in worship of Allah Almighty; praying and prostrating to Him, accepting Him as the Creator and considering oneself His Servant. He is the One Who gives benefit and the One Who can give harm.

If a person bent down to the ground to pick up a stone it does not mean he is performing a prostration to the stone. If a human being prostrated to another human being, held him in the same rank as Allah, considered him to be his creator, and believed that person could harm and benefit him in the same way as Allah, then it is unbelief and no Muslim is doing that.

If anyone claims that it is idolatry (*shirk*) for a child to kiss the feet of his father, for a student to kiss the feet of his teacher, or for Imam Muslim to kiss the feet of Imam Bukhari, then it must also be *shirk* that the angels prostrated to Adam (ﷺ) and Jacob (ﷺ) prostrated to Joseph (ﷺ).

And he placed his parents on the dais and they fell down before him prostrate, and he said: O my father! This is the interpretation of my dream of old. My Lord hath made it true, and He hath shown me kindness, since He took me out of the prison and hath brought you from the desert after satan had made strife between me and my brethren. Lo! my Lord is tender unto whom He will. He is the Knower, the Wise (12:100).

The prostration by the angels and the family of Joseph were mentioned as such (*sajda*), but, in these cases, they were not the prostration of worship, but the prostration of honor. The latter is not the same as the prostration of worship by any means, and is only for the purpose of respect. If it were an indication of worship, Allah would never order it, for Allah never orders something wrong. One cannot say that angels received Allah's permission to worship Adam, nor that Jacob's prostration constituted worship of Joseph. As Allah said, *"Allah does not countenance disbelief for His servants."* Thus it is clear that these two prostrations can only be prostrations of honor and respect, not prostrations that would indicate disbelief.

In the same way, kissing the hands and feet of elders or scholars out of respect can never be considered *shirk* nor *kufr*.

To conclude, Allah said, "*Above every knowledgeable one there is one with more knowledge*" (12:76). Respect for the people of knowledge in Islam, the *ulama*, is based upon the recognition that they stand above us by virtue of their effort (*ijtihad*), and renunciation of worldly pursuits (*zuhd*) towards the acquisition of the highest knowledge (*al-ilm*). The above verse illustrates that there are innumerable ranks and levels of knowledge in the sight of Allah.

The warning for every individual to acknowledge his ignorance in relation to someone more knowledgeable is given, in the Quran, in the form of a rhetorical question: "*Are the knowledgeable equal with the ignorant?*" (39:9). Of course they are not. Allah further addresses the ignorant by telling them to ask those who know: "*Ask the People of Remembrance if you do not know*" (16:43). One cannot ask sincerely and, at the same time, claim equal status with, or withhold respect from, the one who holds the answer. Respect for the people of knowledge is therefore at the foundation of religion, because knowledge is the foundation of religion. Knowledge has been handed down from the more knowledgeable to the less knowledgeable from the time of the Prophet (ﷺ), when he gave his knowledge to the Companions.

The *ulama*, religious scholars, are the guardians of Islamic knowledge from preceding generations. As such, they should be respected, obeyed, and even cherished and revered by Muslims —as they have traditionally been in fourteen centuries of Islamic culture. Kissing their hands is but an elementary and ordinary expression of this system of values. Their fellowship should be sought, their advice heeded, and their supplication requested, because all three are ways of receiving mercy from Allah Most High. They should receive every mark of courtesy and every affordable service, for even a kind look towards a religious scholar's face will receive its reward.

It is not the mark of Muslims to injure or abolish the honor and rank of the *ulama*. Therefore those who scoff at the rank or grade given by Allah to His *ulama*, deny them their extra respect, and consider them ordinary people, are only injuring themselves and those who follow them.

1.7. PRESCRIBED PRAYER (*SALAT*) OTHER THAN IN CONGREGATION (*JAMAA*) IS ACCEPTABLE ACCORDING TO MAINSTREAM ISLAM

Q. Is prayer other than in congregation unacceptable?

The majority of the scholars regard prayer in congregation a strong tradition (*sunna*), not an obligation. Shawkani said, "It [congregational prayer] is neither a *fard ayn*, nor a *fard kifaya*, nor a condition for the validity of one's prescribed prayer (*salat*)."[150]

1.7.1. ALBANI DECLARES THAT PRESCRIBED PRAYER OTHER THAN IN CONGREGATION IN THE MOSQUE IS UNACCEPTABLE

> Prayer in *Jamaaah* is acceptable only if he prays it with the Muslim congregation in the mosque— since Allaah taaalaa did not only order Prayer but also added to it—And bow down your heads with those who bow down (in worship). [2:43] - and he is not allowed to suffice with praying in his home and leave the *Jamaaah* of the Muslims. And the Messenger ordered every fit and well Muslim to pray in the Mosque and desired to burn those who remained in their houses—as occurs in *Saheeh al-Bukhaaree* and *Saheeh Muslim* from Aboo Hurairah (R). He (S) did not burn the houses because of the presence of women and children on whom Prayer in the mosque is not obligatory.

1.7.2. EXPLANATION ACCORDING TO MAINSTREAM ISLAM

The above is by and large incorrect, as the Prophet (ﷺ) did not seek to burn Muslims who remained in their houses, but

---

150 See Shawkani, *Nayl al-awtar* (3:129).

those known as hypocrites. This is established by the detailed explanation of this hadith, its numerous narrations, and by other, similar narrations.[151] As for the hadith of not burning the houses because of women and children, it is *daif*, or weak, as stated by Shawkani.

1.8. PRAYING THE NOON PRESCRIBED PRAYER (*SALAT AL-ZUHR*) AFTER FRIDAY CONGREGATIONAL PRAYER (*SALAT AL-JUMA*) ACCORDING TO MAINSTREAM ISLAM

Q. Is it necessary to pray the noon prescribed prayer (*salat al-zuhr*) after finishing Friday congregational prescribed prayer (*salat al-juma*)? What are the conditions for the validity of Friday congregational prescribed prayer (*salat al-juma*)?

Friday congregational prescribed prayer (*salat al-juma*) pre-empts the regular noon prescribed prayer (*zuhr*). However, in the absence of a valid Friday congregation prescribed prayer (*salat al-juma*), the obligation of the noon prescribed prayer (*zuhr*) stands. Therefore the question is, when is the Friday congregational prescribed prayer (*salat al-juma*) valid? If the Friday congregational prayer (*juma*) is prayed in a single congregation in the country, then it is valid by consensus of the jurists, and the noon prescribed prayer (*zuhr*) is neither required nor even permitted for anyone. However, if there are many Friday congregational prescribed prayers (*juma*) in many different parts of every country and district as is the case nowadays, then doubt arises as to the validity of the Friday congregational prescribed prayer (*salat al-juma*). Therefore it is recommended or rather required to pray the noon prescribed prayer (*zuhr*) after the Friday congregational prescribed prayer (*juma*) according to mainstream Islam.

Ibn Qudama al-Hanbali said:[152]

> Abu Hanifa, Malik, and al-Shafii said, "The Friday congregational prescribed prayer (*juma*) in a single country is impermissible in more than one

---

151 Such as Ibn Hajar in *Fath al-bari* and Shawkani in *Nayl al-awtar*.
152 Al-Hanbali, *al-Mughni* (1994 ed. 2:211).

place." This is because the Prophet (ﷺ) did not have it held except in a single mosque, nor did the rightly-guided caliphs after him. If it were permissible they would not have closed down the mosques [at the time of the Friday congregational prescribed prayer (*juma*)]. Ibn Umar even said, "Friday congregational prescribed prayer (*juma*) is not established except in the greatest mosque in which the Imam [i.e. the ruler] prays."

The Hanbali view is similar. The following is an overview of mainstream Islam's position on this issue as detailed by al-Zuhayli,[153] al-Jaziri,[154] and the jurists of the schools.

In the Hanafi school all Friday congregational prescribed prayers are valid, even if several are prayed in a single area in order not to cause difficulties, but it is better to pray four cycles (*rakat*) with the intention of the noon (*zuhr al-akhira*) afterwards [= "the last *zuhr* due"]. However, if it is ascertained that the Friday congregational prescribed prayer in which one prayed was not the first in one's district or city, then it becomes required (*wajib*) for one to pray four cycles (*rakat*) of the noon prescribed prayer (*zuhr*). It is abominable (*makruh tahrimi*) to pray the noon (*zuhr*) prescribed prayer in congregation in the mosque. The recommended course is therefore two cycles of the Friday congregational prayer, then four cycles of *sunna* after the Friday congregational one and four cycles (*rakat*) for the noon prescribed prayer (individually) and two *sunna* after the noon prescribed prayer (*zuhr*).

The one Friday prayer (*juma*) that has uncontested validity in the Hanafi school is prayed behind the Sultan of Muslims, and this is a pillar (*rukn*) upon which the Friday congregational prescribed prayer (*juma*) is conditional. Al-Sarakhsi said:[155]

> The external conditions of the Friday congregational prescribed prayer (*juma*) are: (1) that it be held in a city; (2) that it be held in its time; (3) that the sermon (*khutba*) be delivered; (4) that there be a congregation (*jamaa*) [minimum Imam and two men]; (5) that the Sultan lead or be represented; (6) that there be general feasibility to hold it.

153 Al-Zuhayli, *al-Fiqh al-islami wa adillatuh* (2:310-311).
154 Al-Jaziri, *al-Fiqh ala al-madhahib al-arbaa* (*Kitab al-salat* p. 385-386).
155 Al-Sarakhsi, *al-Mabsut* (2:23-24).

Al-Sarakhsi also said:[156]

> What is authentically reported from Abu Hanifa and Muhammad is that it is permitted to hold the Friday congregational prayer (*juma*) in two places of the same city, or more. There are two opinions related from Abu Yusuf; the first states that it is permitted to hold *juma* in two places at most, the second states that it is not permitted to hold it in more than one place in the same city unless the city is divided by a huge river, as in Baghdad. This gives each side the legal status of a separate city. The perspective for this narration is that in the time of the Prophet (ﷺ) and the caliphs after him, when the cities were conquered, none of them used more than a single mosque for *juma* in each city.

In the Maliki school, the valid Friday congregational prescribed prayer (*juma*) in a city is the one prayed in the first congregational mosque where the Friday congregational prescribed prayer (*juma*) was ever prayed. All other congregations must pray the noon prescribed prayer (*zuhr*). However, the Friday congregational prescribed prayer (*juma*) may become valid in another mosque if people use it for a good reason; such as: (1) having abandoned the old one; (2) if the old one cannot accommodate the number of worshippers, including those upon whom the Friday congregational prescribed prayer (*juma*) is not incumbent; (3) if there is no fear that dissension or corruption arise from the gathering of all the people in a single spot; (4) if the ruler has decreed the validity of the Friday congregational prescribed prayer (*juma*) in a new mosque.

In the Shafii school, the valid Friday congregational prescribed prayer (*juma*) is the first one as defined by the precedence of *takbirat al-ihram*—in any given city or district. This in accordance with the hadith, "The Friday congregational prescribed prayer goes to the first (*al-jumua li man sabaq*)." The other valid congregations in the city or district are recommended to pray the noon prescribed prayer (*zuhr*) since they were not the first group to pray. However, since none of the valid congregations in a city know who was first to start pray-

156 *Ibid* 2:120-121.

ing, it is therefore recommended for all of the valid congregations in the city to pray the noon prescribed prayer (*zuhr*) also.
A valid congregation is in a large major mosque, but not in the
smaller neighborhood mosques or in homes, etc. When there is
difficulty in reaching the main congregation, *salat al-juma* may
be prayed, but these other small *juma*s are considered invalid
and their congregations must pray the noon prescribed prayer
(*zuhr*) as an obligation.

Al-Rabi said:[157]

> Al-Shafii told us: If the country grows in size and
> its buildings become numerous, and many mosques
> are built, both large and small, it is not granted, in
> my view, to pray [i.e. *juma*] except in the greatest
> mosque in the country. The same applies for the small
> villages which are linked to it: I do not like for them
> except to pray [*juma*] in the largest mosque as well,
> and prayer in other mosques must be four *rakat* of
> *zuhr*. If those still pray *juma* then let them pray it
> over [i.e. as *zuhr*] . . . If someone other than the Imam
> [i.e. the ruler] prays *juma* in the largest mosque while
> the Imam prays it in a smaller one, the latter is
> granted while the other must repeat it [as *zuhr*].

Siraj al-Din al-Bulqini commented on the above: The view
that is relied upon is what Shafii stated elsewhere, namely
that the first *juma* is the valid one.

Al-Misri said:[158]

> In places where having everyone assemble in one
> location is a hardship, as in Cairo or Baghdad, it is
> valid to hold as many Friday prayers as are needed.
> In places where it poses no hardship, such as Makka
> or Madina, if two Friday prayers are held, the first of
> them [to open with *Allahu akbar*] is the Friday
> prayer, and the second is invalid [and must be
> reprayed as a noon prayer]. If two are held in such a
> place and it is not clear which was first, they should
> start over together as one Friday prayer.

In the Hanbali school, the Friday congregational prescribed

---

157 Al-Rabi, *Kitab al-umm* ((Azhar ed.) 1/2:193).
158 Al-Misri, *Umdat al-salik*.

prayer (*juma*) in which the country's ruler is present is the valid one, whether prayed first or not, and all others are invalid and must pray the noon prescribed prayer (*zuhr*). If the number of Friday congregational prescribed prayers is due to a valid reason, such as lack of space, then they are also valid. However, it is still preferable (*awla*) for them to pray the noon prescribed prayer (*zuhr*) afterwards. If the ruler permits other mosques to hold the Friday congregational prescribed prayer (*juma*), or if he gave no explicit permission one way or the other, then whatever Friday congregational prescribed prayer is prayed first is the valid one and others must pray the noon prescribed prayer (*zuhr*). In case of doubt as to precedence they must either repeat the Friday congregational prescribed prayer (*juma*) or else pray the noon prescribed prayer (*zuhr*).

Ibn Qudama said:[159]

> If there is no need for more than one mosque, then the Friday congregational prescribed prayer (*juma*) is not permitted to be held in others. If there is no need for more than two, then it is not permitted in the third, etc. . . . . If they prayed two Friday congregational prescribed prayers in a city unnecessarily, one of them with the Imam [i.e. ruler], then the latter Friday congregational prescribed prayer (*juma*) is the valid one whether it was prayed first or second, and the other is invalid. . . . . This is the more correct view. . . . But if there is no such distinction between the two [i.e. the presence of the Imam], then only the one that is prayed first is the valid one. . . and if both *takbirat al-ihram* are simultaneous then both Friday congregational prescribed prayers are invalid . . . while if they are certain of the validity of one of the two, then the others can only pray the noon prescribed prayer (*zuhr*).

There is no definite evidence on this issue and it is open to *ijtihad*. Consequently there is a variety of different opinions. Ibn Hajar counted sixteen different views among the jurists. The Hanafi school has the two most permissive views: no less than two [for Abu Yusuf and in one opinion of Muhammad] or

159 Ibn Qudama, *al-Mughni* (2:212-213).

three [for Abu Hanifa and another opinion of Muhammad] males + the imam is needed for a valid Friday congregational prescribed prayer (*juma*). The prevailing view considering the evidence (*al-arjah min hayth al-dalil*), according to Ibn Hajar,[160] is probably that the congregation must consist in a very large group without specifics of number.

1.9. SECLUSION (*ITIKAF*) IN OTHER THAN THE THREE HOLY MOSQUES IS ACCEPTABLE IN MAINSTREAM ISLAM

Q. Is seclusion in a mosque during the last ten days of Ramadan (*itikaf*) only to be performed in one of the three mosques (Makka, Madina and Aqsa) and not in any other?

Bukhari said, "*Itikaf* **is possible in ALL mosques**" and made this unambiguous, sweeping statement part of the title of the first chapter of the book of *itikaf* in his *Sahih*. This is also the position of Malik and al-Shafii. Ibn Qudama said Malik said, "*Itikaf* is correct and sound in any mosque whatsoever, because of the generality of Allah's saying, '*While you are in retreat in the mosques*' (2:187)." This is the position of al-Shafii also, as long as one's retreat does not keep him from attending the Friday congregational prescribed prayer (*salat al-juma*).

The Malikis also allowed *itikaf* in the mosque of one's home —both for men and women. The Hanafis restricted the permissibility of *itikaf* in the mosque in the home to women only, although all hold it permissible for them in the mosques as well as the men, since the Prophet's wives performed it.[161]

1.9.1. ALBANI INCORRECTLY RESTRICTS SECLUSION (*ITIKAF*) TO THE THREE HOLY MOSQUES

The "Salafis" misinterpret Itikaf to be restricted to only the three holy mosques. The following is found in the book *The Night Prayer* (*qiyam* and *tarawih*), which is based on the writings of Albani and others.

---

160 As quoted by Shawkani in *Nayl al-awtar* (3:232).

161 Sources besides those quoted: Ibn Rushd, *Bidayat al-mujtahid* (1:202-203); Ibn Hazm, *al-Muhalla* (p. 633); Ibn Qudama, *al-Mughni* (3:169 / 1994 ed. 3:133). The reader is also directed to Shaykh Hasan al-Saqqaf's book *al-Lajif al-dhuaf li al-mutalaib bi ahkam al-itikaf* (The lethal strike against the one who toys with the rulings of *itikaf*).

1.9.1.1. A MOSQUE WHERE FRIDAY CONGREGATIONAL PRAYER IS PERFORMED
A Mosque Of Jumuah

Itikaaf may only be performed in a masjid, as is indicated in the above *aayah* from al-Baqarah (2:187). Also, Aaishah (*radhi Allaahu anh*) said:

It is recommended for the one performing *itikaaf* not to leave (the *masjid*) except for an essential need, not to visit a sick person, and not to touch or sleep with his wife. *Itikaaf* may only be performed in a *masjid* where the *jamaah* prayer is performed [or where *Jumuah* (Friday prayer) is offered]. And it is recommended for the one performing *itikaaf* to fast." [*]

[*] Recorded by al-Bayhaqee with an authentic chain of narrators, and Abu Daawood with a good chain. The part between square brackets is from the latter.

Thus, *itikaaf* must be performed in a *masjid* where the *Jumuah* is held. This insures that one would not need to exit from it to attend the *Jumuah* prayer, which is an obligation on him.

1.9.1.2. THE THREE SACRED MOSQUES

A clear authentic hadeeth further restricts the *masjid*s in the above *aayah* (2:187) to only three: *al-Masjid ul-Haraam* (the Sacred Mosque of Makkah), al-Masjid un-Nabawee (the Prophets mosque at al-Madeenah), and *al-Masjid ul-Aqsaa* (the Furthest Mosque at Jerusalem):

A group of people performed itikaaf in a masjid between the houses of Abdullaah Bin Masood and Aboo Moosaa al-Asharee in al-Koofah. So, Hudhaifah (*radhi Allaahu anhu*) asked Ibn Masood (*radhi Allaahu anhu*):

"Do you hold the opinion that it is permissible to perform *itikaaf* (at the *masjid*) between your house and Aboo Moosaa's? You know that the Prophet (*sal-lallaahu alaihi wa sallam*) said:

Itikaaf should not be performed except in the Three *Masjid*s."

Ibn Masud replied:

"You may have forgotten (the meaning), and they (who are performing *itikaf* at the other mosque) remembered. Or you may be mistaken, and they be right!" [**]

[**] Recorded by at-Tahawi in *Mushkal al-Athar* (4:20), Al-Dhahabi in *Siyaru alam in-nubala* (15:81), al-Ismaili, and al-Bayhaqi in the *Sunan* (3:316), with an authentic chain from Hudhaifah ibn al-Yaman; it is proven authentic by al-Dhahabi and al-Albani in *Silsilat ul-ahadith al-sahihah* (No. 2786). [End of Albani's words].

Commentary: Ibn Masud's response indicates that he does not deny the authenticity of this hadith, but is only uncertain of its correct meaning. The truth in this case is to adhere to the apparent meaning of this hadith.

A number of scholars among the Salaf have adhered to the text of this hadith; among them are Hudhaifah ibn al-Yaman, Said ibn al-Musayyib, and Ata (although Ata did not mention al-Aqsa). Others among the Salaf hold the opinion that itikaaf may be performed at any mosque of jumah.

1.9.1.3. AT HOME?

Some scholars say that one may even perform itikaaf at the part of one's home which is designated as a prayer-place.

It is obvious that one should follow the opinion that agrees best with the authentic hadith. And Allah knows best.[162]

1.9.2. FURTHER DISCUSSION OF MAINSTREAM ISLAM'S POSITION ON *ITIKAF*

The hadith of Hudhayfa clearly shows that Ibn Masud doubted Hudhayfa's report and instead considered *itikaf* permissible in any mosque. Shawkani pointed out that if it were certain that the Prophet (ﷺ) had mentioned only the three mosques, Ibn Masud would not have doubted it; but he strongly doubted it.[163] This is confirmed by Ibn Hajar when he

---

162 Excerpted from *The Night Prayer / Qiyam and Tarawih*, a compilation from works by Muhammad Nasir ud-Deen al-Albani and other scholars by Muhammad al-Jibali, pages 129-131.

163 Shawkani, *Nayl al-awtar* (2:269).

referred to that hadith saying, "Hudhayfa ibn al-Yaman made it specific to the three mosques." He did not attribute the hadith to the Prophet (ﷺ), because the former is certain while the latter is uncertain.[164] This is also the position of the *fuqaha*, who claim that they always ascribe it to Hudhayfa, not to the Prophet (ﷺ), following the caution of Ibn Masud.

Furthermore, there is a different and sound narration from Hudhayfa whereby he replied to Ibn Masud, without attributing his response to the Prophet (ﷺ), "As for myself, I know that there is no *itikaf* except in a congregational mosque (*illa fi masjid jamaa*)."[165] This echoes the doubt expressed by Hudhayfa in yet another of his narrations whereby he said to Ibn Masud, "You know that Allah's Messenger (ﷺ) said, There is no *itikaf* except in the Three Mosques, or he said, except in a congregational mosque."[166] Shawkani commented, "The doubt expressed in the hadith (i.e. "or he said . . .") weakens the probative choice of one of its alternatives over the other."

Another discrepancy is that the version of Hudhayfa's hadith reported by Haythami from Tabarani[167] with a chain of sound narrators, and cited by Ibn Qudama and Shawkani, stops at Hudhayfa, who does not name the Prophet (ﷺ). Namely, Hudhayfa came to Ibn Masud and said:

> 'There are people who perform *itikaf* (in a mosque) between your house and Abu Musa al-Ashari, will you not forbid it?' Ibn Masud replied, 'Perhaps they are right and you are mistaken, and they remembered while you forgot.' Whereupon Hudhayfa said, 'There is no *itikaf* except in these three mosques: the mosque of Madina, the mosque of Makka, and the mosque of Ilya [al-Quds].'

As for the opinion of Ata, it excluded Masjid al-Aqsa. This contradicts the hadith of Hudhayfa, which is the only basis for Albani's ruling in the first place. Ibn al-Musayyib"s opinion contradicts it even further, since he restricted *itikaf* to the Prophet's mosque alone.

164 Ibn Hajar, *Fath al-bari* (1989 ed. 4:342 Bk. 33 ch.1).
165 Haythami narrated it in *Majma al-zawaid* and Ibn Qudama refers to it in the beginning of the book of *itikaf* in his *Mughni*.
166 Cited by Said ibn al-Musayyib in his *Sunan* and related in *Nayl al-awtar* (4:269).
167 Tabarini, *al-Mujam al-kabir*.

Furthermore, the agreement of the scholars is not, as claimed in absolute terms by the *fatwa* in question, that "*itikaaf* must be performed in a mosque where the Friday congregational prescribed prayer is held," but only that *itikaf* must be in a mosque. The vast majority say that any mosque is adequate, while Abu Hanifa and Ahmad stipulated that it must be in any mosque where congregational prayer (*jamaa*) is held. The latter was also the position of Ibn Umar.[168] However, al-Sanani stated that there is a great divergence of opinion as to whether or not *itikaf* was nullified by one leaving the mosque to attend the Friday congregational prescribed prayer (*juma*).[169] That is, *itikaf* may be performed in a mosque where congregational prayer (*jamaa*) is not held.

1.10. MAINSTREAM ISLAM'S VIEW ON ALLEGIANCE TO IMAMS

Q. What is the Islamic view on allegiance (*baya*) to Imams?

Allah said: *O believers! Obey Allah and obey the Prophet and those in authority among you* (4:59).

According to Jabir ibn Abd Allah, Mujahid, Malik ibn Anas, al-Dahhak, and others, "Those in authority among you" are the scholars and the people of knowledge. Qurtubi also says this, but he prefers the meaning "those in charge of the public affairs of Muslims," i.e. the Sultan and governors.[170] The Prophet (ﷺ) said, as related from Abu Hurayra, "One who obeys me obeys Allah, and one who disobeys me disobeys Allah; and the one who obeys the man in authority obeys me, and the one who disobeys the man of authority, disobeys me."[171]

The Prophet (ﷺ) emphasized that allegiance, fealty, pledge (*baya*) to such as are in authority over the Muslims is an obligation upon all. He said:

> . . . 'There will be no Prophet (ﷺ) after me but there will be successors, and many of them.' They asked, 'What is your order for us?' He said, 'Stand by your pledge to the first one, and then to the first one

168 As related in *Kashf al-ghimma* (1:213).
169 Al-Sanani, *Subul al-salam* (2:686 #657).
170 Qurtubi, *Tafsir*.
171 In Bukhari and Muslim.

(who succeeds him; and so forth). Give them their rights, for verily, Allah will be asking them about their custodianship.'[172]

The Prophet (ﷺ) also said:

He has no faith who does not keep his trust, and he has no religion who does not have a covenant (*la imana li man la amanata lahu wa la dina li man la ahda lahu*).[173]

Allah also said, '*And follow the way of those who turned to Me with love*' (31:15).

Abu al-Walid Utba ibn Sad said: "*Bayatu rasulallahi saba bayatin khamsun ala al-taa wa ithnatayni ala al-mahabba* (I pledged seven pledges to Allah's Messenger: five were for utmost obedience, and two were for love)."[174]

Jarir ibn Abd Allah said, "I pledged to Allah's Messenger, that I would hear and obey. He made me add to the utmost of my power, and pure sincerity (*nash*) for every Muslim."[175]

Abd Allah ibn Umar said, "When we pledged to Allah's Messenger, that we would hear and obey, he said, to the utmost of your power."[176]

Anas ibn Malik said, "I pledged to Allah's Messenger, with this hand of mine, that I would hear and obey to the utmost of my power."[177]

When Amr ibn al-As went to Abyssinia, he and those who were with him saw Amr ibn Umayya leave the court of the Negus. He went to the Negus and said, "O Negus, the man who just left your presence is the messenger of an enemy of ours. Give him to us so that we may kill him, for that man has come against our dignitaries and patricians." Amr ibn al-As narrates:

At this the Negus became angry and hit my nose so hard that I thought he had broken it. If a hole in

---

172 It is narrated in *Sahih Bukhari*, in the penultimate chapter of the Book of Prophets.

173 Ahmad narrates it in his *Musnad* with four chains.

174 It is narrated by al-Baghawi, Abu Nuaym, and Ibn Asakir, as cited in *Kanz al-ummal* (1:82) from the *musnad* of Umar. The author of *Hayat al-Sahaba* cites it (Ar. version 1:232; Eng. version 1:299).

175 Bukhari and Muslim narrated it.

176 Bukhari narrates it.

177 Ahmad narrated it in his *Musnad* with three good chains.

the earth had opened for me I would have jumped into
it to get away from him. I said, "O King! by Allah, had
I known it would displease you I would not have
asked it." He said, "How dare you ask me to deliver
you the messenger of a man to whom comes the Arch-
Lawgiver (*al-namus al-akbar* = Gabriel, the angel)
who came to Moses before, so that you may kill him?!"
I said, "O King! Is this how you see it?" He said, "Woe
to you, Amr! Obey me, and follow him. For he is, by
Allah, assuredly on truth, and he shall certainly over-
come whoever opposes him just as Moses overcame
Pharaoh and his armies. Now, give me your pledge
that you will submit to him."

Amr acquiesced and gave him his pledge that he would
accept Islam. He went back to Madina and gave his pledge to
the Prophet (ﷺ) at the same time as Khalid ibn al-Walid. Amr's
words were, "O Messenger of Allah, I pledge you my allegiance
on condition that Allah forgive me all my past sins." The
Prophet (ﷺ) said, "O Amr, go ahead and pledge, for Islam erases whatever came before it, and emigration erases whatever
came before it."[178] The fact that the Negus was Muslim is
established by the Prophet's prayer over him at the news of his
death."[179]

Nafi reported:

> Umar said to me that he heard the Prophet (ﷺ)
> saying, "Whoso takes off his hand of allegiance to
> Allah will meet Him on the Day of Resurrection with-
> out having any proof for him, and whoso dies without
> pledge of allegiance on his neck to the Khalif, he dies
> a death of the Age of Ignorance (*jahiliyya*)."[180]

Shah Wali Allah of Delhi said:

> There are nine types of pledges (*baya*) in the
>   *sunna*:
> Pledge of full acceptance of Islam (*bayat qabul al-
>   islam*)
> Pledge to the leadership (*bayat al-khilafa*)
> Pledge of establishing the pillars of the religion

---

178 It is narrated by Ahmad and Tabarani, and Haythami said in *Majma al-
zawaid* that the narrators in both their chains are trustworthy *(thiqa)*.

179 See the section on *janaza ala al-ghaibin* (funeral prayer in absentia).

180 Muslim reports it in the book of *Imara*.

(*bayat iqamat arkan al-din*)
Pledge of holding fast to the *sunna* with full God-
wariness (*bayat al-tamassuk bi al-sunna wa
al-taqwa*)
Pledge of complete avoidance of innovation (*bayat
al-ijtinab an al-bida*)
Pledge of emigration (*bayat al-hijra*)
Pledge of waging jihad (*bayat al-jihad*)
Pledge of hearing and obeying (*bayat al-sam wa
al-taa*)
Pledge of love (*bayat al-mahabba*).[181]

1.10.1. ALBANI'S DISCORDANT OPINION ON ALLEGIANCE TO IMAMS

Albani says in *Errors in Prayers that must be Avoided*:

> One may perform prayer according to the way he
> was taught by his parents or shaykh, according to
> their *madthhab*. But you should always remember
> that it is only the Messenger of Allah (*sallallaahu
> alaihi wasallam*) who must be followed. The angels
> will not ask you, while in the grave, "Did you follow
> this imaam or that imaam?" Your imaam will not be
> with you then, nor will he defend you on the Day of
> Resurrection. (Footnote: "It should be borne in mind
> that performing prayer correctly means performing it
> in accordance with the traditions only, not according
> to the *madthhab* to which a person adheres.") [182]

1.10.2. CONCLUSION OF MAINSTREAM ISLAM'S VIEW AND REPLY TO ALBANI

Allah says: *On the Day We shall call together all human
beings with their respective Imams* (17:71).

Ibn Abbas said, according to al-Nasafi in his *Tafsir*, this
means they will be raised with their leader in their time,
whether in good or in evil.

It follows that those who follow leaders of innovation and
misguidance will be raised behind them at that time, while
those who followed and obeyed the keepers of the *sunna* and
the callers to good will be raised behind them.

---

181 Shah Wali Allah, *al-Qawl al-jamil*.
182 Found on the website hyperlink http://users.essex.ac.uk/users/rafiam.

Thus, it is established that Muslims are to obey Allah, the Prophet (ﷺ), and those in authority amongst us; that everyone will be raised with their Imam; and that anyone who dies without allegiance to an Imam will die the death of one who died in the Age of Ignorance (*jahiliyya*). Furthermore, it is established that these Imams are both the Imams of guidance in religion, and the Imams of leadership in Muslim public affairs and the administration of justice. There are other types of *baya*, all of which have a bearing on the individual's salvation in Islam.

1.11. FOLLOWING QUALIFIED OPINION (*TAQLID*)

Q. Who is eligible to interpret and explain hadith and deduce *fatawa* according to mainstream Islam?

The mainstream Islamic scholar Ibn Abi Zayd al-Qayrawani said in his *Kitab al-jami fi al-sunan*:

Ibn Uyayna said, "Hadith is liable to misguide all except the jurists (*al-hadithu mudillatun illa li al-fuqaha*)." Ibn Wahb said, "Every memorizer of hadith that does not have an Imam in *fiqh* is misguided (*dall*), and if Allah had not rescued us with Malik and al-Layth (ibn Sad), we would have been misguided."[183]

Ali al-Qari said:

> The early scholars said, "The hadith scholar without knowledge of *fiqh* is like a seller of drugs who is no physician: he has them but he does not know what to do with them; and the *fiqh* scholar without knowledge of hadith is like a physician without drugs: he knows what constitutes a remedy, but he does not dispose of it."[184]

Al-Sakhawi, in his biography of Ibn Hajar entitled *al-Jawahir wa al-durar*, relates similar views:

> Al-Fariqi said, "One who knows chains of hadith but not the legal rulings derived from them cannot be counted among the scholars of the Law." His student

---

183 Ibn Abi Zayd, *al-Jami fi al-sunan* (1982 ed.) p. 118-119.

184 Ali al-Qari, in his book *Mutaqad Abi Hanifa al-Imam fi abaway al-rasul alayhi al-salat wa al-salam* (p. 42).

Ibn Abi Asrun (d. 585) also followed this view in his book *al-Intisar* . . .

Al-Dhahabi said on the authority of Hammad ibn Zayd that Sufyan al-Thawri said, "If hadith were a good thing it would have vanished just as all goodness has vanished." Dhahabi continued, "It is also reported from Sufyan al-Thawri that he said, Pursuing the study of hadith is not part of the preparation for death, but a disease that preoccupies people." Dhahabi comments, "He said this verbatim. He is right in what he said because pursuing the study of hadith is other than the hadith itself."

> Abu Shama related: . . . Al-Amash (the great *tabii* d. 148) said, "The hadith that jurists circulate among themselves is better than that which hadith narrators circulate among themselves." Someone criticized Imam Ahmad ibn Hanbal, may Allah have mercy upon him, for attending the circle of Imam Shafii and leaving the circle of Sufyan ibn Uyayna. Ahmad told him, "Keep quiet. If you miss a hadith with a shorter chain you can find it with a longer chain and it will not harm you. But if you do not have the reasoning of this man (al-Shafii) I am afraid you will not be able to find it."[185]

Some "Salafis" say that "such and such a hadith was not available to this or that Imam," or "you are rejecting a hadith to stick to the saying of your Imam." These claims are not accepted as they are only pretexts for rejecting the *fiqh* of that Imam on the issue raised by the hadith in question, and other issues.

In short, this is a matter in which guidance should be taken only from one who fully understands the sciences that pertain to it such as the following:

• The science of transmission of hadith (*riwayat*) and its defects (*ilal*);

• The sciences of biography (*rijal*) and grades of narrators (*jarh wa tadil*);

185 Sakhawi, *al-Jawahir aw al-durar fi tarjamat shaykh al-islam Ibn Hajar*, ed. Hamid Abd al-Majid and Taha al-Zayni (Cairo: Wizarat al-awqaf, 1986) p. 20-23.

•Extensive knowledge of the Arabic language;
•Science of the questions on which there is differences among the jurisprudents (*ikhtilaf al-fuqaha*) and those on which they all agree (*masail al-ijma*).

All these sciences are part of the curriculum of jurisprudents, the *fuqaha*. In the last analysis, however, it is established that the true *muhaddith* is only one who understands the *fiqh* of all his hadith and their chains, not only their words. That is why someone who does not subscribe to al-Amash's principle that "the hadith that circulate among the *fuqaha* are superior to the hadiths that circulate among the *muhaddithun*" is not someone that should be trusted, for he may have fallen into the *mudilla* that Ibn Uyayna spoke about. The "Salafis" have distinguished themselves as an example of this in our time.

Albani says:

> The traditions quoted here, and in every issue of Ad-Deen an-Naseehah, are authentic. Anyone who rejects the authentic *sunnah* of the Prophet (ﷺ) exposes himself to destruction, as stated by Imaam Ahmed.[186]

As Ta Ha Jabir al-Alwani, a scholar of mainstream Islam, stated:

> The master perpetrators of disagreement in our own times do not have a single plausible basis for justifying their differences. They are not *mujtahidun* or persons capable of independent reasoning or analytical thought. They are, rather, unthinking followers (*muqallidun*) of those among them who raise their voices to proclaim that they are not in fact followers nor do they believe in the duty to follow. They claim that they derive their rulings and opinions directly from the Quran and the *sunnah* of the Prophet (ﷺ). In reality, they cling to some books of hadith and follow in the footsteps of their authors in all matters pertaining to the authenticity of a hadith and the

186 *Errors in Prayers that must be Avoided.*

> trustworthiness and reliability of its narrators . . . On
> the basis of studying a single book on this vast sub-
> ject, a person cannot justifiably elevate himself to the
> position of a *mujtahid*.[187]

One of the "Salafis" cites the sayings of the Imams to the
effect that only the Quran and hadith, not the sayings of the
Imams, must be followed. They neglect to say that the sayings
of the Imams have nothing other than the Quran and hadith as
their source and their goal. The following are examples of the
"Salafis" fallacies:

They quote Abu Hanifa's saying that it is not permissible for
a man to follow his ruling without knowing the source from
which he took it. They neglect to explain that this was Imam
Abu Hanifa's instruction to the scholars, not the mass of the
people. This has been stated again and again by the Hanafi
usuliyyun (scholars of methodology), such as Zafar Uthmani al-
Tahanawi, Yusuf al-Nabahani, and al-Sharani among others.

They quote Imam Shafii's saying that "When the authenticity of the hadith is established, then this is my *madhhab*."
They ignore Nawawi's loud warning that "This most certainly
applies only to the person who has the rank of *mujtahid* in the
madhhab." They quote Imam Malik, who pointed to the
Prophet's grave and said, "Everybody's word can be taken or
rejected, except the dweller of this grave." They neglect to
explain that this was, again, a *faqih* speaking to *fuqaha*. They
quote Imam Shafii's saying to Imam Ahmad, "You know more
hadith than I," but they do not cite Imam Ahmad's acknowl-
edgment of his own dependency on Shafii's expertise in *fiqh*.

Therefore all Muslims are advised not to be misled by
"Salafi" anti-madhhabism such as that found in the books of
Albani and his like. They have cut themselves off from traditional scholarship and innovated a school of self-teaching without precedent in Islam. Allah has misguided such people by the
consensus of the experts of fiqh and hadith among the Imams
of the true Salaf. It is they, therefore, and not the adherents of
mainstream Islam who have exposed themselves to destruction
by straying from the *sunna* of the Prophet (ﷺ) and the methodology of the true Salaf.

---

187 Ta Ha Jabir al-Alwani, *The Ethics of Disagreement in Islam* (p. 119).

Q. What is the understanding of following qualified opinion (*taqlid*) of scholars in Islam?

1.11.1. "SALAFIS" DISTORT STATEMENTS OF THE GREAT SCHOLARS CONCERNING THIS

The introduction of the English edition of Albani's *Prayer* contains some famous statements of the great Imams of *fiqh* that Albani misrepresents as rejecting *taqlid* and encouraging *ijtihad*. This false representation of the Imams original intent is a result of the application of the same principles that Albani applies in his misrepresentation of hadith. Namely, these principles are to sever the texts from their context, and to ignore the statements of the authorities that elucidated those same texts long before Albani was born. The unwary reader, untrained in the methodologies of the Sharia, takes these statements at face value and understands them to apply in absolute and universal terms. Similarly, the young would-be "Salafi" reads the hadiths and the statements of the Imams in Albani's books under the illusion that he can understand their meaning just because he understands the words themselves.

Among the Imams sayings on *fiqh* that the "Salafis" misrepresent are the following:

> When you find in my saying anything contradicting the *sunna* of the Prophet (ﷺ) then take the *sunna* of the Prophet (ﷺ) and leave aside my statement (Imam al-Shafii).

> When the hadith is established as authentic in opposition to my statement, then act according to the hadith and abandon my statement (Imam al-Shafii).

> When the authenticity of the hadith is established, then that is my school of law (*madhhab*) (Imam Abu Hanifa and Imam al-Shafii).

The authenticity of these statements is not contested. However, the "Salafis" who quote these statements misrepresent their real meaning.

1.11.2. MAINSTREAM ISLAM'S VIEW OF FOLLOWING QUALIFIED OPINION

Following are qualified explanations of such statements

according to the mainstream Islamic scholars of mainstream Islam.[188]

Imam Nawawi said:

> What Imam Shafii said does not mean that every-one who sees a *sahih* hadith should say "This is the *madhhab* of Shafii," applying the purely external or apparent meaning of his statement. What he said most certainly applies only to a person who has the rank of *mujtahid* in the *madhhab*. It is a condition for such a person that he overwhelmingly believe that either Imam Shafii was unaware of this hadith or he was unaware of its authenticity. And this is possible only after having made a research of all the books of al-Shafii and similar other books of the companions of al-Shafii, those who took knowledge from him and others similar to them. This is indeed a difficult con-dition to fulfill. Few are those who measure up to this (standard).

What we have explained has been made conditional [i.e. not universally binding] because Imam al-Shafii had abandoned acting purely on the external meaning of many hadiths, which he declared and knew. However, he established proofs for criti-cism of the hadith or its abrogation or specific circumstances or interpretation etc. Due to this, he was constrained by time to leave aside investigating the hadith itself."

Shaykh Abu Amr said: "It is not easy to act according to the apparent meaning of what Imam Shafii said. It is not lawful for every *faqih* to act independently with that which in his opinion constitutes a proof from the hadith."

Zafar Ahmad Uthmani al-Tahanawi said: "Imam Sharani also narrated it [i.e. the statement "When the authenticity of a hadith is established, it is my *madhhab*"], attributing it to the four Imams. It is not hidden from understanding that this is meant only for the one who has competence for insight into the proof-texts and the knowledge of their clear laws and abroga-tions."

Shaykh Yusuf ibn Ismail al-Nabahani said in his book *Hujjatullah ala al-alamin*:

---

188 As quoted in al-Tahanawi's treatise *Ila us-sunan* (2:225-226).

> "Verily, the statement "When the Hadith has been authenticated, then it is my *madhhab*" has been narrated from each of these four Imams who were free from personal opinion. The audience to whom this statement was directed, are the Imams companions [the *fuqaha* of his *madhhab*] who were the great and illustrious Imams among the great *ulama* of his *madhhab*, those who were the People of Precedence. All of them who were masters of the hadith of the Prophet (ﷺ) were fully aware of the proofs of all the schools. These are the one's whom the Imam of the *madhhab* had directed his statement, "When the hadith is *sahih*, it is my *madhhab*." For they are able to reconcile between the hadith from which the Imam had derived proof, and the latest hadith which was established as authentic after the Imam. They can see which of the two hadiths is more authentic and stronger, and which of the two hadiths is the later one so that the later one can be the abrogator for the earlier one."

It is now clear that the statement, "When the hadith is *sahih*, it is my *madhhab*," is directed to an audience of experts in *ijtihad* who have embraced the sciences of the Law; who have mastered the method of their Imam; and who are experts of both narrational (*naqli*) and rational (*aqli*) branches of knowledge. In short, it is addressed to those who were *ulama* and *fuqaha* of the highest caliber, whose likes are few-and-far-between after the first centuries, if they were to be found at all.

Whereas these illustrious *mujtahid* Imams directed their command to their students among the *fuqaha* and *ulama* of early times, the "Salafi" "scholars" take the Imams statements and misdirect them to an audience of ordinary Muslims who are not the intended audience and who do not understand their meaning.

1.12. Mainstream Islam Allows Garments Below the Ankles if Worn Without Arrogance

Q. Can garments hang below the ankles, even trousers?

The hadith of the trailing of garments in Muslim states:

Narrated Abu Dharr: The Messenger of Allah observed, "Three are the (persons) with whom Allah would neither speak on the Day of Resurrection, nor would look at them nor would absolve them, and there is a painful chastisement for them." The Messenger of Allah repeated it three times. Abu Dharr remarked, "They failed and they lost; who are these persons, Messenger of Allah?" Upon this he observed, "They are: the one who makes [his garment] hang down on the ground (al-musbil), the recounter of obligation, and the seller of goods by false oath."[189]

The following are Imam Nawawi, Ibn Qudama, and Ibn Hajar's commentaries on the various hadiths on this chapter. It will be seen that, in light of their views, there is no basis in these hadiths for the "Salafis" statement that "the above and many other traditions indicate clearly that wearing clothes that hang below the ankles for men is a grave sin regardless of whether such garments are worn out of habit or pride."

[Nawawi:] As for the Prophet's saying, "The one who makes his garment hang down on the ground," its meaning is: The one who lets it down and drags its extremity out of arrogance (khayla), as has been mentioned by way of explanation (of the same phrase) in the other hadith [in Bukhari and Muslim]; "Allah will not look at a person who drags his lower garment in arrogance." Khayla is self-aggrandizement (kibar), and this restricted (muqayyad) meaning of letting down the garment as consisting in dragging it (al-jarr) out of arrogance reduces the general sense of the person who lets down the lower garment to a specific sense and indicates that the one meant by the threat of punishment is the one who does so out of arrogance.

The Prophet (ﷺ) permitted Abu Bakr al-Siddiq to do so (i.e. let down his lower garment) and he said to him, "You are not of their number" [Bukhari] because he trailed it for a reason other than arrogance. Imam Abu Jafar Muhammad ibn Jarir al-Tabari and others said, "The letting down of the lower garment was mentioned by itself because it is their most common

---

189 Cf. English version: 1:60-61. Muslim narrates directly afterwards another version from Abu Dharr where the loin-wrap or lower garment (izar) is explicitly mentioned.

garment, but the ruling concerning other garments such as the shirt and others, is the same ruling." I say [Nawawi], This has been made plain to us explicitly in the hadith from the Prophet (ﷺ) on the authority of Salim ibn Abd Allah from his father, "The letting down (*isbal*) pertains to the lower garment, the shirt, and the turban. Whoever drags something out of arrogance Allah will not look at him on the Day of Resurrection." Abu Dawud, al-Nasai, and Ibn Majah narrated it with a fair chain. And Allah knows best.[190]

[Ibn Qudama:] The *isbal* or trailing of the shirt and the pants (i.e. the baggy middle part of the *sarawil*) in the spirit of arrogance is disliked (*makruh*). The Prophet (ﷺ) said . . . [he recounts the evidence already mentioned by Nawawi].[191]

In a hadith narrated by Muslim we find:

Abd Allah ibn Masud said that the Prophet (ﷺ) said, "He will not enter the Garden of Paradise who has an atom's worth of pride in his heart." A man said, "What about someone who likes handsome clothes and handsome sandals?" The Prophet (ﷺ) replied, "Allah is Beautiful and He loves beauty. Pride is refusing to admit the truth and having contempt for people."[192]

1.12.1. ALBANI INCORRECTLY FORBIDS ANY GARMENTS BELOW THE ANKLES

The following are some common errors committed by Muslims in their *salah*. These errors must be avoided hoping that Allah would accept this act of worship and reward us for it.[193]

1) Wearing pants, or garments that hang below the ankles.

This is one of the greatest sins. Abu Dharr reported that the Messenger of Allaah (*sallallaahu alaihi wasallam*) said, There are three people whom Allah shall not speak to on the Day of Resurrection, nor shall he look at them, nor shall he purify them, and they shall have a painful torment: One whose garment hangs down below his ankles, *almanaan* (footnote: "a person who gives out gifts only to reproach

190 Nawawi, *Sharh Sahih Muslim* (3rd ed. al-Mays) 1/2:475-476.
191 Ibn Qudama, *al-Mughni* (1994 ed.) 1:406.
192 Narrated by Muslim and others.
193 *Errors in Prayers that must be Avoided.*

the recipient for what he has given him"), and (a merchant) who sells of his merchandise by means of false oath (footnote: "a merchant who swears falsely that he is not making a profit in his merchandise or that it cost him too much in order to convince the customer to buy it").

Some people think that wearing clothes that hang below the ankles is not a sin if they abstain from doing so while praying only. Others think that wearing such a garment is a sin only if it is worn out of pride; otherwise, they believe there is no harm in doing so. However, the above and many other traditions indicate clearly that wearing clothes that hang below the ankles (for men) is a grave sin regardless of whether such garments are worn out of habit or pride. There are other authentic traditions that emphasize wearing clothing that hangs below the ankles out of pride entails harsher punishment. Abu Hurairah reported that the Messenger of Allah (*sallallaahu alaihi wasallam*) said the part of the garment which hangs below the ankles is (punishable by) Fire (on the Day of Resurrection) (footnote: "*Sahih al-Bukhari*").

It is commonplace to see brothers folding up the hems of their pants for prayer. However, as soon as prayer is completed, they unfold their pants. The belief that wearing garments that hang below the ankles is prohibited during prayers only is a misconception commonly held by many Muslims. Such Muslims are unaware that the Prophet (*sallallaahu alaihi wasallam*) forbade praying with folded clothes (footnote: "*Sahih Muslim*"). Based on this prohibition, scholars have agreed that praying with folded sleeves or pants is unlawful.

1.12.2. MAINSTREAM ISLAM'S REPLY TO ALBANI

As for the "Salafi" statement that "scholars have agreed that praying with folded sleeves or pants is unlawful," it is a falsehood since almost all of them agree that it is *makruh*, not *haram*.[194] Furthermore, Ibn Hajar states that "the prohibition of folding up the clothes in prayer concerns other than the bottom of the lower garment."[195]

---

194 As Nawawi states in his commentary of *Sahih Muslim* quoted below.
195 Ibn Hajar, *Fath al-bari* (1989 ed.) 10:314.

[Nawawi:] The scholars are in agreement that it is forbidden to pray with braided or plaited hair, as well as with folded up garment or sleeves or the like: . . . all this is forbidden and agreed upon as such by the scholars, and the prohibition is that of offensiveness of the lesser type (*karahatu tanzih*), and if one prays in this manner then he has not done well but his prayer is valid. Ibn Jarir al-Tabari has submitted the consensus of the scholars in this question, while Ibn al-Mundhir has related that one must repeat the prayer according to al-Hasan al-Basri.[196]

1.12.3. EVIDENCE FROM SAHIH BUKHARI AND *FATH AL-BARI* ON THIS ISSUE

Imam Bukhari addressed this topic in the first three chapters of the Book of Clothing in his *Sahih*, respectively entitled "Chapter of those who trail their lower garment without arrogance," "Chapter of raising up the bottom of the clothes," "Chapter of what hangs lower than the ankles being in the Fire," and "Chapter of those who trail their cloth out of arrogance." Below are some of the hadiths he included in these chapters,[197] together with some of Ibn Hajar al-Asqalani's commentary on them from his work, *Fath al-bari*.

1.12.3.1. CHAPTER OF THOSE WHO TRAIL THEIR LOWER GARMENT WITHOUT ARROGANCE

Ibn Hajar: Meaning that they are exempted from the threat mentioned in the hadith, but only if there is an excuse, in which case they are not blamed. Otherwise there are considerations that will be mentioned further down.

Narrated Abd Allah bin Umar: The Prophet (ﷺ) said, "Allah will not look, on the Day of Resurrection, at the person who drags his garment (behind him) out of conceit. On that Abu Bakr said, "O Allah's Apostle! One side of my *izar* hangs low if I do not take care of it." The Prophet (ﷺ) said, "You are not one of those who does that out of conceit."

Ibn Hajar: The reason it hanged low was that Abu Bakr was corpulent . . . It seems that its knot would

196 Nawawi, *Sharh Sahih Muslim* 3/4:454.
197 English version: Volume 7, p. 454-459.

loosen when he walked or did other things independently of his will, but that it would not trail if he took
care of it, since he would tie it again every time he
noticed it . . . The Prophet's words indicate that there
is unconditionally no blame on those whose *izar* trails
on the ground without their will. As for Ibn Abi
Shayba's report whereby Ibn Umar disliked it in any
case, Ibn Battal said, "This is part of his strictness.
Besides, he narrated this hadith himself and so the
ruling (of toleration) was not unknown to him." I say,
Rather, Ibn Umar's dislike signifies those who deliberately trail it whether out of arrogance or not, and it
is in conformity with his narration mentioned by Ibn
Battal. Surely Ibn Umar would not blame those who
did not intend anything. By declaring it disliked he
only meant those who trail their *izar* without their
will and then continue doing so after they realize it.
This is agreed upon. They only disagreed whether the
offensiveness is of a near-forbidden or of a slight type.

Narrated Abu Bakrah: The solar eclipse occurred
while we were sitting with the Prophet. He got up
dragging his garment (on the ground) hurriedly until
he reached the mosque. The people turned (to the
mosque) and he offered a two cycle (*rakat*) prayer
until the eclipse was over. Then he faced us and said,
"The sun and the moon are two signs among the signs
of Allah, so if you see a thing like this (eclipse) then
offer the prayer and invoke Allah until He removes
that state."

Ibn Hajar: This hadith shows that if the trailing
of the *izar* is due to haste then it does not enter under
the prohibition. It intimates that the prohibition is
specific to what is done out of arrogance. Yet it provides no proof for those who restrict the prohibition to
arrogance only to the point that they permit the long
shirts that trail on the ground.[198]

1.12.3.2. CHAPTER ON RAISING OR TUCKING UP (*TASHAMMUR*) ONE'S CLOTHES

Ibn Hajar: *tashammur* is the raising up of the bottom of one's clothes.

Narrated Abu Juhayfa: I saw Bilal bringing an
anaza or small spear and fixing it in the ground, then

198 Ibn Hajar, *Fath al-bari* (1989 ed.) 10:313-314.

he called for the start of the prayer (*iqama*) and I saw Allah's Messenger coming out in a suit of clothes having tucked up its end (*mushammiran*). He then offered a two cycle (*rakat*) prayer while facing the spear, and I saw the people and animals passing in front of him but behind the spear.

Ibn Hajar: al-Ismaili did not have *mushammir* in his narration but related it as, "and the Prophet (ﷺ) came out and I can almost see the gleaming of his shanks" then he said, al-Thawri narrated it in the terms, "I can almost see the glistening of his shanks" which al-Ismaili commented, "This is the *tashmir* in question." It can be concluded from it that the prohibition of folding up the clothes in prayer concerns other than the bottom of the lower garment].

1.12.3.3. CHAPTER OF "WHAT HANGS BELOW THE TWO ANKLES IS IN THE FIRE."

Ibn Hajar: Bukhari in the chapter-title did not restrict the subject to the part of the *izar* as in the hadith he cites in the body of the chapter. This is a reference to the generalization of the prohibition to include the lower garment, the shirt, and others. It seems he was referring to the wording of the hadith of Abu Said al-Khudri narrated by Malik, Abu Dawud, al-Nasai, and Ibn Majah, which Abu Awana and Ibn Hibban declared sound, all through al-Ala ibn Abd al-Rahman . . . Abu Dawud, Nasai, and al-Hakim who declared it sound [also Ahmad] cited the hadith of Abu Jurayy [Jabir ibn Sulaym] whereby the Prophet (ﷺ) said, "Lift up your lower garment to the middle of your shank, and if you don't wish to, then to the ankles. Beware the trailing of the lower garment, for it is arrogance, and Allah does not like arrogance." Nasai also cited, as well as al-Hakim who declared it sound, the hadith of Hudhayfa with the wording, "The lower garment is let down to the middle of the two shanks, and if you don't wish to, then lower, and if you don't wish to, then lower than the shanks, but there is no right to the lower garment for the ankles."

Narrated Abu Hurayra: The Prophet (ﷺ) said, "The part of an *izar* which hangs below the ankles is in the fire."

Ibn Hajar: al-Khattabi said, "He means that the spot which the lower garment reaches below the ankles is in the Fire, and he has named the cloth to refer to the body of its wearer (i.e. by metonymy) . . . its principle being in what Abd al-Razzaq has cited from Abd al-Aziz ibn Abi Dawud whereby Nafi was asked about this and he said: What wrong did the clothes do? Rather, it concerns the feet." However, Tabarani narrated from Ibn Umar through Abd Allah ibn Muhammad ibn Aqil: The Prophet (ﷺ) saw me trailing my lower garment and he said, "O Ibn Umar, every part of the clothes that touches the ground is in the Fire." Tabarani also narrated with a fair chain from Ibn Masud that he saw a Bedouin praying with a trailing garment and he said, "What trails in the prayer is neither lawful nor unlawful in the eyes of Allah." Such a statement is not made on the basis of opinion (i.e. it is related from the Prophet (ﷺ)). Based on the above there is no impediment to understanding the hadith literally (i.e. as referring to the cloth alone) . . .

The warning in absolute terms is in fact understood as specific to arrogance according to the other evidence that has been narrated, and it is agreed upon that the threat concerns arrogance . . .

Exempt from the absolute understanding of lowering the garment is that which is done out of necessity, as for instance when one suffers an ankle-wound which the flies would harm if it were not covered with one's lower garment for lack of something else. Our shaykh [al-Iraqi] has pointed this out in his Commentary on Tirmidhi, and he has cited as a proof the Prophet's dispensation to Abd al-Rahman ibn Awf in wearing a silk shirt because of itching.

1.12.3.4. CHAPTER ON THE ONE WHO TRAILS HIS CLOTHES IN ARROGANCE

Narrated Abu Hurayra: The Prophet (ﷺ) said, "Allah will not look, on the Day of Resurrection, at a person who trails his *izar* out of pride."

[Ibn Hajar disagrees with Nawawi's limitation of the general prohibition against trailing the lower garment as being specific to trailing it out of pride. He then says:] In conclusion there are two cases for men: one of desirability, which is to shorten the lower garment to the middle of the shanks; and one of permissibility, which is to lower it to the ankles. Similarly there are two cases for women: one of desirability, which is to add a handspan to what is permissible for men; and one of permissibility, which is to add an arms length instead of a handspan . . ."

It is inferred from the narrations that:

•What is highlighted in the majority of cases is the specific meaning of dragging the garment behind.

•Conceit and strutting is abhorrent even for one who lifts up his garment.

•The comprehensive understanding of the evidence is that whoever means, by dressing well, to show Allah's favor upon him, in thankful awareness of it and without despising those who do not possess what he has: then it does not harm him in the least to wear whatever is permitted, even if it is extremely costly.

Narrated Abd Allah ibn Umar: Allah's Messenger said, "While a man was trailing his *izar* on the ground, suddenly Allah made him sink into the earth and he will go on wailing in the earth until the Day of Resurrection."

Shuba said: I met Muharib ibn Dithar on horseback as he was riding to the place where he sat to judge cases and I asked him about this hadith. He said: I heard Abd Allah ibn Umar say: Allah's Apostle said, "Whoever drags his clothes on the ground out of conceit, Allah will not look at him on the Day of Resurrection." I said to Muharib: Did he mention the man's *izar*? He replied, He specified neither the *izar* nor the shirt . . . Musa ibn Uqba, Umar ibn Muhammad, and Qudama ibn Musa add to it from Salim from Ibn Umar, "Whoever drags his *izar* out of arrogance."

Ibn Hajar: He mentioned the lower garment because in the majority of cases it is the lower garment which shows one's conceit . . . In these hadith is evidence that the trailing of one's lower garment on the ground is an enormity. As for letting it down for other than arrogance then the apparent meaning of the narrations is that it is also forbidden. However: the restriction of these narrations to the meaning of arrogance furnishes proof that the unqualified criticism in the abhorrence of letting down garments must be understood in terms of its specific meaning here. Therefore neither dragging the garment nor letting it down is forbidden if one is safe from arrogance.

Ibn Abd al-Barr said, "What is understood from the hadith is that trailing for other than arrogance is not sanctioned by the threat, but trailing the shirt and other than the shirt among garments is abhorrent in every case."

Nawawi said: Letting down one's garment below the ankles is due to arrogance. If it is done for other than that then it is merely disliked. This is what Shafii declared about the difference between the trailing due to arrogance and that due to another reason. His words are: What is desirable is that the lower garment reach to the middle of the shanks, and what is permitted without offensiveness (*bi la karaha*) is between that point and down to the ankles. Whatever is below the ankles, if due to arrogance, is prohibited (*mamnu*) with the prohibitiveness of what is strictly forbidden (*tahrim*), otherwise it is prohibited with the prohibitiveness of the lesser kind (*tanzih*), because the hadith that are extant concerning the prevention (*zajr*) of trailing are unqualified and must therefore be restricted to trailing out of arrogance.

Buwayti referred in his abridgment to the text of Shafii that Nawawi mentioned. He said:

> *Sadl*–letting down a loose cloth–is not allowed in prayer nor elsewhere out of arrogance; but it is less (of a prohibition) if done for another reason because of the Prophet's saying to Abu Bakr.

His expression "it is less" implicitly precludes strict forbiddance. The latter is definitely understood to apply for trailing out of arrogance. Other than that the case varies. If the length of the garment fits the wearer but he lets it hang down then it seems there is no *tahrim* of it, especially if this is unintended as happened to Abu Bakr. But if the length of the garment exceeds the size of the wearer then this may become prohibited from the perspective of waste (*israf*) and end up as strictly forbidden; or it may become prohibited from the perspective of resemblance to female fashion, and this is more likely than the former . . .

In conclusion, letting down the garment supposes dragging it behind oneself, and dragging it behind oneself supposes arrogance.[199]

1.12.3.5. A DUBIOUS PASSAGE FROM *FIQH AL-SUNNA* ON THIS ISSUE

Concerning the related passage in the English translation of *Fiqh al-sunna*:

> Chapter entitled: "Disliked Acts in Prayer #7: Covering The Mouth and Letting One's Garment Down" whereby Abu Hurayra said, "The Messenger of Allah prohibited as-sadl in the prayer and covering one's mouth" which is "reported by the Five" and by Hakim who says that it is sahih according to Muslims conditions. Al-Khattabi explains, "As-sadl is to lower one's garment until it reaches the ground." Al-Kamal ibn al-Humam adds, "This also applies to wearing a cloak without putting one's arms through its sleeves."

The author of *Fiqh al-sunna* neglects to clarify several respects of the paragraph above:

> 1 The hadith of Abu Hurayra is actually only reported by four: Abu Dawud, Tirmidhi, Ahmad, and Darimi, and all of their chains contain Isl ibn Sufyan al-Yarbui, who is weak. This is pointed out by Tirmidhi when he says, "We do not know this hadith through the chain from Ata [ibn Abi Rabah] from Abu Hurayra from the Prophet (ﷺ) except through Isl." Also Abu Dawud, directly after citing this hadith, cites Ibn Jurayj's report that "Most of the time I saw Ata pray as he let down his garment." Abu Dawud comments, "This weakens the previous narration"

---

199 Ibn Hajar, *Fath al-bari* (1989 ed.) 10:312-324.

because Ata is in all the chains. Furthermore, only
Abu Dawud's narration mentions the covering of the
mouth.

2 The author seems to imply that *sadl* in the weak
hadith of Abu Hurayra is the same as *isbal* in the
sound hadiths of Muslim previously quoted. It should
have been made clearer that *sadl* in the hadith of Abu
Hurayra means the letting down of a single loose garment from the head, as the Wahhabis and uneducated who imitate them do, and as Tirmidhi reports is
the manner of the Jews. The narration also implies
that in some cases it is done without wearing any
other garment. It is different from the *isbal*, which
consists in trailing the *izar* or lower garment behind
oneself while walking. This is confirmed by the explanations of the authorities cited below.

a) Tirmidhi said, after citing the hadith in his *Sunan*:

The People of Knowledge differ concerning letting
down the garment. They said it is the fashion of the
Jews. Others said it is only disliked when, in prayer,
one does not wear other than a single garment. If he
is also wearing a shirt then there is no harm in it.
This is the position of Ahmad ibn Hanbal. As for Ibn
al-Mubarak, he dislikes it in prayer (unconditionally).[200]

b) Abū Bakr ibn al-Arabi said in his commentary on Tirmidhi concerning the hadith of Abu Hurayra:

It requires further consideration (i.e. its meaning
is not evident). Al-Shafii and others disliked it (unconditionally) while Malik said it is permissible, but
there is difference as to its interpretation.

Some said it refers to the trailing of one's clothing
on the ground. Those who allowed the letting down in
the prayer said that in such a case one neither walks
nor trails it because at that time one stands firmly on
the ground whereas what is forbidden is pomposity or
conceit (*tabakhtur*) while walking, and arrogance
(*khayla*).

Others said what is forbidden is letting down the

---

200 Tirmidhi, Book of Prayer, Chapter on what has been cited concerning the disliked nature of letting down the garment in prayer.

garment without wearing a shirt (i.e. letting down a
sleeveless garment from the head). In this case if one
lets it down (loose) over the chest then he remains
uncovered, whereas if he is wearing a shirt then it is
permitted for him to let down a cloak and he does not
need to tie it to himself.[201]

Muwaffaq al-Din ibn Qudama said in his *Mughni*:

Sadl is disliked, and it consists in letting down
the two extremities of a garment on both sides of oneself without throwing either extremity on the opposite shoulder nor gathering them up in one's hand. It
is disliked by Ibn Masud, al-Nakhi, al-Thawri, al-
Shafii, Mujahid, and Ata. It is reported that Jabir and
Ibn Umar permitted it, and that al-Hasan and Ibn
Sirin used to let down a garment over their shirt. Ibn
al-Mundhir said, "I don't know of a single hadith that
can be established concerning it," while it is narrated
from Abu Hurayra that the Prophet (ﷺ) "prohibited
letting down the garment in the prayer and covering
one's mouth." Abu Dawud narrated it through the
narration of Ata, then he narrated from Ibn
Jurayj:,"Most of the time I saw Ata pray as he let
down his garment."
[Also] disliked is the *isbal* or trailing of the shirt
and the pants . . . [already cited above].[202]

It is correct that Umar permitted *sadl* as Ibn Qudama said;
however, he considered it offensive because it resembled the
manner of Jews, as reported from him by Ibn Abi Shayba and
confirmed by Shawkani.[203] Still, it is known that he permitted
it because Ibn Abi Shayba reports and Nawawi confirms that
he was seen doing it at least once.[204] The apparent contradiction between the reports that he disliked it and yet practiced it,
as in Ata's report concerning his dislike of *sadl* and the fact
that he did it, is resolved by the fact that they were prone to do
it even though they considered it offensive. This is established
by Ibn Umar himself when he was seen leaning against a wall
in prayer, although he had declared it offensive to do so. When

---

201 Ibn al-Arabi, *Tuhfat al-ahwadhi* 2:170-171.
202 Ibn Qudama, *al-Mughni* (1994 ed.) 1:406.
203 Ibn Abi Shayba, *Musannaf* 1:94; Shawkani, *Nayl al-awtar* 2:81.
204 Ibn Abi Shayba, *Musannaf* 1:94; Nawawi, *al-Majmu* 3:184.

asked about it he said, "Yes, we do it, but it diminishes the reward."[205]

1.13. ENUNCIATING ONE'S INTENTION BEFORE OFFERING THE PRESCRIBED PRAYER (*SALAT*)

Q. Must one enunciate the intention to pray before *salat*?

1.13.1. MAINSTREAM ISLAM'S VIEW

The view of mainstream Islam on pronouncing the intention for prayer is presented below.

Hanafi school:

> Pronouncing the intention with the tongue is not a pre-condition for *salat* but is desirable (*mustahabb*) so as to assist the heart in allying its intention with the speech of the tongue. See: al-Kasani's *Badai al-sanai* (1:127); al-Haskafi's *al-Durr al-mukhtar* (1:496); al-Zaylai's *Tabyin al-haqaiq* (1:99); Ibn al-Humam's, *Fath al-qadir* (1:185); Ghunaymi's commentary on al-Quduri's *Mukhtasar*, entitled *al-Lubab fi sharh al-kitab* (1:66).

Maliki school:

> The seat of the intention is the heart. Pronouncing the intention is desirable (*mustahabb*) only for the one who whispers (*waswasa*) to remove his mistake, otherwise it is best to leave it. See: al-Dardir's *al-Sharh al-kabir* with Muhammad al-Dasuqi's commentary (1:233); al-Dardir's *al-Sharh al-saghir* with al-Sawi's commentary (1:303-305); Ibn Juzayy, *al-Qawanin al-fiqhiyya* (p. 57); Ibn Rushd, *Bidayat al-mujtahid* (1:116).

Shafii school:

> The seat of the intention is the heart, and it is praiseworthy that it be uttered (*yundab al-natq*) shortly before the *takbir*. See: *Hashiyat al-bajuri*

---

205 Ata, *Musannaf Ibn Abd al-Razzaq* 2:277.

(1:149); al-Shirbini's commentary on Nawawi's *Minhaj al-talibin* entitled *Mughni al-muhtaj* (1:148-150); Abu Ishaq al-Shirazi, *al-Muhadhdhab fi fiqh al-imam al-Shafii* (1:70); Nawawi's commentary on the latter entitled *al-Majmu* (2:243-252).

Hanbali school:

> The seat of the intention is the heart in obligation, and the tongue in desirability. See: Ibn Qudama, *al-Mughni* (1:464-469); Buhuti's *Kashshaf al-qina* (1:364-370).

1.13.2. ALBANI SAYS NOT TO ENUNCIATE THE INTENTION

> Mumbling the *niyyah* or intention, and uttering it in a low audible voice. The heart is the place of intention. Mumbling words such as "I intend to pray such prayer or such number of rakaat, or I intend to fast, or do such act of worship or another," just before starting prayer is a *bidah* which was practiced neither by the Prophet (ﷺ) nor his companions, nor by their followers. Uttering the above words of *niyyah* allows *shaitaan* to put irrelevant words in the mouth of the person who utters the *niyyah*. Do you remember at one time or another that once you stood up for *zuhr* and discovered yourself saying, "I intend to pray four cycles (*rakat*) of night prescribed prayer (*isha*)," or when you were standing for *asr* prescribed prayer you made your intention to pray *fajr* instead? This confusion is from *shaitan*. Had you kept silent, *shaitan* would have no chance of confusing you.[206]

1.13.3. DISCUSSION OF PRONOUNCING THE INTENTION ACCORDING TO MAINSTREAM ISLAM

To this it is answered: The example given above is a proof for, not against, pronouncing the intention. It is not the utterance that causes the mistake, but the fact that one is acting out of habit and without thinking, and this takes place in the heart. Had that person not pronounced his intention, he would not have realized his mistake, and so would have proceeded

---

206 *Errors in Prayers that must be Avoided.*

with his prescribed prayer (*salat*) unaware that it was based on the wrong intention and therefore invalid.

The intention is precisely what differentiates *salat* and all acts of worship from habit, and it is a pre-condition for *salat*, without which *salat* is invalid. Intention must include naming the *salat* in question, specifying its quantity, type, time, and the status of the person making prayer. For example, "I intend to pray at this time the four rakat of the obligatory (*fard*) prayer of the noon prescribed prayer (*zuhr*) as an individual, facing the noble Kabah, for Allah Almighty." In Arabic: *nawaytu usalli arba rakat hadir fard salat al-zuhr fardan mustaqbil al-kaba al-sharifa lillahi taala.*

The Prophet (🕌) stressed in many hadiths the necessity of coordinating the acts of the tongue with those of the heart and vice-versa. It should be understood that the seat of the intention is the heart, and the majority of scholars outside the Maliki school said it is praiseworthy (*mandub*) to pronounce the intention before *salat*. The Malikis only allow it if one fears the whispering of satan and if it helps one's concentration to pronounce it.

1.14. RAISING ONE'S HANDS AFTER
TAKBIRAT AL-IHRAM
Q. May one raise the hands after *takbirat al-ihram*?

1.14.1. MAINSTREAM ISLAM'S VIEW
On the issue of not raising the hands except at the opening of *salat*, the Hanafis and Malikis base their position on sound and authentic evidence that the Prophet (🕌) did not raise his hands in *salat*, except for the first *takbira*.[207] The evidence also shows that this was also the practice of many of the Companions, Umar, Ali, Abu Hurayra, and the early Muslims of Madina and Kufa. It is therefore futile to question the validity of not raising the hands or to claim that it is an error.[208]

1.14.2. ALBANI SAYS HANDS MUST BE RAISED
Neglecting raising the hands in the opening tak-

---

207 Ibn Masud, Ibn Abbas, Ibn Umar in some reports, and al-Bara ibn Azib.

208 Those who are interested in reviewing the evidence for the above should look up the excellent presentation of the issue in Abd al-Rahman ibn Yusuf's recent book *Fiqhul Imaaam* (p. 91-110). Another good discussion of the issue in English is available in Sayf al-Din Ahmad ibn Muhammad's book *al-Albani Unveiled* (p. 35-48).

beer of *salah* and before and after *rukoo*, and upon standing up for the third *rakah*. Abdullah bin Umar said: "I saw the Prophet (*sallallaahu alaihi wasallam*) raising his hands to the level of his shoulders, upon starting prayer, and before bending for *rukoo* and when he stood up again (Footnote: Bukhari and Muslim). Raising hands with every *takbeer*, subsequent to the first *takbeer* in *janaza*, *Eed* or rain prayers is not recommended. The Messenger of Allah (*sallallaahu alaihi wasallam*) used to put his hands on his chest (while standing in prayer) (Footnote: Bukhari and Abu Dawud).[209]

1.15. ONE MAY ENUNCIATE THE *BASMALA* AND *AMIN* IN THE RECITATION OF *SURAH AL-FATIHA*

Q. May one enunciate the *Basmala* and *AMIN* in *Fatiha*?

1.15.1. MAINSTREAM ISLAM'S VIEW

The Hanafis and Malikis do not consider the *basmala* part of the *Fatiha* and therefore do not recite it. This is not incorrect. However, the Hanafis require that those praying behind the imam recite it silently. The Malikis allow it, but for blessing, not because it is obligatory.

Among their proofs are the following:

> Anas said, "I prayed with Allah's Messenger, Abu Bakr, Umar, and Uthman, and I never heard one of them reciting: *Bismillah al-rahman al-rahim*."[210]

The Companion Abd Allah ibn Mughaffal al-Muzani saw his son pronounce the *tasmiya* in his prayer and he forbade him to do so and said, "O my son, keep away from innovation in Islam. I prayed behind Allah's Messenger, behind Abu Bakr and behind Umar, and they did not pronounce the *tasmiya*. Therefore do not say it. When you pray, say (directly): *al-hamdu lillah rabb al-alamin*." Tirmidhi narrates it and says:

---

209 *Ibid.*
210 Muslim and Ahmad narrated it.

It is *hasan*, and that is the practice of the majority of the People of Knowledge among the Companions of the Prophet (ﷺ), among them: Abu Bakr, Umar, Uthman, Ali, and other than them as well as those after them from among the Tabiin. That is also the position of Sufyan al-Thawri, Ibn al-Mubarak, Ahmad, and Ishaq: they do not consider that one should say "B*ismillah al-rahman al-rahim*" out loud, but they said he should say it to himself.[211]

Abu Hurayra said the Prophet (ﷺ) said:

Allah says, "I divided the prayer into two halves between Myself and My servant (i.e. one half for Me, one half for him), and My servant shall have what he asked for." When the servant says, "*Al-hamdu lillahi rabb al-alamin*) praise belongs to the Lord of the worlds)," Allah says, "My servant has praised Me." When he says,"*Al-rahman al-rahim* (the Merciful, the Compassionate)," Allah says, "My servant has glorified Me." When he says, "*Maliki yawm al-din* (Master of the Day of Judgment)," Allah says, "My servant has exalted Me." And when he says, "*Iyyaka nabudu wa iyyaka nastain* (Thee alone do we worship and to Thee alone do we seek help)," Allah says, "This is (one half) between Me and My servant, and he shall have what he asked for." Therefore when he says, "*Ihdina al-sirat al-mustaqim sirat al-ladhina anamta alayhim ghayri al-maghdubi alayhim wa la al-dallin* (guide us on the straight path, the way upon which Thou hast bestowed Thy Grace, not the path of those who have gone astray)," Allah says, "This is for My servant, and My servant shall have what he asked for."[212]

Sarakhsi said, "The fact that he begins with *al-hamdu lillahi rabb al-alamin* is proof that the *tasmiya* is not a verse in the beginning of the *Fatiha*, and if it were a verse, then the division into two halves would not be realized."

Aisha said, "Allah's Messenger used to open the prayer with *takbir*, and he used to open the recitation with *al-hamdu lillahi rabb al-alamin*."[213] Al-Sarakhsi said, "Its interpretation is that

---

211 Tirmidhi, *Kitab al-salat*.

212 Narrated by Muslim, Tirmidhi, Abu Dawud, Nasai, Ibn Majah, and Ahmad.

213 Muslim narrates it in the book of *salat*, chapter entitled: "The Proof of those who say the *Basmala* is not to be pronounced."

he used to pronounce the *tasmiya* silently (*kana yakhfi al-tas-miya*), and this is the position of our school and the saying of Ali and Ibn Masud."[214]

Ibn Masud said, "Let the Imam not pronounce four things: *taawwudh, tasmiya* [i.e. *basmala*], *tamin* [saying *AMIN*], and *tahmid* [saying *rabbana laka al-hamd*]."[215]

1.15.2. ALBANI SAYS TO OMIT THE *BASMALA* IS AN ERROR

Neglecting the opening dua of prayer, *tawwudth*, and *basmala*. *Tawwudth* is saying "*Aoudhu billahi min ashshaitan ir-rajim*" and *basmala* is saying "*Bismillah hirRahmaan irRaheem*."[216]

1.15.3. MAINSTREAM ISLAM LEAVES THE ISSUE OF PRONOUNCING THE *BASMALA* OPEN TO *IJTIHAD*

Of those who say that the *basmala* must be recited are Ibn Umar, al-Zuhri, Shafii, Ahmad, Ishaq, Abu Thawr, and Abu Ubayd. This indicates that this is a matter of *ijtihad* and not a decisive conclusion, as some who claim some knowledge of *fiqh*, yet do not have it, make it appear to be. To declare millions of Muslims to have erred because of this is rejected and condemned.

1.15.4. TO SAY *AMIN* SILENTLY IS INCORRECT ACCORDING TO ALBANI

As for saying or not saying *AMIN*, there is no disagreement; all agree that it is a *sunna*–not an integral requirement of *salat*–but there is disagreement as to saying it aloud. As Tabari said, there are sound (*sahih*) reports supporting both sides of the issue. The position of the Hanafis and Malikis, who hold that it should be said silently by both imam and follower, is that the context of the hadith in which the Prophet (ﷺ) said it aloud was didactic and temporary. Among the evidence they adduce in support of this is the following:

Abu Hurayra narrates that the Prophet (ﷺ) said, "When the Imam says, "*Ghayri al-maghdubi alayhim wa la al-dallin*," say, "*AMIN*," for the angels say *AMIN* and the Imam says

---

214 Al-Sarakhsi, *al-Mabsut* (1:15).
215 Ibn Abi Shayba narrated it in his *Musannaf* from Ibrahim al-Nakhi. Ibn al-Humam cited it in *Fath al-qadir* (1:204).
216 *Ibid.*

AMIN, and he whose *AMIN* coincides with that of the angels, his previous sins are forgiven."[217]

Al-Sarakhsi said, "The wording: and the Imam says *AMIN* indicates that the Imam is not saying it out loud. That is the position of our scholars (i.e. in the Hanafi school), and that of Ali and Ibn Masud."[218]

Samura ibn Jundub and Ubay ibn Kab stated that there were two moments in the *salat* [which were prayed aloud] in which the Prophet (ﷺ) would be silent: after the initial *takbir*, and after *wa la al-dallin* (i.e. at the end of the *Fatiha*).[219]

Ibn Masud's saying, which has already been cited, "Let the Imam not pronounce four things: *taawwudh, tasmiya* [i.e. basmala], *tamin* [saying AMIN], and *tahmid* [saying *rabbana laka al-hamd*]."[220]

> Neglecting *tameen* (to say *Aameen*) loudly when the imam recites the concluding verse of *surat al-Fatiha*, "*waladh-dhalleen*". The Prophet (*sallallaahu alaihi wasallam*) commanded: When the imam says, *waladh-dhalleen*, say *Aameen*, because the angels also say, *Aameen*, and the imam says, *Aameen*. He whose *aameen* coincides with the *aameen* of the angels, Allah forgives his past sins [Bukhari and Muslim]. In another narration, the Prophet (*sallallaahu alaihi wasallam*) said: Then say, *Aameen*, Allah loves you [Muslim].[221]

1.15.5. MAINSTREAM ISLAM'S APPROACH TO
AMIN AND THE BASMALA ETC.

To all of the above it is answered: All these questions pertain to matters that are open to *ijtihad* among the scholars, and are *sunna* and not obligatory in *salat*. It is impermissible for anyone to say that to do or not do one of them is an "error that should be avoided." It is a wonder that anyone dare claim that Ali and Ibn Masud erred in their *salat*, since it is narrated from Abu Wail that they did not pronounce the *basmala* or the

---

217 Ahmad and al-Nasai narrate it.

218 Al-Sarakhsi, *al-Mabsut* (1:32).

219 It is narrated by Tirmidhi who said it is *hasan*, also by Abu Dawud and Ahmad.

220 Ibn Abi Shayba narrated it in his *Musannaf* from Ibrahim al-Nakhi. Ibn al-Humam cited it in *Fath al-qadir* (1:204).

221 *Ibid.*

taawwudh at the beginning of *salat*, nor the *Amin* at the end of the *Fatiha*.[222]

The compilers of the so-called "Errors in Prayer that should be avoided" stand much to gain from the words of Ibn al-Qayyim: "This is merely a common difference of opinion in which there should be no criticism leveled at the one who says *AMIN* aloud nor at the one who says it silently. This issue is like that of *raf al-yadayn*."[223]

1.15.5.1. THE MEANING OF THE ARABIC WORD *AMIN*

Imam Bukhari has a chapter in his *Sahih* entitled "The Imam's Saying *Amin* aloud."[224] He says in the subtitle:[225]

> Ata said, "*Amin* is an invocation." Ibn al-Zubayr said *Amin*, and all those who were behind him, until the whole mosque was filed with sound. Abu Hurayra used to call to the Imam, "Don't finish saying *Amin* before me." Nafi said, "Ibn Umar never omitted it, and he used to press them to say it; I hear many good things about it from him."

Then Bukhari relates the following from Abu Hurayra: The Prophet (ﷺ) said, "When the Imam says *AMIN*, say *AMIN*, for he whose *AMIN* coincides with the *AMIN* of the angels, his past sins are forgiven." al-Zuhri said, "The Prophet (ﷺ) used to say *AMIN*."

Bukhari relates the same hadith as reported by Abu Hurayra but through Said ibn al-Musayyib.[226]

Shawkani stated that the vast majority of the scholars understand the words When the Imam says *AMIN* to mean: "When he intends to say it."[227]

Ibn Hajar, in his commentary on these two chapters, says the following:

> Its meaning according to the vast majority of the

---

222 Tabarani narrated it in *al-Mujam al-kabir* with a good chain as shown by Haythami in *Majma al-zawaid*.

223 Ibn al-Qayyim, *Zad al-maad* (70:1) cited by the author of *Fiqh al-imam* (p. 78).

224 Bukhari, *Sahih*, # 111.

225 Ibid. Book of *Adhan* (#10).

226 Ibid., Book of *Daawat* (#80: Invocations), chapter on saying *Amin* (#63).

227 Shawkani, *Nayl al-awtar* (2:223).

scholars is: "*Allahumma istajib* (O Allah, answer this plea)." Other meanings are given, which all go back to this one, such as:

O Allah, keep us safe with Your goodness;

So be it;

It is a level in Paradise which answers to him who says it;

It will be answered as the angels *AMIN* is answered;

It is one of the names of Allah [Abd al-Razzaq relates it from Abu Hurayra with a weak chain], and Hilal ibn Yasaf the Tabii also states it;[228]

It means "We are coming to You," as related from Jafar al-Sadiq;

It is a word in Hebrew or Aramaic;

Abu Dawud relates from the Companion Abu Zuhayr al-Numayri that *AMIN* is like the stamp on a page, and he then mentions that the Prophet (ﷺ) looked at a man making invocation and said, "If he seals it with *AMIN*, then he has been answered." Then the man came to the Prophet (ﷺ) and the latter said to him, "O so-and-so, seal it with *AMIN* and be happy with the good news."

Aisha said, "The Jews do not envy you for anything more than giving *salam* and saying *AMIN*." Ibn Majah relates it and Abu Khuzayma declared it sound (*sahih*).

Ibn Majah relates through Abu Hurayra, "They envy you for nothing more than saying AMIN, so say it a lot."

Al-Hakim relates from Habib ibn Muslima al-Fihri: I heard Allah's Messenger say, "No people gather while some of them make invocation and others say AMIN except Allah answers them."

Ibn al-Athir writes in his dictionary, under the word "*amin*":[229]

AMIN: Pronounced either AAmEEn or amEEn but the former is more frequent. Regarding it the

---

228 Also, the author of *al-Qamus* from al-Wahidi, as stated by Shawkani in *Nayl al-awtar* 2:223.

229 Ibn al-Athir, *al-Nihaya fi gharib al-hadith wa atharih*.

hadith is narrated: "Amin is the seal of the Lord of the Worlds."[230] It means that it is the seal of Allah on His servants, because disasters and afflictions are repelled by it, so it acts like the seal of the book that preserves it from corruption and exposure . . . Its meaning is "*Allahumma istajib li* (O Allah, answer my plea)." It has also been said that its meaning is: So be it, in reference to the invocation made . . . There is also the hadith "*Amin* is one of the levels of paradise," that is, he who says it obtains a certain level in paradise. And the hadith of Bilal whereby he asked the Prophet (ﷺ), "O Messenger of Allah, do not finish saying *Amin* before me."[231] It suggests that Bilal was reciting the *Fatiha* in one of two silent prayer-cycles behind the Imam, and for fear that the Prophet (ﷺ) would finish reciting it before him, he asked him to delay pronouncing *amin* so that his own *amin* would coincide with that of the Prophet.

1.16. PLACING ONE'S FOOT NEXT TO HIS NEIGHBOR'S FOOT IN PRESCRIBED PRAYER (*SALAT*)

Q. Must one place one's foot next to his neighbor's foot in *salat*?

1.16.1. MAINSTREAM ISLAM'S VIEW

The Prophet (ﷺ) never said that the feet should touch. He did mention the shoulders however, since he said *hadhu bayn al-manakib*, or "Close in your shoulders."[232] Some quote Abu Dawud's narration from another Companion, al-Numan ibn Bashir, that the Companions legs touched when they stood for *salat* behind the Prophet (ﷺ), and they incorrectly conclude by that it is *wajib*–obligatory. However, what is *wajib* can only be based on the explicit statement of Allah or the Prophet (ﷺ). Shawkani pointed out *la yastadillu bi mithli qawli sahabi ala al-wujub*, "The *wajib* cannot be inferred from something like the saying of a Companion."[233] Furthermore, the said narration only signifies that the rows were extremely straight, not

---

230 Ibn Adi, Tabarani in the chapter on *Dua*, and Suyuti in *al-Jami al-saghir*, who mentioned that it is weak.

231 Abu Dawud, and Ibn Hajar authenticates it: *Fath al-bari*, Adhan Ch. 111 #780; also Bayhaqi, *Sunan* 2:23, 56; Tabarani 1:352, 6:311; *Majma al-zawaid* 2:113.

232 It is narrated by Ahmad and his student Abu Dawud, and Malik narrates that Uthman ibn Affan also ordered it in his *khutba*.

233 Shawkani, *Nayl al-awtar* (3:126).

that the feet necessarily touched. That is how the Imams of *fiqh* and hadith understood it, and the scholars of mainstream Islam understand it this way.

1.16.2. ALBANI SAYS FEET MUST TOUCH

Leaving gaps in lines of congregational prayer. The Messenger of Allah commanded: Straighten your lines, level your shoulders and block the gaps. *Shaitan* passes through [line] gaps (footnote: Imam Ahmad and others).[234]

1.16.3. REFUTATION OF "SALAFI" STANCE BY MAINSTREAM ISLAMIC SCHOLARS

The following is taken from a book written in refutation of the innovations of "Salafis" and their wayward criticism of the Hanafi madhhab. The book is by Abdur-Rahman ibn Yusuf and is entitled *Fiqhul Imaam*:

A hadith of Abu Dawud does describe the Companions joining their feet with each other to form straight rows. The hadith is:

Abu al-Qasim al-Jadali reports: I heard Numan ibn Bashir relating that Rasoolullah (*sallallahu alayhi wa sallam*) faced the people and ordered, "Straighten your rows. By Allah, you will certainly straighten your rows, otherwise Allah will cause contradiction among your hearts." Numan ibn Bashir stated, "I saw each person join his shoulders to his neighbor's and his knees and ankle-bones to the person next to him."

This is the hadith that is put forward as evidence by those people who say that everyone's feet should be joined to the next persons while in congregation. Some of these people also make a great fuss about it. If the person standing next to him happens to draw his feet inwards then this person usually widens his legs more, to maintain the contact. Similarly, they criticize those who do not leave much of a gap between their feet as though it is only their way that is the *sunnah* of the Prophet (⸙).

However, their attempts to prove their point from

---

234 *Errors in Prayers that must be Avoided.*

this or similar ahadith are in vain, for a number of simple reasons:

The words that describe the joining of the feet are not at all the words of the Prophet (ﷺ) . . .

The hadith merely tells us of the behavior of the Companions before prayer had begun . . . The hadith does not indicate that this was done inside prayer . . . Whether this connection was continued throughout the *salaah* or not once it had begun, is not mentioned.

If it is taken for a moment to imply that the joining of the feet was maintained throughout the *salaah* then a number of questions arise. The first is, should the feet and shoulders be joined in all postures of the *salaah* or only in *qiyaam*? If the answer is "only in *qiyaam*" then what is the proof of that? How have you confined this to *qiyaam* and not to any other posture? On the other hand, if the answer is the opposite and they reply that it is an obligation in all parts of *salaah* then how will one go about joining his feet, shoulders, etc. to the people next to him while in *sajdah* or *qadah*? It is quite impossible to do so . . .

If you treat it as obligatory to join the shoulders and feet together then why have the knees been excluded? As it mentions in the hadith that the Companions also joined the knees together, then to join them should also be treated as a necessary act... But be warned that to stand with one's knees joined to the next person's can be very difficult.

The real concept that the Companion wants to present to us is that they attempted to make extremely straight rows. They did not join their feet, shoulders and ankles together literally. It is for this reason that *Hafiz* Ibn Hajar has termed the title of a chapter in Bukhari that says, "Joining of the shoulders and feet together" to be based on exaggeration. He said, "Imaam Bukhari's aim in choosing this specific title is to portray the emphasis upon straightening the rows and filling the gaps."[235]

Imam Shawkani, one of the "Salafi" Imaams, did not take it for its literal interpretation either. He writes in *Naylul-awtar*:

It (the Companion's statement) means, place the parts of the body (shoulders, etc.) in line with each

---

235 Ibn Hajar, *Fath al-bari* 2:247.

other so that the shoulder of each *musalli* is level with the shoulders of the rest. In this way everyone's shoulder, knees and feet will be in a single straight line. In clear words, this indicates that the real motive for joining the shoulders etc., was to straighten the rows. Therefore, the joining itself will not be treated as an obligatory act.[236] . . .

A question should be posed at this point to the people who assert that the shoulders and feet should be joined together: if they believe the joining of the shoulders and feet, etc. to be necessary, then the feet should not be widened more than a shoulder width. The reason for this is that when everyone's shoulders are joined together, then the feet will without doubt also have to be opened to the same width only. It would be quite impossible to spread them any more. If this is the case then why do these people stretch their legs beyond the width of the shoulders and make it seem as though one is in the East and the other in the West?

Furthermore, the hadith only mentions a congregational situation, in which the Sahaba joined their feet together. Why do these people also widen their feet the same distance, whilst performing *salaah* individually and where is the evidence for that? . . . They cannot say that it is necessary or even *sunnah* whilst performing salaah alone. [End of excerpt from *Fiqhul Imaam*.][237]

1.17. RECITING *SURAH AL-FATIHA* WITHOUT PAUSING AFTER EVERY VERSE

Q. May one recite the *Fatiha* without pausing after every verse?

The mainstream Islamic position of *Ahl al-sunna* regarding the correct recitation of *al-Fatiha* is that stated in the Hanafi scholar al-Haskafi's *Manual of fiqh*, entitled *al-Durr al-mukhtar*, where he says:

The following is a poem written by Ahmad Ibn Kamal Pasha on the *sejawands* (marks of subdivision) in the Quran:

---

236 Shawkani, *Nayl al-awtar* 3:65.
237 Abdur-Rahman ibn Yusuf, *Fiqhul Imaam* (p. 64-67).

Jeem: [*waqf Jaiz*] Permissible to pass by it, and proper too, better to stop when you see it, though.

Zaa: [*waqf mujawwaZ*] You are free to stop, and so have they done. But they have deemed it better to read on.

Tah: [*waqf muTlaq*] It is an absolute sign of stop; wherever you see it be sure to stop!

Saad: [*waqf murakhkhaS*] "Stopping is permissible," they have said; so they have allowed you to take a breath.

Meem: [*waqf laziM*] Absolutely necessary to stop for it; fear of disbelief is in passing by it!

Laa: [*nahy*] "No pause!" is its meaning, everywhere; never stop! Nor breathe, anywhere! Now perfect your reading with this recipe, and gift its *thawab* to Muslims before thee![238]

Below are the recitation-marks of the *Fatiha* as found in the *mushaf*s of mainstream Islam:

[*Bismillah al-Rahman al-Rahim*],
al-hamdu lillahi rabbi al-alamin,
al-rahmani al-rahimi,
maliki yawmi al-din,
iyyaka nabudu wa iyyaka nastain,
ihdina al-sirata al-mustaqimi,
sirata al-ladhina anamta alayhim,
ghayri al-maghdubi alayhim wa la al-dallin.

Even if one does not always recite according to the above instructions, at least let him make sure that his *mushaf* has them so that he can take advantage of them and avail himself of their benefit, as there are many *mushaf*s being circulated nowadays from which these marks have been removed.

1.17.1. ALBANI SAYS RECITING *AL-FATIHA* WITHOUT PAUSING IS WRONG

Reciting *Surah al-Fatiha* fast without pausing after each verse. The Prophet (ﷺ) used to pause after each verse of this *surah* (Footnote: Abu Dawood).[239]

---

238 Al-Haskafi, *al-Durr al-mukhtar*. The letter **ayn** means *ruku*. It means that when conducting prayer in *jamaa*, Hadrat Umar al-Faruq used to stop reciting the Quran while standing and bow for the *ruku*. This sign, *ayn*, always comes at the end of *ayat*s. If you stop at the place where the sign is, you must begin reading with the previous word. When you stop at the end of a verse, you do not have to repeat the previous word.

239 *Errors in Prayers that must be Avoided.*

1.17.2. ONE MAY RECITE *AL-FATIHA* WITH OR WITHOUT PAUSING ACCORDING TO MAINSTREAM ISLAM

The *sunna* is to recite clearly and deliberately with a beautiful voice, not necessarily to pause between each verse. The two pauses dictated by meaning are clearly marked in the *mushaf*s of *Ahl al-sunna*, whether according to Imam Warsh or Hafs: one pause after *maliki yawm al-din*, and another pause after *iyyaka nabudu wa iyyaka nastain*. Not pausing certainly does not mean that one is reciting fast.

Furthermore, the hadith the "Salafis" have quoted is *ghayr muttasil*; that is, missing a link. Abu Dawud narrated it thus:[240]

> Said ibn Yahya narrated to us: My father narrated to me: Ibn Jurayj narrated to us from Abd Allah ibn Abi Mulayka from Umm Salama that she mentioned that the recitation–or some other word–of the Prophet (ﷺ) was *Bismillah al-Rahman al-Rahim / al-Hamdu lillah rabb al-alamin al-rahman al-rahim maliki yawm al-din*, and that he would separate his recitation, reciting verse by verse (*ayatan ayatan*) . . .

Tirmidhi said of the above chain *laysa isnaduhu bi muttasil* –"its chain is not firmly linked."[241] This is because a sounder chain has al-Layth ibn Sad narrating from Ibn Abi Mulayka from Yala ibn Mamlak from Umm Salam that she described the Prophet's recitation as being harfan harfan, or "letter by letter" – i.e. not verse by verse. The meaning of the Prophet's example is that he was articulating each letter, not necessarily pausing between each verse. This is firmly established by the sound (*sahih*) hadith that states it explicitly.[242]

1.18. SITTING IN *TAWARRUK* IN THE LAST CYCLE OF DAWN AND FRIDAY CONGREGATIONAL (*JUMA*) PRESCRIBED PRAYER (*SALAT*)

Q. May one sit in *tawarruk* in the last *rakat* of *fajr* and *juma*?

240 Abu Dawud, *Sunan*, book of al-*Huruf wa al-qiraat*.
241 Tirmidhi, his *Sunan* (book of *Qiraat*).
242 Narrated by Tirmidhi in the book of *salat*, Ahmad in his *Musnad* (3:237), Ibn

1.18.1. MAINSTREAM ISLAM"S VIEW

There are several views on this issue among the scholars; therefore it is impermissible to fault all views other than the one "Salafis" have chosen. Imam Malik's view is that *tawarruk* is always the position for sitting, whether in the first, or the second, or the only *tashahhud*. The view of Imam Shafii and his school is that *tawarruk* is the position for the final *tashahhud*, whether one prayed two or four *rakat*. The view of Imam Ahmad and the Hanbali school, which is falsely being claimed by the "Salafis" as the only valid view, is that *tawarruk* is the position for the final *tashahhud* only if one prayed four *rakat*. In the Hanbali school if one prayed only two, as in *fajr* (dawn) or *juma* (Friday), then he must sit in *iftirash*. The view of Imam Abu Hanifa and his school is that one must sit in *iftirash* every time, and that *tawarruk* is only permissible, not praiseworthy, in case of difficulty in sitting in *iftirash*.[243]

Imam Shafii's position is sound. It is established from the hadith of Abu Humayd al-Saidi in *Sahih Bukhari* (book of *Adhan*) that the Prophet (ﷺ) sat in *tawarruk* in his last *tashahhud*. This hadith does not specify whether it was at the end of two or four *rakat*, but simply says, "*Wa idha jalasa fi al-raka al-akhira qaddama rijlahu al-yusra wa nasaba al-ukhra, wa qaada ala maqadatihi* (whenever he sat after his last *raka* he would put forward his left leg, set up the other, and sit on his posterior)." There is no basis, therefore, for those who claim that *tawarruk* is for sitting after four *rakat* and not two. Shawkani said, "The stipulation that Ahmad made is refuted by the words of Abu Humayd."[244]

1.18.2. ALBANI ONLY ACCEPTS HANBALI VIEW ON *TAWARRUK*

Sitting in *tawarruk* position in the last *rakat* of *fajr* and *juma* prescribed prayers. It is praiseworthy to take *tawarruk* position only in the last *rakah* of *Dhuhr, Asr, Maghrib* and *Isha* prayers. *Tawarruk* is described in *Sahih al-Bukhari* as resting the body, during sitting position, on the left thigh and putting

Abi Shayba in his *Musannaf* (*Fadail* #524), Nasai, and Abu Dawud in the book of *salat*, chapter entitled *Istihbab al-tartil fi al-qiraa*: "The desirability of making one's recitation deliberate/articulate."

243 See, *Al-Mudawwana* (1:74), Nawawi's *Sharh al-muhadhdhab* (3:450), Ibn Qudama's *al-Mughni* (1:571), and Marghinani's *al-Hidaya* (1:55).

244 Shawkani, *Nayl al-awtar* (2:274).

the left foot under the right leg, while setting the right foot upright; and supporting the body by the left hand with which the left knee is grasped.[245]

1.19. COUNTING *TASBIH* WITH BOTH HANDS
Q. May one count *tasbih* with both hands?

1.19.1. MAINSTREAM ISLAM'S VIEW

It is established that the Prophet (ﷺ) said, "Count *tasbih* on your fingers, for they will be called to witness." He never said to use the right hand only. Therefore we may count *tasbih* on all our fingers, beginning with the right hand, as the Prophet (ﷺ) always began everything with the right side.

1.19.2. ALBANI REJECTS COUNTING *TASBIH* WITH BOTH HANDS

COUNTING *TASBEEH* WITH THE LEFT HAND

> The Prophet (*sallallaahu alaihi wa sallam*) used to count *tasbeeh* on the fingers of his right hand after *salah*. Abdullah bin Amr reported that the Messenger of Allah (*sallallaahu alaihi wasallam*) said, (There are) two good deeds, any Muslim who does them shall enter *Jannah* but few are those who do them: to say, "*subhanAllah*" ten times, and "*alHamdulillah*" ten times, and "*AllahuAkbar*" ten times. And I have seen the Messenger of Allah (*sallallaahu alaihi wasallam*) counting them on his hand. lbn Qudamah said: The Messenger of Allah (*sallallaahu alaihi wasallam*) used his right hand for *tasbeeh* [Abu Dawood]. The above *hadeeth* indicates clearly that the Prophet (*sallallaahu alaihi wasallam*) used only one hand for counting *tasbeeh*. No Muslim with sound mind would imagine that the Prophet (*sallallaahu alaihi wasallam*) used his left hand for counting *tasbeeh*. Aaishah, with whom Allah is pleased, said that the Prophet (*sallallaahu alaihi wasallam*) used his left hand only for *Istinjaa*, or cleaning himself after responding to the call of nature. He never used it for *tasbeeh*.

---

245 *Errors in Prayers that must be Avoided.*

Yasirah reported: "The Prophet (*sallallaahu alaihi wasallam*) commanded women to count *tasbeeh* on their fingers." The Messenger of Allah (*sallallaahu alaihi wasallam*) said: "They (the fingers) will be made to speak, and will be questioned (on the Day of Resurrection)" [Tirmidhi]. The above *hadeeth* indicates that it is preferable to count *tasbeeh* on the fingers of the right hand than to do so on *masbahah* (rosary).[246]

As for using a *masbaha* or *dhikr*-beads, it is established as a *sunna*. This has been amply demonstrated above, in the section on remembrance of Allah (*dhikr*).

1.20. SUPPLICATION (*DUA*) AFTER PRESCRIBED PRAYER (*SALAT*)

Q. May one supplicate after prescribed prayer (*salat*)?

1.20.1. MAINSTREAM ISLAM'S VIEW

Bukhari in his *Sahih*, book of *Daawat*, named a chapter *al-dua bad al-salat* [247] "*Dua* after prayer." Ibn Hajar comments: "In this chapter-title is a refutation of those who claim that *dua* after prayer is unlawful."[248]

The fact is that the Prophet (peace be upon him) did make *dua* directly after salat. This is established from the following hadith, among others, which Ibn Hajar cites in refuting the above claim:

Muadh ibn Jabal said that the Prophet (peace be upon him) said to him, "O Muadh, by Allah, I love you! So never forget after every prayer (*dubura kulli salat*) to say, "*Allahumma ainni ala dhikrika wa shukrika wa husni ibadatik* (O Allah! help me to remember You, to thank You, and to worship You well)."[249]

Abu Bakrah said, "*Allahumma inni audhu bika min al-kufri wa al-faqri wa adhab al-qabr* (O Allah, I seek refuge in You from disbelief and poverty and the punishment of the

---

246 *Errors in Prayers that must be Avoided.*
247 Bukhari, *Sahih,* #18.
248 Ibn Hajar, *Fath al-bari* (1989 ed. 11:160).
249 Narrated by Ahmad, Abu Dawud, and Nasai, and both Ibn Hibban and al-Hakim declared it *sahih*. The narrations also mention that each of the narrators renewed the Prophet's advice to his student, including Muadh to the one who took the hadith from him.

grave. The Prophet (ﷺ) used to supplicate with these words after every prayer (*dubura kulli salat*))."[250]

Suhayb said, "The Prophet used to say when he finished his prayer (*idha insarafa min salatihi*), "*Allahumma aslih liya dini* (O Allah! straighten my way in religion for me)."[251]

Zayd ibn Arqam said, "I hear Allah's Messenger supplicating after every prayer (*dubura kulli salat*): '*Allahumma rabbana wa rabba kulli shay* (O Allah! our Lord and the Lord of everything)!'"[252]

Fadala ibn Ubayd said he heard the Prophet (ﷺ) say, "Whenever one of you has prayed, then he should begin by invoking Allah, thanking Him and praising Him and then he should make praise of the Prophet (ﷺ) and then he may invoke Allah as he wishes."[253]

The complete text of the Prophet's supplication after prayer in Zayd's narration is as follows:

> *allahumma rabbana wa rabba kulli shay*
> O Allah! our Lord and the Lord of everything.
> *ana shahidun annaka anta al-rabbu wahdaka la sharika lak*
> I am witness that You are the Lord, alone, without partner.
> *allahumma rabbana wa rabba kulli shay*
> O Allah! our Lord and the Lord of everything.
> *ana shahidun anna muhammadan abduka wa rasuluk*
> I am witness that Muhammad is Your servant and messenger.
> *allahumma rabbana wa rabba kulli shay*
> O Allah! our Lord and the Lord of everything.
> *ana shahidun anna al-ibada kulluhum ikhwa*
> I am witness that Your servants are all brethren.
> *allahumma rabbana wa rabba kulli shay*
> O Allah! our Lord and the Lord of everything.
> *ijalni mukhlisan laka wa ahli fi kulli saatin fi al-*

---

250 Narrated by Ahmad, Nasai, and al-Hakim who declared it *sahih*.
251 Narrated by Nasai with a strong chain, and Ibn Hibban declared it *sahih*.
252 Narrated by Abu Dawud and Ahmad with a good chain.
253 Abu Dawud narrated it with a strong chain.

dunya wa al-akhira

Make me and my family pure and truthful with You in every moment in this world and the next.

ya dha al-jalali wa al-ikrami isma wa istajib allahu akbar al-akbar

O Lord of majesty and nobility hear and answer! Allah is greater, greater!

allahumma nura al-samawati wa al-ard allahu akbar al-akbar

O Allah! light of the heavens and the earth, Allah is greater, greater!

hasbiya allahu wa nima al-wakil allahu akbar al-akbar

Enough for me is Allah, the best of advocates. Allah is greater, greater!

Ibn Hajar continues:

If it is said, "What is meant by *dubur kulli salat*– after every prayer–is actually at the end of the salat i.e. in *tashahhud*," we say, "The reports mention the Prophet's order to perform *dhikr* "after every prayer" (*dubur kulli salat*), and the meaning of this is after giving *salam* by the consensus of the scholars." The same applies to this until the contrary is firmly established. Indeed, Tirmidhi narrates from Abu Umama that he asked the Prophet (ﷺ), "O Messenger of Allah, which supplication is best answered?" He replied, "That made in the second half of the night and that after the prescribed prayers." Tirmidhi said it is *hasan*.

Ibn Hajar continues:

Many of those whom we met among the Hanbalis have understood from Ibn Qayyim's words that *dua* is completely forbidden after *salat* and this is not so. The gist of his words is that what he forbade is the continuation of facing the *qibla* by the imam in making *dua* after *salat*. However, if he faces another direction, or offers the *adhkar* stipulated by the Law, then there is no objection to make *dua* at that time.

1.20.2. ALBANI REJECTS SUPPLICATION
AFTER PRESCRIBED PRAYER
RAISING HANDS FOR *DUA* SOON AS PRAYER IS OVER

This was not the practice of the Messenger of
Allah (*sallallaahu alaihi wa sallam*). The *sunnah* is
to start with *dhikr* soon after *salah* is over. The
Prophet (*sallallaahu alaihi wasallam*) said: When
you recite, "At-tahiyyat . . ." (just before *tasleem*),
choose whichever *dua* you like (Footnote: al-Nasai).
The best forms of *dua* are those authentically related
to the Prophet, (*sallallaahu alaihi wasallam*) . . .
Insha Allah, we will publish the authentic *dua mas-
noon*, soon.[254]

1.20.3. MAINSTREAM ISLAM'S ANSWER
The above claims are from Ibn Qayyim, who said, "Making
dua after giving *salam* ending *salat* . . . was not the practice of
the Messenger, etc."[255] Ibn Hajar said, "His claim, which completely negates the *dua* after *salat*, is rejected."

1.21. COLLECTIVE SUPPLICATION
Q. May one make collective supplication (*dua*)?

1.21.1. MAINSTREAM ISLAM'S VIEW
Some "Salafis" also try to propagate the notion that collective *dua* is wrong; that is, *dua* led by the imam to which the
congregation responds *Amin*. This is a false notion, as just
proven by the mention of the hadith of Zayd ibn Arqam whereby the Prophet (ﷺ) said, "O Allah! Our Lord" after every
prayer.

The principle for collective *dua* is entirely based on the
Quran and *sunna*. There is decisive evidence (*hujja qatia*) for
loud *dua* in *jamaa*:

Al-Hakim relates from Habib ibn Muslima al-
Fihri: I heard Allah's Messenger say, "No people gath-
er while some of them make invocation and others say
AMIN except Allah answers them."

---

254 *Ibid.*
255 Ibn Qayyim, *al-Hadi al-nabawi.*

The *sunna* of collective invocations specifically after the salat is established from the *sunna* of *dhikr* directly after the *salat*. This is described by the hadith of Ibn Abbas whereby he knew from outside the mosque that the *salat* had ended by the sound of the collective *takbir*.[256] *Dhikr* is a form of *dua* as are all forms of worship according to the sahih hadith in Tirmidhi, "Supplication (*dua*) is worship (*ibada*) itself."

The Quran is replete with collective invocations by a group of Muslims, such as the following verse, which Anas said the Prophet (ﷺ) repeated the most,[257] *"O our Lord, grant us goodness in this life, and grant us goodness in the next life, and protect us from the fire"* (2:201). Also, the dua of the Hawariyyun or disciples of Jesus, *"O our Lord, we believe in what you have revealed, therefore write us among the witnesses"* (3:53); and the dua of the young men of the *ashab al-kahf*, *"Our Lord! Give us mercy from Thy presence, and shape for us right conduct in our plight"* (18:10).

The congregational supplication hinges on the supplication of the imam. Tirmidhi narrates from Thawban that the Prophet (ﷺ) said that the imam who makes his *dua* particular to himself has betrayed his people.[258]

When Umar, as the Imam of Muslims, supplicated through al-Abbas, it was a collective *dua* as established by the use of plural wording.

The evidence clarifies that congregational *dua* is ordered by the Prophet (ﷺ) in the hadith that says, "When you hear in (loud) congregational prayer the Imam say *"Wa la al-dallin,"* say, *"Amin."*[259] Ibn Hajar said, in commenting on this hadith, "The meaning of the unmodified order "say" is "say out loud.""" This does not make it incorrect to say it silently, as according to other interpretations. At any rate, this is clearly congregational *dua*, as the noble *Fatiha* is the highest and best *dua* of all. The fact that it is or is not a part of *salat* is irrelevant, as words of *dhikr* and *dua* that are *halal* inside *salat* do not become *haram* outside it.

Another clear evidence is the *dua* of *qunut* in the congregational *fajr* prayer, whereby the Imam stands after *ruku* in the

---

256 Bukhari and Muslim.
257 Bukhari.
258 Tirmidhi—*hasan*—Abu Dawud, Ibn Majah, and Ahmad also narrate it.
259 Bukhari, Muslim and others.

second *rakat* and supplicates out loud with his hands raised palms up, and the congregation repeatedly says *AMIN* until he goes into prostration. This is the position of the Shafii school as set forth by al-Nawawi and elsewhere.[260] It is recommended to make the same kind of *qunut* out loud in prayers other than *fajr* in certain circumstances. Nawawi cites the hadith of Anas whereby "The Prophet (ﷺ) did not cease to make *qunut* in the dawn (*fajr* prescribed prayer) until he left the world."[261]

1.22. RAISING ONE'S HANDS IN SUPPLICATION AND WIPING ONE'S FACE AFTERWARDS

Q. May one raise the hands in supplication (*dua*) and wipe the face afterwards?

1.22.1. MAINSTREAM ISLAM'S VIEW

Scholars agree that it is *sunna* to raise one's hands in *dua*. It is stated explicitly by Nawawi in *al-Majmu* and by Ibn Hajar in *Fath al-bari*. The latters words were "Nawawi said the scholars said, 'The *sunna* in every *dua* . . . wherein one asks for something is to raise one's hands towards the heaven.'"[262]

It is related through many different chains that the Prophet (ﷺ) raised his hands in *dua* and that he did not rest them before wiping his face with them.[263]

Al-Hafiz Ibn Hajar, after citing the different *daif* (weak) narrations regarding this, says "*Wa majmuuha yaqtadi annahu hasan* (from their collated weight it is concluded that the hadith is *hasan* (fair))."[264] This explains why it is considered *sunna*, as found in many of the books of *fiqh*.

---

260 Nawawi, *Adhkar* (Chapter of *Qunut* at *Fajr*).

261 Al-Hakim narrates it and said it is *sahih*, and Ibn Hajar: *hasan*. He then cites the *sahih* hadith of al-Hasan ibn Ali stipulating the words taught by the Prophet for that *qunut*.

262 Ibn Hajar, *Fath al-bari*, 1989 ed. 2:658. This ruling has been established at length by Shaykh Muhammad al-Ahdal in his book entitled *Sunniyyat raf al-yadayn fi al-dua bad al-salawat al-maktuba*, which the late Shaykh Abd al-Fattah Abu Ghudda edited. Also noteworthy is Bakr Abu Zayd's monograph on the topic, entitled *Juz fi mash al-yadayn bad al-dua*.

263 It is narrated by Tirmidhi in the book of *Daawat*, from Umar ibn al-Khattab, and he said: *gharib* (very rare).

264 Ibn Hajar, *Bulugh al-maram* (#1343).

Ibn Hajar also lists many sound hadiths to that effect, in commenting upon Bukhari:[265]

> Bukhari narrates in his *Sahih*, Book of invocations (*daawat*), chapter 23, "Raising hands in *dua*," Abu Musa al-Ashari said, "The Prophet (🖋) supplicated then he raised his hands and I saw the whiteness of his armpits." Ibn Umar said, "The Prophet (🖋) raised his hands and said, "O Allah, I am innocent before you of Khalid [ibn al-Walid]'s doing." Bukhari said: "Al-Uwaysi said: 'Muhammad ibn Jafar narrated to me from Yahya ibn Said and Sharik that they both heard Anas say, "The Prophet (🖋) raised his two hands until I saw the whiteness of his armpits."'"
>
> Ibn Hajar said: "There is in the first and second hadiths a refutation of those who say that the Prophet (🖋) did not raise his hands other than in the prayer for rain (*istisqa*). They adduce as their evidence the hadith of Anas whereby 'The Prophet (🖋) did not raise his hands in any part of his *dua* except in *istisqa*. which is sound (*sahih*). However, what makes it and the others compatible is that what is negated by him is a specific aspect of raising hands, not the act itself . . . Namely, the raising in *istisqa* differs from other types of raising. This difference is either in the fact that in *istisqa* the hands are raised all the way, for example next to the face, while in other *dua* they are raised to the shoulders only. There is no discrepancy in the fact that in both cases the whiteness of his armpits was seen, and what harmonizes between them is that in *istisqa* the whiteness is more visible than at any other time. Or, the difference is in the fact that in *istisqa* the hands are turned downwards and face the earth, while they are otherwise turned upwards and face the sky."

Al-Mundhiri said, "Insofar as allying [between the negation of raising hands and the hadiths that establish it] is unfeasible, then affirming [the raising of the hands in *dua*] is more correct." I say, This is true, especially in the light of the many hadiths supporting the latter, and al-Mundhiri collected them in a monograph from which Nawawi cited several in his

265 Ibn Hajar, *Fath al-bari* (11:170-172).

Adhkar and *Sharh al-muhadhdhab*. Bukhari also devoted a chapter to them in *al-Adab al-mufrad* in which he mentioned Abu Hurayra's narration:

Al-Tufayl ibn Amr came to the Prophet (ﷺ) and said, "Daws rebelled, invoke Allah against them!" whereby the Prophet (ﷺ) turned to the *qibla*, raised his hands, and said, "O Allah, guide Daws!" It is narrated in the two *Sahih* collections without the words "raised his hands."

Also the narration of Jabir whereby al-Tufayl ibn Amr emigrated, in which he mentions the man who emigrated with him and in which the Prophet (ﷺ) says, "O Allah, forgive even his hands!" and he raised his own hands. Its chain is sound and Muslim narrates it.

Also Aisha's narration whereby she saw the Prophet (ﷺ) with hands raised in supplication saying, "O Allah, I am only a human being" etc. Its chain is sound.

Among the sound narrations which Bukhari collected in his monograph on raising hands (*raf al-yadayn*) is, "I saw the Prophet (ﷺ) with his hands raised, invoking on behalf of Uthman."

Muslim narrates from Abd al-Rahman ibn Samura in the story of the eclipse, "I reached the Prophet (ﷺ) and saw that he had his hands raised and was supplicating."

Also in Muslim is Aisha's narration of the eclipse to the same effect, "Then he raised his hands in supplication."

Also in Muslim, the narration of both Aisha and ibn Samura concerning the Prophet's invocation for the people of Baqi, "He raised his hands three times," etc.

Abu Hurayra's long narration of the conquest of Makka in which he says, "He raised his hands and began to supplicate."

Abu Humayd's narration in Bukhari and Muslim whereby "He raised his hands until I saw the paleness of his armpits and he said, O Allah! Have I delivered the message?"

The hadith of Abd Allah ibn Amr: the Prophet (ﷺ) mentioned the sayings of Ibrahim and Isa then he raised his hands and said, "O Allah! My Community!"

The hadith of Umar, "Whenever revelation descended on the Prophet (ﷺ), a sound was heard around his face like the buzzing of bees. One day Allah sent down His revelation on him, and after he regained his composure he faced the *qibla*, raised his hands, and supplicated." Tirmidhi narrated it thus, and also Nasai and Hakim.

Usama's hadith, "I was riding behind the Prophet (ﷺ) in Arafat when he raised his hands in *dua* whereupon his camel leaned forward and its halter slipped, so the Prophet (ﷺ) grasped it with his hand while he kept the other raised." al-Nasai narrated it with a good chain.

The hadith of Qays ibn Sad narrated by Abu Dawud: Then the Prophet (ﷺ) raised his hand in *dua* saying, "O Allah, send your blessings and peace on the family of Sad ibn Ubada" etc. and its chain is good . . .

Both Abu Dawud and Tirmidhi among others narrated, and the latter declared it fair (*hasan*), from Salman from the Prophet (ﷺ), "Verily, your Lord is magnanimous and generous, He is unwilling to let His servant who raises his hands to Him, take them back empty." Its chain is good. [End of Ibn Hajar's words.]

In addition Bukhari, Muslim, Tirmidhi, Abu Dawud, Nasai, and Ibn Majah narrate from Aisha that the Prophet (ﷺ) would recite into his two hands three *surahs* before sleeping at night: *Ikhlas, Falaq,* and *Nas*, then wipe himself with them beginning with his face and head. Bukhari and Muslim also relate that the Prophet (ﷺ) did this whenever he was sick. Thus, the "Salafi" objection to wiping with the hands after prayer is unfounded and contradicted by the teachings of mainstream Islam.

1.23 MEN AND WOMEN SHAKING HANDS WITH NON-*MAHRAM*

Q. What is the ruling on men shaking hands with non-*mahram* women who are either distant relatives or co-workers in the work place?

While the author of this work does not recommend men and women who are non-*mahram* shaking hands, it is a question asked more and more by Muslims living in the West as well as in the Middle and Far East where it has become a common practice. The author feels duty-bound to present a scholar's view here. This question was asked of Dr. Ahmad at-Tayyib who responded with the following:

Some hadith have often been cited from which people MIGHT assume that it is forbidden for men to shake hands with non-*mahram* women like the hadith of Tabarani where he said that the Prophet (ﷺ) said that it would be better to be stabbed with an iron spike than to TOUCH (*lamasa*) a non-*mahram* woman.

This hadith was not well-known at the time of the Companions and their students, and scholars do not consider that it forbids the shaking of hands because the word *yamus* does not refer to shaking hands as can be seen in the Quran. *Yamus* comes from *lams* which relates to being alone with and touching a non-*mahram* woman for the purpose of sexual pleasure.

The Quran and the *sunna* use the word *lams* with that meaning. Explaining the Quranic verse *"If you divorce women while you have not yet touched them,"*(2:236-237), Ibn Abbas said, *"Al-mass, al-lams* and *wal malamasa* in these Quranic verses refer to *al-jimaa. Malamasa* means to make love and to seclude onself with non-*mahram* women. Mary says in *Surah Maryam, "How shall I have a son when no mortal has touched me"* (19:20). From here it is evident that touching differs from shaking hands. The Tabarani hadith says *al-mass* which means private seclusion and satisfying sexual desires, not shaking hands.

The most significant point showing that shaking hands is allowed are two authentic hadith from Bukhari. In the first, Bukhari narrates from Anas that the women of Madina used to take the hand of the Prophet in theirs and pass it over their bodies wherever they wished to be blessed by the Prophet. In the second authentic narration, Bukhari says that the Prophet never took his hand away from their hand until the woman had put his hand wherever she wanted for blessings.

These two narrations show that men shaking the hands of non-*mahram* women is allowed. Scholars say that if shaking hands is only with the intention of extending greetings, giving respect and following common practice, there is nothing forbidden in doing it. However if it is done with the intention of seeking pleasure, it is completely forbidden like other things forbidden by the Prophet (ﷺ).[266]

---

266 *Al-Ahram*, North American Edition, #4048, March 13, 1998.

2. FOLLOWING QUALIFIED OPINION (*TAQLID*), CONSENSUS (*IJMA*), AND DIFFERENCES OF JURISTS (*IKHTILAF AL-FUQAHA*)

Questions addressed in this chapter include among others:

What is the position of mainstream Islamic scholars on following qualified opinion (*taqlid*) and consensus (*ijma*)?

What exactly does *taqlid* (following qualified opinion) and *ijma* (consensus) mean?

Do the scholars' differences of opinion in religion constitute a blessing or a curse?

Can differences in opinion expel one from the religion? What is the opinion of Ibn Taymiyya on the question?

Are we allowed to follow other scholars or to follow *ijma* (the consensus of the scholars) since *taqlid* (following qualified opinion) is characterized by the "Salafis" as reprehensible, and some of them say, "We do not worship men" to support their opinion?

2.1. THE ROLE OF FOLLOWING QUALIFIED OPINION (*TAQLID*)

The obligation to follow the opinion of those more knowledgeable than us is reported by Ibn Qayyim in his discussion of the different kinds of *taqlid*. He said:

> There is an obligatory (*wajib*) *taqlid*, a forbidden *taqlid*, and a permitted *taqlid* . . . The obligatory *taqlid* is the *taqlid* of those who know better than us, as when a person has not obtained knowledge of an evidence from the Quran or the *sunna* concerning something. Such a *taqlid* has been reported from Imam al-Shafii in many places where he would say, 'I said this in *taqlid* of Umar' or 'I said that in *taqlid* of Uthman' or 'I said that in *taqlid* of Ata. As al-Shafii said concerning the Companions—may Allah be well pleased with all of them, 'Their opinion for us is better than our opinion to ourselves."[1]

This is the meaning of Imam Ahmad's frequent warning, "Beware of speaking on a matter regarding which you do not stand on as imam (as your precedent) (*iyyaka an tatakallama fi masalatin laysa laka fiha imam*)." Albani says:

> This is a frequent saying of Imam Ahmad: see our editions of his responses to various questions, such as *Masail* Abd Allah ibn Ahmad, *Masail* Ibn Hani al-Nisaburi, and *Masail* al-Kharqi.

One of Ibn Taymiyya's sayings under al-Mamun's Inquisition quoted by Albani, was, "How can I say what was never said before (*kayfa aqulu ma lam yuqal*)?"[2]

Jamil Effendi Sidqi al-Zahawi of Baghdad (d. 1930 CE) wrote in *al-Fajr al-sadiq*, a refutation of the Wahhabi heresy:[3]

> Among the evidence for the probative value of *ijma* is the Prophet's statement, on him be peace, "My Community will never agree on error." The content of this hadith is so well-known that it is impossible to lie about it [*mutawatir*] simply because it is produced in so many narrations, for example, "My Community will not come together on misguidance;" "A group of my Community will continue on truth until the coming of the Hour;." "The hand of Allah is with the

---

1 Ibn Qayyim, *Alam al-muwaqqiin an rabb al-alamin* (2:186-187).

2 Cited by Ibn Taymiyya in his *Majmu al-fatawa* (19:320-341). See Albani's edition of Sanani's *Raf al-astar li ibtali adillat al-qailina bi fanai al-nar* (Beirut and Damascus: al-Maktab al-islami, 1405/1984), p. 41.

3 See *The Doctrine of Ahl al-Sunna Versus the "Salafi" Movement*, translated with introduction and notes by Shaykh M. Hisham Kabbani (As-Sunna Foundation of America, 1996).

Congregation;" "Whoever separates from the
Congregation . . .;" "Whoever leaves the Community
or separates himself from it by the length of a span,
dies the death of the Age of Ignorance (*jahiliyya*)" etc.

Abd Allah ibn Masud said:

Whatever the Muslims deem to be good is good in
the eyes of Allah and whatever they consider bad is
bad in Allah's view.[4]

It is not true that the chain of this hadith, as related by
Ahmad, contains Sulayman ibn Amr al-Nakhai as claimed by
Abd al-Wahhab Abd al-Latif;[5] nor that it is not contained in
Ahmad's *Musnad*, as Abd al-Latif further claims. This is a mistake on the part of *hafiz* al-Sakhawi, as he says, "Ahmad narrated it in *al-Sunna* and whoever ascribes it to the *Musnad* is
mistaken [it is in the *Musnad*] . . . It is extracted by al-Bazzar,
al-Tayalisi, al-Tabarani, and Abu Nuaym in his biography of
Ibn Maud in the *Hilya*, also by Bayhaqi in *al-Itiqad*."[6]

Imam al-Tahawi said: "*Wa la nukhalifu jamaat al-muslimin* (we do not separate [in belief and practice] from the largest
group of the Muslims)."[7]

The commentators have explained that the "largest group
of the Muslims" here refers to the *ijma al-mujtahidin*, or consensus of the majority of scholars.

Both knowledge of the questions on which there is
Consensus, and of the differences of opinions on the questions
on which there is not, are requirements of Islamic scholarship.
The first scholar to compile a list of questions on which there
was consensus was Ibn al-Mundhir (d. 318).[8] He lists 765 ques-

---

4 This is an authentic saying of Ibn Masud. Ahmad related it in his *Musnad* (1:379
#3599), also al-Bazzar and Tabarani in the *Mujam al-Kabir* as Haythami said in
Majma al-zawaid, and he adds: "Its narrators are trustworthy." Al-Amidi considered
this to be a hadith whose chain of narration goes back to the Prophet (*al-Ihkam fi usul
al-ahkam* 2nd ed. Beirut, 1401/1982, 1:214).   Ahmad Hasan points out that Abu
Hanifa's disciple Imam Muhammad ibn Hasan al-Shaybani initially reported this as a
hadith, but that later it was attributed to Ibn Masud. Ahmad Hasan, *The Doctrine of
Ijma in Islam*, Islamabad: Islamic Research Institute, 1976, p. 37.

5 The commentator to Malik's *Muwatta* as narrated by Muhammad ibn al-Hasan
al-Shaybani" in his notes (p. 91).

6 Al-Sakhawi, *al-Maqasid al-hasana* (p. 368).

7 Al-Tahawi, *Aqida al-tahawiyya*.

8 Ibn al-Mundhir, *Kitab al-ijma*. Published in 1401 H by Fouad Abd al-Munim
Ahmad at Dar al-dawa in Doha, Qatar.

tions of worship and social transactions–leaving out doctrine –
on which there is agreement not among 100 percent, but among
the majority of scholars. This is enough to form Consensus
according to the definition of Shafii, and others such as Tabari
(d. 310) and Abu Bakr al-Razi (d. 370).[9] Then Ibn Hazm (d. 456)
authored *Maratib al-ijma*, in which he included matters of doctrine but for which he was criticized for claiming that he had
compiled the questions on which there was unanimous agreement, although he himself contradicts it many times.[10]
Suyuti's (d. 911) *Tashnif al-asma bi masail al-ijma* was unfor-
tunately lost.

Tirmidhi reports Ibn al-Mubarak's view that *jamaa* means
the concentration of the manners and knowledge of the *sunna*
in a living person (or group of persons) at any given time, i.e.
without the necessity of their forming the congregation of
Muslims. Abu Bakr ibn al-Arabi remarks that this is one of the
many meanings of the word, and that the most common meaning is that of Congregation in the large sense.[11]

Ibn Taymiyya has two contradictory views about *ijma*. He
says, "*Al-aimma ijtimauhum hujjatun qatiatun wa ikhtilafuhum rahmatun wasia* (the consensus of the Imams [of *fiqh*]
on a question is a definitive proof, and their divergence of opinion is a vast mercy)."[12] and, "If one does not follow any of the
four Imams [of *fiqh*] . . . then he is completely in error, for the
truth is not found outside of these four in the whole Sharia."[13]

In the second view, Ibn Taymiyya departs from the above
and divides the definition of *ijma* into two kinds: a general one
as expressed in views similar to the above, and a particular
one, to which he reserves particular adherence, and which is
that of the Salaf (Pious Predecessors). He says in his *Aqida
wasitiyya*:

> The Sunnis . . . are also called People of the
> Community (*ahl al-jamaa*) because *jamaa*
> (Community) implies *ijtima* (gathering), its opposite

---

9 Abu Ishaq al-Isfarayini said that the questions on which there was Consensus
exceeded 20,000. However, the author of the more recent *Mawsuat al-ijma fi al-fiqh al-
islami* [Encyclopedia of Consensus in Islamic Law] compiled a total of 9,588 questions.
  10 Ibn Taymiyya in his *Naqd maratib al-ijma* (pub. 1357 H).
  11 Ibn al-Arabi al-Maliki, *Aridat al-ahwadhi* 9:11.
  12 Ibn Taymiyya. *Mukhtasar al-fatawa al-misriyya*. (Cairo, 1980). p. 35.
  13 *Ibid.* p. 54.

being *furqa* (separation), and the expression *jamaa* has become a name for people who share the same conviction, while *ijma* (consensus) is the third principle (*asl*) on which knowledge of divine law (*ilm*) and religion (*din*) rest . . . *Ijma* is defined as everything that people follow (*jami ma alayh al-nas*) in matters of religion. But the *ijma* to which there is to be meticulous adherence is what the first pious generations (*al-salaf al-salih*) agreed upon, for after them divergences became numerous and the Community became spread out.[14]

Note that he scatters the concept of *ijma* between two diametrically opposed areas: the amorphous, inimitable mass of "the people" on the one hand, and the bygone, crystallized era of the Salaf on the other. The above departs from the position of all the major schools, for whom the notion of *ijma* rests on two foundations:

•The consensus of Muslim <u>scholars</u>
•The consensus of Muslim scholars <u>at any given time in history</u>

That Ibn Taymiyya particularly departed from the Hanbali school's position is clear from Muwaffaq al-Din Ibn Qudama's concept of *ijma* as providing categorical proof that permits neither abrogation nor allegorical interpretation–unlike the Quran and the *sunna*, while Ibn Taymiyya rejects the notion that the Community is incapable of agreeing on an error.[15] Perhaps this explains why he himself departed from *ijma* on more questions than anyone else among those considered among mainstream Islam before him. This is despite the fact that Imam Ahmad said that for the single scholar to leave *ijma* constitutes *shudhudh*, or dissent and deviation.[16] Ibn Taymiyya was severely brought to task for this by scholars including Shaykh al-Islam *al-hafiz* Taqi al-Din al-Subki, *al-hafiz* al-Izz ibn Jamaa, Shaykh al-Islam Imam Ibn Hajar al-Haytami, Taqi al-Din al-Hisni al-Dimashqi, Imam al-Sanani (in *Raf al-astar*), and others.

14 Ibn Taymiyya, *Aqida wasitiyya.*
15 Ibn Qudama, *al-Rawda fi usul al-fiqh.*
16 Ahmad, *Rawdat al-nazir* 2:143.

2.1.1. *TAQLID* IS PERMISSIBLE BY CONSENSUS[17]
Dr. Salah al-Sawi wrote:[18]

Among the constants in *ijtihad* and *taqlid* is the tenet that *taqlid* is permissible for the one who is incapable of *ijtihad*. Allah the Exalted has said, "*So, ask the ahl al-dhikr (People of Remembrance / Knowledge) if you yourselves do not know.*"(16:43).

Ibn Majah, Abu Dawud and Ahmad have narrated, through their chains of narration, on the authority of Ibn Abbas, that a man sustained an injury to his head during the time of the Prophet (ﷺ). Then, he became sexually impure, and was ordered (by people) to perform *ghusl*. He did, and later contracted tetanus and died. This was then conveyed to the Prophet (ﷺ), who said, "They killed him, may Allah kill them! Could they not have asked, since they did not know? The only remedy for incompetence is asking."

Shaykh al-Islam Ibn Taymiyya said, "That which the majority of the Community is agreed upon, is that *ijtihad* is totally permissible, and *taqlid* is totally permissible. They do not compel *ijtihad* on everyone, forbidding *taqlid*, nor do they compel *taqlid* upon everyone, forbidding *ijtihad*. They are also agreed that *ijtihad* is permissible for the one capable of *ijtihad*, and *taqlid* is permissible for one incapable of *ijtihad*."[19]

Ibn Qudama said, "*Taqlid* in the branches of the Law is permissible by consensus (*ijma*), and so the proof therein is the consensus."[20]

Shaykh Albani said, as reported from him by Muhammad Id Abbasi in the book *Bidat al-taassub al-madhhabi* (The innovation of school partisanship) (2:112):

It is worth mentioning that this is the opinion of our teacher himself. He has mentioned more than once that what is obligatory on people in this age of ours, is that they start with learning *fiqh* by way of one of the four schools, and that they study the reli-

---

17 Excerpted from Salah al-Sawi's *al-Thawabit wa al-mutaghayyirat* (Cairo: al-muntada al-Islami, 1414 /1994) p. 66, as translated by Suhail I. Laher on his website hyperlink http://webpages.marshall.edu/~laher1/taqlid.html.

18 Salah al-Sawi, *al-Thawabit wa al-mutaghayyirat*.

19 Taymiyya, *Majmu fatawa Ibn Taymiyya* (20:204). Ibn Taymiyya also said in *al-Fatawa al-kubra* that the lay person who is incapable of *ijtihad* and who therefore follows a *madhhab*, can expected to be rewarded rather then incurring sin, and is to be praised rather than condemned.

20 Ibn Qudama, *Rawdat an-Nazir*, p. 206.

gion from its books. Then, they should progress grad-
ually in knowledge. . . Thus, our shaykh is of the view
that this is the correct path, which it is possible to
pursue in this age. This is because pursuing the obligatory path which the Pious Predecessors were upon is
impetuosity, and not possible today, because *mujtahid*
scholars are not present among the people, and so
they cannot teach them the *fiqh* of the Book and
sunna. Therefore, there are only two choices before
people: either they should be left without learning
and understanding, and wander in blind aimlessness,
or they should learn their religion and gain understanding of its regulations by way of one of the four
madhahib. And I do not doubt that this latter path is
less harmful and less evil than the first path!
Therefore we direct people towards it and support it.

Abbasi said in another place (1:62), "The synopsis
is that we do not prevent people, in the current times,
from studying *fiqh* according to the *madhhabi* way,
but on one condition, which is the absence of fanaticism. *Madhhabi* fanaticism is what we wage war
against and dislike."

[Dr. Sawi comments:] It is not apparent to me on
what basis the two dignified shaykhs–Albani and
Abbasi–regard the study of *fiqh* according to the *madhhabi* method for students of knowledge, in the starting stages, and without fanaticism, as one of those
things which are permissible as an exception, by way
of necessity! Has acquisition of initial knowledge,
throughout history, ever been in any manner other
than this? In fact, are most students of hadith today
not constrained by the choices of our Shaykh Albani
and his scholarly preferences, to the extent that they
almost have a fifth *madhhab*? However, they are not
to be censured for that, as long as they merely follow,
without acting fanatical.[21]

---

21 This confirms what we said before, namely, that the Four *Madhahib* must be
followed in our time, although some people have started a fifth *madhhab* on the pretense that they are not following any of the *madhahib*. We must take into consideration that *taqlid* and *qiyas* are a necessity because these methods facilitate for us the
process of *nasiha* and *fatwa* in different geographical and cultural areas of Islam,
instead of the rigid uniformity of a fifth – "Salafi" – *madhhab* which imposes a supposedly unified view on Muslims, when in reality such a fifth *madhhab* constitutes
intolerance and tyranny. Furthermore, the supposed *mujtahids* of the pseudo-fifth
madhhab are themselves *muqallids* in the guise of non-*muqallids*. This was brought
to light by Dr. Ta Ha Jabir al-Alwani in his book *The Ethics of Disagreement in Islam*
which we already quoted: "They are not *mujtahidun* or persons capable of independent
reasoning or analytical thought. They are, rather, unthinking followers *(muqallidun)*

Shaykh Dihlawi said (*Bidat al-taassub al-mad-hhabi* 1:112), "The Community (*umma*)– or at least those who are worthy of reckoning among them – has unanimously accepted, up to this day, the permissibility of applying *taqlid* of the four established *madhahib*. This [*taqlid*] contains benefits which are not hidden, especially in this time when energies have dwindled severely, souls have been dampened with caprice, and each revels in his own opinion."[22]

[Also among the constants in *ijtihad* and *taqlid* is:] Mention of the evidences to the lay person does not remove him from the province of *taqlid* from the jurisprudential point of view . . . We have already mentioned the words of Shatibi: "The *fatawa* of the *mujtahid*s are to the laymen what the Sharia evidences are to the *mujtahid*s." . . .

As for that which has appeared from among the sayings of the Imams regarding prohibition of making *taqlid* of them it is true, but it must be put in its proper context:

It prohibits people from following them in those things to which the evidence is established to the contrary;

It prohibits the Imams counterparts, *mujtahid*s, from making *taqlid* of them, for *mujtahid*s must take from the sources from which the Imams took.

This specification–that the ordinary people are not concerned by these sayings – is indicated by that which has been reported from these Imams themselves, and others of the People of Knowledge, for example what Imam Malik said, "It is obligatory upon the laymen to make *taqlid* to the *mujtahid*s, just as it is obligatory for the *mujtahid*s to make *ijtihad* in the evidences themselves."

This is the verdict of the majority of scholars.

2.2. DEFINITION OF CONSENSUS (*IJMA*)

Imam al-Shafii defines the *ijma* thus:

The adherence of the Congregation (*jamaa*) of Muslims to the conclusions of a given ruling pertain-

---

of those among them who raise their voices to proclaim that they are not in fact 'followers' nor do they believe in the 'duty to follow.' They claim that they derive their rulings and opinions directly from the Quran and the *Sunnah* of the Prophet, peace be upon him. In reality, they cling to some books of hadith and follow in the footsteps of their authors in all matters pertaining to the authenticity of a hadith and the trustworthiness and reliability of its narrators."

22 *Ibid.*, vol. II, p. 112.

ing to what is permitted and what is forbidden after the passing of the Prophet (ﷺ), blessings and peace be upon him.[23]

By the "Congregation of Muslims" he actually means the experts of independent reasoning (*ahl al-ijtihad*) and legal answers in the obscure matters that require insight and investigation, as well as the agreement of the Community of Muslims concerning what is obligatorily known of the religion with its decisive proofs.[24]

Shafii continues, "The Prophet's order that men should follow the Muslim Community is a proof that the consensus (*ijma*) of the Muslims is binding."[25] Later on he quotes the hadith whereby the Prophet (ﷺ) said:

> Believe my Companions, then those who succeed them, and after that those who succeed the Successors. But after them falsehood will prevail when people will swear to the truth without having been asked to swear, and testify without having been asked to testify. Only those who seek the pleasures of paradise will keep to the Congregation . . ."[26]

Shafii comments:

He who holds what the Muslim Congregation (*jamaa*) holds shall be regarded as following the Congregation, and he who holds differently shall be regarded as opposing the Congregation he was ordered to follow. So the error comes from separation; but in the Congregation as a whole there is no error concerning the meaning of the Quran, the *sunna*, and analogy (*qiyas*).

2.2.1. TEXTS ON CONSENSUS (*IJMA*)

1 "*Fatasimu bi hablillahi jamian wa la tafarraqu* (*hold fast to the rope of Allah, all of you, and do not split into factions*)" (3:103).

2 "*Wa la tafarraqu illa min badi ma jaahum al-ilmu baghyan baynahum* (*and they were not divided until after the knowledge came unto them, through rivalry among them-*

---

23 Al-Shafii, *Risala.*
24 See Imam Abu Zahra's *Usul al-fiqh* p. 191 ff.
25 Shafii, *Risala* p. 253.
26 Shafii, *Risala* p. 286; Ahmad, *Musnad* 2:187; 1:112-113, 176-181.

selves)" (42:14).

3 "Ya ayyuha al-ladhina amanu atiullaha wa atiu al-rasula wa uli al-amri minkum (O you who believe, obey Allah and
obey the Prophet and those of authority among you)" (4:59).

4. "Wa man yushaqiq al-rasula min badi ma tabayyana
lahu al-huda wa yattabi ghayra sabil al-muminin nuwallihi
ma tawalla wa nuslihi jahannama wa saat masira (whoever
contraverts the Messenger after guidance has become clear to
him and follows other than the believers way, We shall give him
over to what he has turned to and expose him unto hell, and how
evil an outcome)!" (4:115).

5. 'Wa asbir nafsaka ma al-ladhina yaduna rabbahum bi al-
ghadati wa al-ashiyyi yuriduna wajhah wa la tadu aynaka
anhum turidu zinat al-hayat al-dunya wa la tuti man aghfalna
qalbahu an dhikrina wa ittabaa hawahu wa kana amruhu
furutan (restrain thyself along with those who call upon their
Lord at morning and evening, seeking His pleasure; and let not
thine eyes overlook them, desiring the pomp of this worldly life;
and obey not him whose heart We have made heedless of Our
remembrance, who followeth his own lust and whose case has
gone beyond all bounds)." (18:28).

6 "Alaykum bi al-jamaa fa innallaha la yajmau ummata
Muhammadin ala dalala (you have to follow the Congregation
for verily Allah will not make the largest group of Muhammad's
Community agree on error)."27

7. "La yajmaullahu ummata Muhammadin ala dalala (verily Allah will not make Muhammad's Community agree on
error)."28

8a. "La yajmaullahu ummati ala dalala (verily Allah will
not make my Community agree on error)."29

8b. "Inna Allaha la yajmau ummati–aw qala: ummata
Muhammadin–ala dalalatin wa yadullahi ma al-jamaa (verily
Allah will not make my Community–or Muhammad's
Community–agree on error, and Allah's hand is with the largest
Congregation)." Tirmidhi said, "And the meaning of "jamaa"
according to the people of knowledge is: the people of jurispru-
dence, learning, and hadith."30

27 Ibn Abi Shayba relates it with a sound chain.
28 Al-Hakim narrated it in the *Mustadrak* (1:116, 177) with a sound (*sahih*) chain.
29 Tirmidhi with a fair (*hasan*) chain.
30 Tirmidhi (*gharib*) #2256, Cairo ed. *Aridat al-ahwadhi* (11:9).

There are several views about the meaning of *umma* expressed in the preceding hadith:

It means the overwhelming majority of the Muslims. This is the prevailing view, confirmed by many hadiths of the Companions, and also by the hadiths of the Prophet (ﷺ) on *jamaa* and *al-sawad al-azam*.

It refers to the scholars only. It is the position of the majority of the *fuqaha* that this is what is meant in such hadith, and also in the saying of al-Qasim ibn Muhammad, "Difference in the Community is a mercy," i.e. among the scholars. Abu Bakr ibn al-Arabi gave the same restricted meaning to *jamaa*.

It refers, like *jamaa*, only to the Companions themselves. This is the view of Ibn Taymiyya and a handful of scholars.

It refers to all of the Muslims and not to any particular section of them. This is the view of Imam Shafii who said in his *Risala*, "We know that the people at large cannot agree on an error and on what may contradict the *sunna* of the Prophet (ﷺ)." It is also the view of the scholars of hadith regarding the authentication of a weak hadith: if the people at large do it, then it becomes *sahih* and even *mutawatir*. An example is *talqin al-amwat*, which Imam Ahmad accepted on the basis of its universal acceptance rather than on the basis of *isnad* as stated by Ibn al-Qayyim in *Kitab al-ruh*.

9. *Man arada minkum bi habuhat al-jannati fal yulzim al-jamaat* (whoever among you wants to be in the middle of Paradise, let him cling to the Congregation."[31]

10 *Inna al-shaytana dhaybun ka dhayb al-ghanam yakhudh al-shat al-qasiya wa al-najiya fa iyyakum wa al-shuaab wa alaykum bil-jamaati wa al-aammati wa al-masjid* (satan is a wolf like the wolf that preys on sheep, taking the isolated and the stray among them; therefore, avoid factionalism and keep to the Congregation and the collective and the mosque)."[32]

11 "*Inna ummati la tajtamiu ala dalalatin fa idha raaytum al-ikhtilaf fa alaykum bi al-sawad al-azam* (my Community shall never agree upon misguidance, therefore, if you see divergences, you must follow the greater mass or larger group)."[33]

31 Tirmidhi related it and said it is sound (*sahih*).
32 Ahmad relates it through Muadh and through Abu Dharr, the two chains being respectively fair [*hasan*] and sound [*sahih*] according to Haythami in *Majma al-zawaid*.
33 Ibn Majah (2:1303 #3950) from Anas with a weak chain. Ahmad narrates it *mawquf* through three sound chains to Abu Umama al-Bahili and Ibn Abi Awfa.

11a *"Lan tajtamia ummati ala dalalatin fa alaykum bi al-jamaati fa inna yadullahi ala al-jamaa* (my Community shall not agree upon misguidance. Therefore, you must stay with the Congregation, and Allah's hand is over the Congregation)."[34]

12 *"Innallaha qad ajara ummati min an tajtamia ala dalala* (verily Allah has protected my Community from agreeing upon error)."[35]

13 *"Kana al-nasu yasaluna rasulallahi an al-khayr wa kuntu asaluhu an al-sharr . . . qultu ya rasulallahi sifhum lana [ayy al-duat ala abwabi jahannam] qala hum min jildatina wa yatakallamuna bi alsinatina qultu fa ma tamurni in adrakani dhalik al-yawm? qala tulzim jamaat al-muslimin wa imamahum* (people used to ask the Prophet (ﷺ) about the good and I used to ask him about the evil . . . I said, O Messenger of Allah, describe them to us [the callers at the door of the fire]. He said, They are of our complexion and they speak our very language. I said, What do you order me to do if that day reaches me? He said, You must keep to the Congregation of Muslims and to their leader)."[36]

14 *"Yadu Allah ala al-jamaa* (Allah's hand is over the group)."[37]

Al-Munawi said:

> Allah's hand is over the group means His protection and preservation for them, signifying that the collectivity of the people of Islam are in Allah's fold, so be also in Allah's shelter, in the midst of them, and do not separate yourselves from them. Whoever diverges from the overwhelming majority concerning what is lawful and unlawful and on which the Community does not differ has slipped off the path of guidance and this will lead him to hell.[38]

However, it is *marfu* to the Prophet from Abu Umama by Ibn Abi Shayba in his *Musannaf* as well as Ibn Jarir al-Tabari and al-Tabarani with a sound chain, the latter three's narrations stating that Abu Umama heard this from the Prophet up to seven times. Bayhaqi in *al-Madkhal* narrates something similar from Ibn Abbas.

34 Tabarani narrated it with two chains from Ibn Umar, one of which is sound (*sahih*). See Haythami, *Majma al-zawaid*, chapter on the obligation to stay with the Congregation.

35 Ibn Abi Asim narrated it in the *Sunna* and Albani declared it *hasan* in his *Silsila sahiha* (3:319).

36 Bukhari and Muslim on the authority of Hudhayfa ibn al-Yaman.

37 Tirmidhi (*hasan*).

38 Al-Munawi, *Sharh al-Jami al-saghir* 3:449.

14a. *"Yadu Allah ala al-jamaat wa man shadhdha shadhd-ha ila al-nar* (Allah's hand is over the group, and whoever dissents from them departs to hell)."[39]

14b. *"Yadu Allah ala al-jamaa, ittabiu al-sawad al-azam fa innahu man shadhdha shadhdha ila al-nar* (Allah's hand is over the group, follow the largest mass, for verily whoever dissents from them departs to hell)."[40]

14c. *"Man faraqa al-jamaata shibran mata maytatan jahiliyya* (whoever leaves the Community or separates himself from it by the length of a span, dies the death of the Jahiliyya (period of ignorance prior to Islam)."[41]

15. Abu Ghalib said that during the crisis with the Khawarij in Damascus, he saw Abu Umama one day and he was crying. He asked him what made him cry and he replied, "They followed our religion," then he mentioned what was going to happen to them tomorrow. Abu Ghalib said, "Are you saying this according to your opinion or from something you heard the Prophet (ﷺ) say?" Abu Umama said, "What I just told you I did not hear from the Prophet (ﷺ) only once, or twice, or three times, but more than seven times. Did you not read this verse in *Al-Imran,,* *'The day faces will be white and faces will be dark . . .?'* (3:106) Then he said, "I heard the Prophet (ﷺ) say, The Jews separated into 71 sects, 70 of which are in the fire; the Christians into 72 sects, 71 of which are in the fire; and this Community will separate into 73 sects, all of them are in the fire except one which will enter Paradise. We said, "Describe it for us." He said, 'The *sawad al-azam.'"*[42]

16. *"Ma raahu al-muslimuna hasanan fa huwa ind Allahi hasanun* (hat which the Muslims consider good, Allah considers good)."[43]

17. *"Sataftariqu ummati ala thalathat wa sabina firqatin kulluhum fil nari ila millatin wahidat, qalu man hiya ya rasulallah, qala ma ana alayhi wa as-habi* ('my Community will

39 Tirmidhi (*gharib*) from Ibn Umar, al-Hakim both from Ibn Umar and Ibn Abbas, and Ibn Jarir from Ibn Umar.

40 Narrated by al-Hakim and al-Tabari from Ibn Abbas, and al-Lalikai in *al-Sunna* and al-Hakim also narrated it from Ibn Umar.

41 Muslim (*Imara* #55) through Ibn Abbas. Muslim relates it with slight variations through three more chains. Ibn Abi Shayba also relates it in his *Musannaf.*

42 Haythami said in *Majma al-zawaid*: Tabarani narrated it in *al-Mujam al-kabir* and *al-Awsat*, and its narrators are trustworthy (*thiqa*).

43 Ahmad in the *Musnad* (#3599) relates it from the words of Ibn Masud

split into seventy-three sects. All of them will be in the fire except one group." They asked, 'Who are they, O Messenger of Allah?" He said, 'Those that follow my way and that of my companions.'"44

18. "*La tazalu taifatun min ummati yuqatiluna ala al-haqqi zahirina ila yawm al-qiyama* (there will always be a group from my Community that fight for truth and remain victorious until Judgment Day)."45

2.3. THE MEANING OF *AL-SAWAD AL-AZAM*

The *sawad al-azam* means a "massive gathering of human beings." This meaning is established by the following sound hadith:

> Ibn Abbas narrated: When the Prophet (ﷺ) was taken up to heaven he passed by prophets followed by their nations and he passed by prophets followed by their groups and he passed by prophets followed by no one until he saw a tremendous throng of people (*sawad azim*). So he said, "Who are these?" and the answer was, "This is Moses and his nation, but raise your head and look up," whereupon the Prophet said, "(I raised my head and saw) a tremendous throng (*sawad azim*) that had blocked up the entire firmament from this side and that!" And it was said, "They are your Community . . ."46

2.4. CONCLUSION OF *TAQLID* AND *IJMA* ACCORDING TO MAINSTREAM ISLAM

When the "Salafis" say, "We do not worship men," it is *kalimatu haqqin yuradu biha al-batil* (a word of truth spoken in the pursuit of error). For it is only a pretense for their desire to follow a path other than the path of guidance clarified by the Imams and the *fuqaha*, on certain questions. Thus they will falsely characterize *taqlid* as blind imitation. This is the method used in a pernicious book of theirs entitled *Blind-Following of Madhaahib*. They will further falsely characterize *ijma* as a thing of the past, claiming that it is unverifiable at

(mawquf) with a sound chain.
    44 Tirmidhi, Abu Dawud, and al-Darimi related it.
    45 Bukhari, Muslim etc. related it. Hadith *mutawatir*.
    46 Tirmidhi *(hasan sahih)*.

present due to the great scattering of scholars and the multi-farious character of modern communication.

The truth is that *taqlid* is obligatory on the majority of the Muslim Community, since the majority are not qualified scholars. Secondly, knowledge of the questions that enjoy *ijma* and those that fall under *khilaf* has always been part of the obligatory curriculum of the scholars of mainstream Islam, who strived to make themselves familiar with other schools at all times, although for them communication and education were not nearly as developed as they are today. Yet, they were the most intellectually accomplished, most dynamic and scholarly communicative people, spurring their mounts in the vanguard of other riders in the pursuit of knowledge even past the age of sixty.[47] The "Salafi" pretense that there is no *ijma* today only reveals their incapacity to keep abreast of required knowledge, and their estrangement from the scholarly community.

---

47 As *al-hafiz* al-Sakhawi reports of his master *al-hafiz* al-Asqalani.

3. Differences in Schools of Law (*MADHHAB*) in Islam and the Differences Among the Jurists (*IKHTILAF*)

*A*l-Hafiz al-Bayhaqi[1] and al-Zarkashi relate:[2]

> Imam al-Qasim ibn Muhammad ibn Abi Bakr al-Siddiq said, "The differences among the Companions of Muhammad are a mercy for Allah's servants."

Al-Hafiz al-Iraqi, the teacher of Ibn Hajar al-Asqalani, said:

> This is a saying of al-Qasim ibn Muhammad who said, "The difference of opinion among the Companions of Muhammad is a mercy."

Al-Hafiz Ibn al-Athir relates the above saying from Imam Malik.[3]

Bayhaqi and Zarkashi also said:

> Qatada said: Umar ibn Abd al-Aziz used to say, "I would dislike it if the Companions of Muhammad did not differ among them, because had they not differed there would be no leeway (for us)."

---

1 Al-Bayhaqi, *al-Madkhal.*

2 Al-Zarkashi, *Tadhkirah fi al-ahadith al-mushtaharah.*

3 Ibn al-Athir, in the introduction to his *Jami al-usul fi ahadith al-rasul.* According to *al-Hafiz* Ibn al-Mulaqqin in his *Tuhfat al-muhtaj ila adillat al-Minhaj* and Ibn al-Subki in his *Tabaqat al-Shafiiyya.*

Bayhaqi and Zarkashi also relate:[4]

> Al-Layth ibn Sad said on the authority of Yahya ibn Said: "The people of knowledge are the people of flexibility (*tawsia*). Those who give *fatawa* never cease to differ, and so this one permits something while that one forbids it, without one finding fault with the other when he knows of his position."

Al-Hafiz al-Sakhawi said after quoting the above:[5]

I have read the following written in my shaykh's (*al-Hafiz* ibn Hajar) handwriting, "The hadith of Layth is a reference to a very famous hadith of the Prophet (ﷺ), cited by Ibn al-Hajib in the *Mukhtasar* in the section on *qiyas* (analogy), which says, "Difference of opinion in my Community is a mercy for people." (*ikhtilafu ummati rahmatun li al-nas*). There is a lot of questioning about its authenticity, and many of the imams of learning have claimed that it has no basis (*la asla lahu*). However, al-Khattabi mentions it in the context of a digression in *gharib al-hadith* . . . and what he says concerning the tracing of the hadith is not free from imperfection, but he makes it known that it does have a basis in his opinion."

Al-Iraqi mentions all of the above (1-5) and adds:[6]

> What is meant by "the Community" in this saying is those competent for practicing legal reasoning (*al-muhtajidun*) in the branches of the law, wherein reasoning is permissible.

What Iraqi meant, in saying "the branches wherein reasoning is permissible," is that difference is not allowed in matters of doctrine. There is agreement that there is only one truth in the essentials of belief, and anyone, whether a *muhtajid* or otherwise, who takes a different view automatically renounces Islam.[7]

---

4 Bayhaqi, *al-Madkhal* and Zarkashi, *Tadhkira*.
5 Al-Sakhawi, *Maqasid al-hasana* p. 49 #39.
6 Al-Iraqi, *Mughni an haml al-asfar*.
7 Al-Shawkani, *Irshad al-Fuhul* p. 259 as quoted in Mohammad Hashim Kamali, *Principles of Islamic Jurisprudence* p. 383.

Albani, in his attack on the hadith "Difference of opinion in my Community is a mercy," ignores this distinction. He even adduces the verse *"If it had been from other than Allah they would have found therein much discrepancy"* (4:82) to prove that differences can never be a mercy in any case but are always a curse.[8] His point is directed entirely against those who are content to follow a *madhhab*. The only scholar he quotes in support of his position is Ibn Hazm al-Zahiri, whose mistake in this was denounced by Nawawi.

Ibn Hazm said:[9]

> The saying "Difference of opinion in my Community is a mercy" is the most perverse saying possible, because if difference were mercy, agreement would be anger. It is impossible for a Muslim to say this, because there can only be either agreement, or difference, and there can only be either mercy, or anger.

Imam Nawawi refuted this view in his commentary on *Sahih Muslim*:

> If something (i.e. agreement) is a mercy it is not necessary for its opposite to be the opposite of mercy. No one makes this binding, and no one even says this except an ignoramus or one who affects ignorance. Allah the Exalted said, *"And of His mercy He has made night for you so that you would rest in it"* (28:73), and He has named night a mercy; it does not necessarily ensue from this that the day is a punishment.

Al-Khattabi said:[10]

> Difference of opinion in religion is of three kinds:
> • In affirming the Creator and His Oneness: to deny it is disbelief;
> •In His attributes and will: to deny them is innovation;

---

8 Albani, *Silsila daifa* 1:76 #57.
9 Ibn Hazm, *al-Ihkam fi usul al-ahkam* (5:64).
10 Al-Khattabi, *Gharib al-hadith*.

•In the different rulings of the branches of the
law (ahkam al-furu): Allah has made them
mercy and generosity for the scholars, and
that is the meaning of the hadith: "Difference
of Opinion in my Community is a mercy."[11]

9 *Al-Hafiz* al-Suyuti says:[12]

The hadith "Difference of opinion in my
Community is a mercy for people" has many benefits
among which are the fact that the Prophet (ﷺ) fore-
told of the differences that would arise after his time
among the *madhahib* in the branches of the law. This
is one of his miracles because it is a foretelling of
things unseen. Another benefit is his approval of
these differences and his confirmation of them
because he characterizes them as a mercy. Another
benefit is that the legally responsible person can
choose to follow whichever he likes among them.
[After citing the saying of Umar ibn Abd al-Aziz
already quoted (#3 above), Suyuti continues:] This
indicates that what is meant is their differences in the
rulings in the branches of the law.

The *muhaddith* al-Samhudi relates *al-Hafiz* Ibn al-Salah's
discussion of Imam Malik's saying concerning difference of
opinion among the Companions: "Among them is the one that
is wrong and the one that is right: therefore you must exercise
ijtihad." Samhudi said:

Clearly, it refers to differences in legal rulings
(ahkam). Ibn al-Salah said, "This is different from
what Layth said concerning the flexibility allowed for
the Community, since this applies exclusively to the
muhtajid as he said, you must exercise *ijtihad*,
because the *muhtajids* competence makes him legally
responsible (*mukallaf*) to exercise *ijtihad* and there is
no flexibility allowed for him over the matter of their
difference. The flexibility applies exclusively to the
unqualified follower (*muqallid*). The people meant in
the saying, "Difference of opinion in my Community is
a mercy for people" are those unqualified followers. As

---

11 Al-Jarrahi cited it in *Kashf al-khafa* 1:64 #153.
12 Al-Suyuti, in his short treatise *Jazil al-mawahib fi ikhtilaf al-madhahib* (The
abundant grants concerning the differences among the schools).

for the import of Malik's saying: Among the Companions is the one that is wrong and the one that is right, it is meant only as an answer to those who say that the *muhtajid* is able to follow the Companions. It is not meant for others."

11 Imam Abu Hanifa said:[13]

Difference of opinion in the Community is a token of divine mercy.

12 Ibn Qudama al-Hanbali said:[14]

The difference in opinion in the Community is a mercy, and their agreement is a proof.

13 Ibn Taymiyya says:[15]

Al-aimma ijtimauhum hujjatun qatiatun wa ikhtilafuhum rahmatun wasia (the consensus of the Imams [of *fiqh*] on a question is a definitive proof, and their divergence of opinion is a vast mercy . . . If one does not follow any of the four Imams [of *fiqh*] . . . then he is completely in error, for the truth is not found outside of these four in the whole Sharia).[16]

Al-Shatibi said:[17]
   A large group of the Salaf deemed the differences of the Community in the branches of the Law to be one of the paths of Allah's mercy . . .
   The exposition of the fact that the aforesaid difference is a mercy is what is narrated from al-Qasim ibn Muhammad ibn Abi Bakr al-Siddiq's words, "Allah has made us gain through the differences among the Companions of Allah's Messenger in their practice." No one practices according to the practice of one of them except he (al-Qasim) considered it to be within the fold of correctness.
   Dumra ibn Raja narrated: Umar ibn Abd al-Aziz and al-Qasim ibn Muhammad met and began to

13 Abu Hanifa, in the shorter version of *al-Fiqh al-Akbar*.
14 Ibn Qudama al-Hanbali, *al-Aqaid*.
15 Ibn Taymiyya, *Mukhtasar al-fatawa al-misriyya,* (Cairo, 1980) p. 35, 54.
16 *Ibid.*
17 Al-Shatibi, *Kitab al-itisam.*

review the hadith. Umar then began to mention things which differed from what al-Qasim mentioned, and al-Qasim would give him trouble regarding it until the matter became clearer. Umar said to him, "Don't do that! (i.e. don't question the difference). I dislike stripping the favors (of Allah) from their differences."

Ibn Wahb also narrated from al-Qasim that he said, "I was pleased by the saying of Umar ibn Abd al-Aziz: I would dislike it if the Companions of Muhammad did not differ among them, because if there were only one view then the people would be in difficulty. Verily the Companions are Imams which one uses for guidance (*innahum aimmatun yuqtada bihim*). If someone follows the saying of one of them, that is *sunna*."

The meaning of this is that they (the Companions) have opened wide for people the door of scholarly striving (*ijtihad*) and of the permissibility of difference in striving. If they had not opened it, the *muhta-jid*s would be in a bind, because the extent of *ijtihad* and that of opinions do not generally agree; the people who exert striving would then, despite their obligation to follow what they are convinced of, be obliged to follow what differs with them, and this is a kind of unbearable legal obligation and one of the greatest binds.

Allah therefore gave the Community generous leeway in the existence of disagreement in the branches of the law among them. This is the door that He opened for the Community to enter into this mercy. How then could they possibly not be meant by "those on whom thy Lord has mercy" in the verses "*Yet they cease not differing, save those on whom thy Lord has mercy*" (11:118-119)?! Therefore, their difference in the branches of the Law are like their agreement in them (in the fact that both consist in mercy), and praise belongs to Allah.[18]

Al-Shatibi also said, "Whatever is open to *ijtihad* is open to difference of opinion among those who make *ijtihad*, due to differences in circumstances or perspective."[19]

---

18 Al-Shatibi, *al-Itisam* 3:11; or (1995 Beirut ed.) p. 395.
19 Al-Shatibi, *al-Muwafaqat* (4:119).

Ibn Abd al-Barr said:[20]

> The *ulama* are in agreement that it is permissi-
> ble, for whoever looks into the differing opinions of
> the Prophet's Companions, to follow the position of
> whomever he likes among them. The same holds for
> whoever looks into the positions of the Imams other
> than the Companions, as long as he does not know
> that he has erred by contradicting the text of the
> Quran or *sunna* or the Consensus of the scholars, in
> which case he cannot follow the above position.
> However, if this contradiction is not clear to him in
> any of the three respects mentioned, then it is per-
> missible for him to follow the saying in question even
> if he does not know whether it is right or wrong, for
> he is in the realm of the common people (*al-amma*) for
> whom it is permissible to imitate the scholar upon
> asking him something, even without knowing the
> bases of the answer . . .
>
> Al-Uqayli mentioned that Muhammad ibn Abd al-
> Rahman al-Sayrafi said: I asked Ahmad ibn Hanbal,
> "If the Companions of the Prophet (ﷺ) differed
> regarding a certain question, is it permissible for us
> to check their positions to see who among them is
> right so that we may follow him?" He replied, "It is
> not permissible to check on the Prophet's Companions
> (*la yajuz al-nazar bayna ashabi rasulillah*)." I said,
> "Then what is the procedure in this?" He replied, "You
> follow whichever of them you like."[21]

Abu Dawud narrates that Ibn Masud had censured
Uthman for completing the prayer while travelling (i.e. rather
than shortening it to two cycles instead of four), yet when he
prayed behind Uthman he performed four cycles and did not
shorten it. When this was pointed out to him he said, "Dissent
is an evil" (*al-khilafu sharr*). That is, dissent in the lines of
prayer, or in the unity of Muslims. Abu Dawud mentioned al-
Zuhri's explanation that Uthman had prayed four *rakat* at
Mina instead of two because that year the bedouins had come

---

20 Ibn Abd al-Barr, *Jami bayan al-ilm*, (Cairo: dar al-tibaa al-muniriyya) 2:78-83,
181.
   21 *Ibid.*

in great numbers and he wished to teach them that the prayer consisted in four cycles.[22]

Ibn Abi Zayd al-Qayrawani related that Ibn Masud said:[23]

> Whoever wishes to follow the *sunna*, let him fol-
> low the *sunna* of those that died (i.e. keep to the prac-
> tice of the Companions). Those are the Prophet's
> Companions. They were the best of this Community,
> the purest of heart, the deepest in knowledge, and the
> scarcest in discourse. They were a people Allah chose
> for His Prophet's company and the establishment of
> His religion. Therefore be aware of their superiority
> and follow them in their views, and hold fast to what-
> ever you are able from their manners and their lives.
> Verily they were on a straight path.[24]

Ibn Qudama al-Hanbali relates the following examples of the great Imams occasional practice of positions contrary to their *ijtihad*:[25]

> Abu Hanifa, Muhammad al-Shaybani, and Abu
> Yusuf's position is that ablution is nullified by bleed-
> ing. Yet when Abu Yusuf saw that Harun al-Rashid
> stood for prayer after being cupped without perform-
> ing ablution, based on Malik's *fatwa* for him–since
> bleeding does not annul ablution in Malik's view–he
> prayed behind al-Rashid, and did not repeat his
> prayer. That is, he considered the prayer valid, and
> that therefore, the ablution is not nullified for one
> who follows Malik's *fatwa*.
>
> Another time Abu Yusuf performed *ghusl* and
> prayed *juma* in congregation, then he was told that a
> dead mouse had been found in the tank of the bath
> water. He did not repeat the prayer but said, "We
> shall follow in the matter the opinion of our brothers
> from the Hijaz (i.e. school of Malik): If the quantity of
> water is more than two pitchers worth, the water is
> still pure (if a dead mouse is found in it)."
>
> When Shafii prayed the dawn prayer with the
> Hanafis at the grave of Abu Hanifa in Baghdad, he
> did not make the supplication after rising from bow-

---

22 Abu Dawud, *Manasik*, Chapter on Prayer #1960.
23 Ibn Abi Zayd al-Qayrawani, *Jami fi al-sunan*.
24 Ibn Abi Zayd, *al-Jami fi al-sunan* (1982 ed.) p. 118-119.
25 Ibn Qudama al-Hanbali, in the introduction to his manual of *fiqh* entitled *al-Mughni* (1:22f).

ing in the second cycle of prayer as is required in his own school but not in the Hanafi.

Imam Ahmad's opinion is similar to the Hanafis concerning the necessity of ablution after cupping. Yet when he was asked, "Can one pray behind the Imam who stands up to lead prayer after being cupped without having renewed his ablution?" he replied, "How could I not pray behind Malik and Said al-Musayyib?" And, in another narration, "Can I forbid you from praying behind so-and-so?" That is, behind the Imams who do not consider it necessary to renew ablution.[26]

Imam Ahmad also declared that one must pronounce the *basmala* aloud when leading the prayer in Madina–although this is contrary to his general view in the matter – due to the fact that the majority of the people of Madina follow the school of Malik, which requires it. Ibn Taymiyya mentions it in his *Qaida fi tawahhud al-milla*.[27]

Bukhari and Muslim relate from Ibn Umar: On the day of the battle of al-Ahzab (the battle of the Trench) the Prophet (ﷺ) said (to a travelling party), "Let none of you pray the afternoon prescribed prayer (*asr*) prayer [in Muslim also: the noon prescribed prayer (*zuhr*)] except after reaching the Banu Qurayza." The *asr* prayer became due for some of them on the way. Some of those said, "We will not offer it till we reach the Banu Qurayza," while others said, "Rather, we will pray at this spot, for the Prophet (ﷺ) did not mean that for us." Later on it was mentioned to the Prophet (ﷺ) and he did not take to task any of the two groups.

Following are Imam Nawawi's and Ibn Hajar's views of this hadith. Imam Nawawi said, in commenting on the hadith of the Companions difference in praying *asr* and following the Prophet's order, he believes every *muhtajid* can be correct. He said:[28]

> In this hadith there is evidence for those who act upon the understanding and according to analogy and in attending to the meaning of words, and also to

26 Ibn Qudama, *Muqaddimat al-Mughni* 1:22.
27 Ibn Taymiyya, *Qaida fi tawahhud al-milla* p. 174.
28 Nawawi, *Sharh Sahih Muslim. Kitab al-Jihad,* Ch.23, al-Mays ed.

those who stick to the external letter; there is also evidence that the *mujtahid* must not be taken to task in what he did through his *ijtihad* if he did his best. And it can be inferred from this that every *mujtahid* is correct (*wa qad yustadallu bihi ala an kulla mujtahidin musib*). Those who take the opposite view can say that the Prophet (☸) did not manifest which of the two sides was correct, but he did not take them to task. There is no disagreement that the *mujtahid* is not taken to task even if he was mistaken, if he did his utmost in striving. And Allah knows best.

The same position is taken by Ibn Hajar in commenting upon the same hadith in Bukhari:[29]

In this hadith is evidence that each one of the two *mujtahid*s that differ in a matter of the branches, is correct (*wa fihi anna kulla mukhtalifayni fi al-furu min al-mujtahidina musib*).

Some ask about the discrepancy about which prayer was actually mentioned, since it is related in Bukhari as *asr* and in Muslim as *zuhr*. Both reports are authentic and confirmed by other sound chains. Nawawi and Ibn Hajar said that the discrepancy is solved by the possibility that the travellers left in two groups, to each of whom was given a different order: the first group had not prayed *zuhr* yet; while the second had prayed *zuhr*, but not *asr*. Or it is solved by the possibility that one single group left together, containing those who had already prayed *zuhr* and those who had not. The import of the hadith is to make haste and not dismount to pray nor anything else.

Jamal al-Din al-Qasimi said, "It is required by justice that differences of opinion not be a pretext for disaffection. Enmity that stems from religious quarrels typifies the ignorant, not the knowledgeable; it typifies the people of folly, not the fair-minded."[30]

3.1. COMMENTARY

Some mention the account of Umar's position over the dif-

---

29 Ibn Hajar, *Fath al-Bari. Kitab al-maghazi*, ch 31, 1989 ed. 7:520.
30 Jamal al-Din al-Qasimi, *Risalat al-jarh wa al-tadil*.

ference of opinion that took place between Ubayy ibn Kab and Abd Allah ibn Masud over the matter of praying in a single garment. Ibn Abd al-Barr said in his book *Jami bayan al-ilm*:

> Umar ibn al-Khattab was angry about the disagreement between Ubayy ibn Kab and Ibn Masud on the question of praying in a single cloth: Ubayy said that it was fine and good, while Ibn Masud said that this was done only when clothes were scarce. Umar said, "Two men disagreeing from among the Prophet's Companions who are those one looks at and takes [knowledge] from?!"–and this supports the import of the hadith which they have declared weak whereby "My Companions are like the stars; whoever among them you use for guidance, you will be rightly guided." Umar continued, "Ubayy has told the truth, nor has Ibn Masud fallen short of it: but don't let me hear anyone disagree about this matter after this point, or I will do such-and-such with them!"[31]

Al-Qari said in his commentary on *al-Shifa*:[32]

> It is narrated from the Prophet (ﷺ) by Abd ibn Humayd from Ibn Umar; "My Companions are like the stars" refers to the totality of the guidance of the stars, for by the stars is one guided in the darkest nights, and by the Companions is one guided to the beauties and the highest levels of the lights of the Sharia. The hadith may be deduced from Allah's saying, "*Ask the People of dhikr*," (16:43) and it is strengthened by the Prophet's saying, "The scholars of knowledge are the inheritors of the prophets."[33]
>
> But you must know that "My Companions are like the stars" is another hadith narrated by al-Daraqutni in the *Fadail* and Ibn Abd al-Barr through his chain

31 Ibn Abd al-Barr, *Jami bayan al-ilm* 2:84.
32 *Ibid.* 2:91.
33 It is narrated from Abu al-Darda by Tirmidhi, Abu Dawud, Ibn Majah, Ahmad (5:196), Ibn Hibban in his *Sahih*, Bayhaqi in the *Shuab al-iman*, Darimi in the *Muqaddima* of his *Sunan*, and Bukhari in the Book of Knowledge in his *Sahih* in *muallaq* form (i.e. without chain). Al-Raghib al-Asfahani (d. 425) said in his dictionary *Mufradat alfaz al-quran* under the entry *w-r-th*: "Suyuti said: Shaykh Muhyiddin al-Nawawi was asked about it and he said it was weak *(daif)* – that is: in its chain – even if it is true *(sahih)* – that is: in its meaning. al-Mizzi said: This hadith has been narrated through chains which attain the rank of *hasan*. It is as al-Mizzi said, and I have seen fifty chains for it, which I collected in a monograph. Here end Suyuti's words."

from Jabir. He said, "This is a chain through which no proof can be established firmly." Al-Bazzar said of Abd ibn Humayd's narration, "It is denounced (*munkar*) and unsound." Ibn Adi narrated it in *al-Kamil* from Nafi from Ibn Umar with a weak chain. Bayhaqi narrated something similar in *al-Madkhal* from Umar and Ibn Abbas and he said, "Its text is well-known (*mashhur*) and its chains are weak." al-Halabi said, "'The author should not have cited it as if it were definitely a hadith of the Prophet (ﷺ) due to what is known about it among the scholars of this science, and he has done the same thing several times before." I say that it is possible that he had established a chain for it, or that he considered the multiplicity of its chains to raise its grade from weak to that of *hasan*, due to his good opinion of it, although even the weak hadith may be put into practice for meritorious acts (*fadail al-amal*), and Allah knows best.

The author of *Kanz al-ummal* cited the similar hadith, *mahma utitum min kitabillah. . . :*[34]

> Whatever is brought to you from Allah's Book, it is obligatory to practice it, there is no excuse for leaving it; if it is not from Allah's book, then a *sunna* established by me; if not one of my *sunna*s, then what my Companions said; verily, my Companions are equivalent to the stars in the sky: whichever of them you pinpoint, you will be guided, and the differences among my Companions are a mercy for you.[35]

Anas relates that the Prophet (ﷺ) said, "The simile of the scholars of knowledge (*al-ulama*) on the earth is the stars in the sky by which one is guided in the darkness of the land and the sea. When the stars are clouded over, the guides are about to be lost." Ahmad narrated it with a chain containing Rishdin ibn Sad who is weak.[36] However, it is confirmed by the hadith in Muslim and Ahmad narrated by Abu Musa al-Ashari whereby the Prophet (ﷺ) said:

34 *Kanz al-ummal* (#1002).

35 Narrated by Bayhaqi in *al-Madkhal* and Abu al-Nasr al-Sajzi in al-*Ibana*, and he said: It is very rare (*gharib*); also al-Khatib, Ibn Asakir, and al-Daylami from Sulayman ibn Abi Karima from Juwaybir al-Dahhak from Ibn Abbas. The former two are both weak.

36 Ahmad, *Musnad* (3:157 #12606).

The stars are trust-keepers for the heaven, and when the stars wane, the heaven is brought what was promised (i.e. of the corruption of the world and the coming of the Day of Judgment); and I am a trust-keeper for my Companions, so when I go my Companions will be brought what was promised them (i.e. of *fitna* and division); and my Companions are trustkeepers for my Community, so when they go my Community will be brought what was promised to you (i.e. following *hawa* and vying for *dunya*)."

This trust-keeping is what Umar meant when he named the Companions "Those whom people look at and take (knowledge) from" when he disapproved of the difference of opinion between Ubayy ibn Kab and Abd Allah ibn Masud.[37]

This is further confirmed by al-Zuhri's saying:

Beware of evaluating things for yourself. By the One in Whose hand is my soul, if you evaluate things for yourself you will assuredly declare lawful the unlawful and declare unlawful the lawful. Rather, whatever reaches you from those who learned from the Companions of Muhammad–peace be upon him–put it into practice.[38]

Similar to this is al-Awzai's saying, "Knowledge is what comes from the Companions of Muhammad (ﷺ) and whatever does not come from one of them is not knowledge."[39] This also extends to the *sunna*, according to the Prophet's injunctions in Bukhari and Muslim, "You must follow my *sunna* and the *sunna* of my rightly-guided successors" and "You must follow those after me: Abu Bakr and Umar."

According to Asim:

They took out Khubayb as far as al-Tamim to crucify him. He asked them to give him time to make a couple of prayer-cycles, and they agreed. He performed two excellent bowings and then turned to the people saying, "Were it not that you would think that I only delayed out of fear of death I would have prolonged my prayer." Khubayb ibn Adi was the first to

---

37 As related in Ibn Abd al-Barr's *Jami bayan al-ilm* (2:84).
38 Related by Darimi in the introduction to his *Sunan*.
39 Narrated by Ibn Abd al-Barr in his *Jami bayan al-ilm* (2:36).

establish the custom of performing two bowings at
death. Then they raised him on the wood and when
they had bound him he said, "O Allah, we have delivered the message of Thy Messenger, so tell him tomorrow what has been done to us." Then he said, "O
Allah, reckon them by number and kill them one by
one, let none of them escape." Then they killed him,
Allah have mercy on him."[40]

Umar considered neither Ubayy nor Ibn Masud to be
wrong, as illustrated by his answer in the following hadith:[41]

Narrated Abu Hurayra: A man stood up and asked
the Prophet (﷽) about praying in a single garment.
The Prophet (﷽) said, "Has everyone of you two garments?" A man put a similar question to Umar whereupon he replied, "When Allah makes you wealthier
then you should act wealthier. Let a man gather up
his clothes about himself. One can pray in a loinwrap
and mantle, or a loinwrap and shirt, or in a loinwrap
and long sleeves, or in trousers and a cloak, or in
trousers and a shirt, or in trousers and long sleeves,
or in legless breeches and long sleeves, or in shorts
and a shirt." The narrator added, "And I think he
said, Or in shorts and a cloak."[42]

Ibn Hajar relates that the second inquirer in the above
hadith—that is, the man who asked Umar—was Abd Allah ibn
Masud.[43] He mentions Abd al-Razzaq's report that Ibn Masud
approached Umar as a result of his difference with Ubayy, who
permitted prayer in a single garment and did not consider it
offensive (*makruh*). Ibn Masud held that this was the case only
when there was a dearth of clothing. Umar went up to the pul-
pit and said, "What is right is what Ubayy said, and Ibn Masud
certainly did not fall short" (*al-qawlu ma qala ubayy wa lam
yail ibnu masud*).[44]
Thus Umar's decision to authorize praying in a single gar-

---

40 From *The Life of Muhammad: A Translation of Ishaq's Sirat Rasul Allah,*
trans. A. Guillaume, p. 428.

41 Book of Prayer in *Sahih al-Bukhari.*

42 Cf. English version vol. 1, Bk. 8, #361.

43 Ibn Hajar, *Fath al-bari.*

44 Ibn Qayyim, *Ilam al-muwaqqiin* 2:186-187.

ment is not a proof that "one was right and the other was wrong," as more superficial observers understand. Rather, it is a proof that Umar exercised his own *ijtihad* and authority as the Greater Imam in settling the question. He ruled without dismissing any view. Furthermore, if Ibn Masud adopted his position from the Prophet (ﷺ), he cannot change it even after the ruling of the Greater Imam. This is true of every true *mujtahid* at any time: he is obligated to follow the result of his own *ijtihad* even if it should differ with that of every other *mujtahid* of the past and present, unless he becomes convinced that he was mistaken in his previous *ijtihad*.

According to all the scholars, it is incumbent upon the leader of Muslims to be a *mujtahid*, and it is his responsibility, in such cases, to settle the question for the sake of the people of his time. That is the proper context of Imam Malik's injunction, "Exercise *ijtihad*." It is addressed to the *mufti*, who must establish what is correct in clear-cut fashion, not to the *muqallid* or follower, who is only interested in "a way to follow" (= *madhhab*) without having to verify its proofs and inferences. The *muqallid* is not free to follow anything other than what he accepts as correct; nor is the *ijtihad* of the unqualified ever considered valid for others. However, another *mufti* may reach a separate conclusion and be followed, He is not bound by that of the first, nor are those who take their *fatwa* from him. No one finds fault with the other, as stated by al-Layth ibn Sad. Those who condemn *taqlid* unconditionally are innovating in religion. As Ibn Qayyim said, there is a kind of *taqlid* that is even obligatory:

> There is an obligatory (*wajib*) *taqlid*, a forbidden *taqlid*, and a permitted *taqlid* . . . The obligatory *taqlid* is the *taqlid* of those who know better than us, as when a person has not obtained knowledge of an evidence from the Quran or the *sunna* concerning something. Such a *taqlid* has been reported from Imam al-Shafii in many places, where he would say, "I said this in *taqlid* of Umar" or "I said that in *taqlid* of Uthman" or "I said that in *taqlid* of Ata." As al-Shafii said concerning the Companions–may Allah be

well pleased with all of them, "Their opinion for us is better than our opinion to ourselves."[45]

A clear proof that the leader's *fatwa* overrules, but does not invalidate, the opinion of the Companions even if it directly contradicts it, is the fact that when Umar ibn al-Khattab proposed to have all the hadith collected and written down, he consulted the Companions. They unanimously agreed to his proposal. Later, he disapproved of it and ordered everyone who had written a collection to burn it. Yet, Umar ibn Abd al-Aziz later ordered that hadith be collected and written.[46]

Those who think they are *mujtahid*, but are actually unqualified, camouflage their deviation from mainstream Islam using the claim, "We must follow Quran and *sunna*, not *madhahib*." When it is pointed out to them that to follow a *madhhab* is to follow Quran and *sunna* through true *ijtihad*, they become upset: "How can the major schools differ and be right at the same time? I have heard that only one may be right, and the others wrong." The answer is that a person follows only the ruling that he believes is right, but cannot pretend to invalidate the following of other rulings by other *madhahib*, as they too are based on the sound principles of *ijtihad*. At this they rebel and number the mistakes of the *mujtahid*s: "Imam Shafii was right in this, but he was wrong in that. Imam Abu Hanifa was right in this, but he was wrong in that..." They do not spare even the Companions. When they are rebuked for this blatant disrespect, *"They become arrogant in their sin"* (2:206). And this is the legacy of the "Salafi" movement.

3.2. IBN TAYMIYYA ON LABELING MUSLIM SCHOLARS UNBELIEVERS ON THE BASIS OF DIFFERENCES IN OPINION

Ibn Taymiyya said:[47]

The scholars of Islam cannot be labeled as unbelievers, despite whatever mistakes they might fall

---

45 Ibn Hajar, *Fath al-Bari* (1989 ed.) 1:627. in the *Musannaf.*
46 Al-Baghdadi relates it in his *Taqyid al-ilm* 49, 52-53, 105-106, and Ibn Sad in his *Tabaqat* 3(1):206, 8:353.
47 Ibn Taymiyya, *Majmua Fatawa Ibn Taymiyya* (35:99).

into in their approach or point of view. To authorize ignorant people to label Muslim scholars unbelievers is one of the biggest sins.

Sunnis agree that the scholars of Islam may not be labeled *kafir* no matter what mistake they make. You may take what you like from what they said and you may leave what you don't like. Whatever you neglect from their discourse and guidance cannot be the basis for labeling them as *kafir*s and they will not be considered sinners in Allah's sight for a mistake they did without a bad intention, because Allah said: *"Our Lord! Do not take us to task if we forget or make a mistake"* (2:285).

And Muslim scholars agreed that no one has the right to label as *kafir* anyone from the scholars of Islam, even if they are in dissent concerning the infallibility of the prophets.

And if we are going to begin labeling as *kafir* scholars of Islam for their point of view, we are then going to declare as unbelievers many of the Shafii school, of the Maliki School, of the Hanafi school, of the Ashari school, of the people of hadith, of the people of *tafsir*, and of the Sufi school, all of which, according to the consensus of the Muslims, and on top of that, by the agreement of the scholars of the Muslims, are not unbelievers!"

4. THE VINDICATION OF IMAM ABU HANIFA FROM THE "SALAFI" CLAIM THAT HE WAS WEAK (*DAIF*) IN HADITH

Imam Abu Hanifa was acknowledged by Imam al-Shafii and others as the founder of *fiqh*. Yet certain "Salafi" scholars, among them Albani, claim that he was *daif* (weak) as a narrator of the hadith of the Prophet (ﷺ). Is this claim true?

4.1. ABU HANIFA'S RANK IN HADITH

4.1.1. IMAM ABU HANIFA IS HIGHLY TRUSTWORTHY (*THIQA*) AND HE IS INCLUDED AMONG THE HADITH MASTERS (*HUFFAZ*)

Shaykh Hasan al-Saqqaf wrote in his book about Albani's attacks on the great scholars:

> He [Albani] says of Imam Abu Hanifa, "The imams have declared him weak for his poor memorization" (in his commentary of Ibn Abi Asim's *Kitab al-sunna* 1:76) although no such position is reported, see for example Ibn Hajar Asqalani's biography of Abu Hanifa in *Tahdhib al-tahdhib*.[1]

A "Salafi" and follower of Albani:

> The statement that no such position is reported is a lie, it was the position of Muslim (*al-Kunaa wal*

1 Shaykh Hasan al-Saqqaf, *Qamus shataim al-Albani* [Dictionary of Albani's Insults of the Scholars].

Asmaa), Nasaaee (ad-Duafaa) ibn Adee (al-Kaamil
2/403), ibn Sad (Tabaqaat 6/256), al-Uqailee (ad-
Duafaa p.432), ibn Abee Haatim (al-Jarh wat Tadil),
Daaruqutnee (as-Sunan p132), al-Haakim (Marifa
Ulum al-Hadeeth), Abdul Haqq al-Ishbelee (al-
Ahkaam al-Kubraa q.17/2), adh-Dhahabee (ad-
Duafaa q. 215/1-2), Bukharee (at-Taareekh al-
Kabeer), ibn Hibbaan (al-Majrooheen)

Albani has shown enmity toward scholars, of a kind that
passes all bounds and is unbefitting of a person with knowledge
in Islam. As mentioned in the first volume, Saqqaf documented
an instance where Albani compares Hanafi *fiqh* to the
Christian Gospels in respect to its distance from Quran and
sunna.[2] As this would be unacceptable coming from a
Christian, it is even more disturbing from a Muslim. Albani
and his following have pushed even the gentlest of scholars, the
late Abd al-Fattah Abu Ghudda, to take pen to paper to oppose
such aberrations.[3]

Albani's supporters claim that "The statement that no such
position is reported is a lie" is itself a lie. None of the references
he adduces contains a single authentic proof for Albani's claim
that, "The imams have declared him weak for his poor memorization." For such a claim to be even remotely true, it would
have to be modified to read "He was graded weak by some
scholars but this grading was rejected by the Imams." This is
supported by the fact that the reports against Abu Hanifa are
all weak, rejected, and often inauthentic. In the end, they
amount to nothing. Therefore, even though there is some criticism reported, it does not constitute a "declaration of weakness
by the Imams," as Albani asserts.

The example Saqqaf offers as proof, Ibn Hajar Asqalani's
notice on Abu Hanifa,[4] confirms that the Imams of hadith
never declared Abu Hanifa weak, for Ibn Hajar would have had
to report this declaration if it held true. Rather, he states the

---

2 In his commentary of Mundhiri's *Mukhtasar Sahih Muslim*, 3rd ed. (al-Maktab
al-islami 1977) p. 548. The comparison was removed from later editions.

3 Abd al-Fattah Abu Ghudda, *Radd ala abatil wa iftiraat Nasir al-Albani wa
sahibihi sabiqan Zuhayr al-Shawish wa muazirihima* (Refutation of the falsehoods and
fabrications of Nasir al-Din Albani and his former friend Zuhayr al-Shawish and their
supporters). This book received two editions recently.

4 Ibn Hajar Asqalani, *Tahdhib al-tahdhib*.

reverse, as is clear from the translation of Ibn Hajar's notice, excerpted below, which cites Ibn Main's declaration that Abu Hanifa was *thiqa* (highly trustworthy). Saqqaf's statement is correct, since Ibn Hajar accurately reflects the opinions of the Imams in hadith criticism and methodology concerning the weakness or poor memorization of any given narrator or scholar.

Moreover, Ibn Hajar calls Abu Hanifah *al-imam* and *al-faqih al-mashhur* (the well-known jurisprudent), and Dhahabi includes him in his list of hadith masters.[5] These titles are not given to anyone who is declared weak in hadith. Dhahabi, before Ibn Hajar, and al-Mizzi, before Dhahabi, concurred that no report purporting Abu Hanifa's weakness should be retained. As Dhahabi, "Our shaykh Abu al-Hajjaj [al-Mizzi] did well when he did not cite anything [in *Tahdhib al-kamal*] whereby he [Abu Hanifa] should be deemed weak as a narrator."[6]

The remainder of the supposed support for "Salafi" claims is therefore irrelevant and over-ruled, especially in view of Ibn Abd al-Barr's statement that "Those who narrated from Abu Hanifa, who declared him trustworthy (*waththaquhu*), and who praised him, outnumber those who criticized him."[7] Nevertheless, the sources that Albani introduces will be examined to show the extent to which these sources all suffer from various problems. It is the wont of "Salafis," seen time and time again, to adduce false or weak evidence to promote their aberrant opinions.

4.1.2. HAFIZ IBN HAJAR'S RANK IN HADITH IS HIGHLY TRUSTWORTHY (*THIQA*) AND HE IS INCLUDED AMONG THE HADITH MASTERS (*HUFFAZ*)

4.1.2.1. IBN HAJAR'S NOTICE ON ABU HANIFA IN *TAHDHIB AL-TAHDHIB*

The following is excerpted from *Tahdhib al-tahdhib*.[8]

---

5 Ibn Hajar, *Taqrib al-tahdhib* (1993 ed. 2:248 #7179). Dhahabi, in his *Tadhkirat al-huffaz* [Memorial of the Hadith Masters].

6 Dhahabi, *Tadhhib al-tahdhib* (4:101).

7 As related by Ibn Hajar al-Haytami in his book *al-Khayrat al-hisan fi manaqib Abi Hanifa al-Numan* (p. 74).

8 Ibn Hajar, *Tahdhib al-tahdhib*. 1st ed. (Hyderabad: Dairat al-maarif al-nizamiyya, 1327) Vol. 10 p. 449-452 #817 (10:45f. of the later edition).

Al-Numan ibn Thabit al-Taymi, Abu Hanifa, al-Kufi, mawla Bani Taym Allah ibn Thalaba. It is said that he was Persian. He saw Anas. He narrated hadith from Ata ibn Abi Rabah, Asim ibn Abi al-Nujud, Alqama ibn Marthad, Hammad ibn Abi Sulayman, al-Hakam ibn Utayba, Salama ibn Kuhayl, Abu Jafar Muhammad ibn Ali, Ali ibn al-Aqmar, Ziyad ibn Alaqa, Said ibn Masruq al-Thawri, Adi ibn Thabit al-Ansari, Atiyya ibn Said al-Awfi, Abu Sufyan al-Sadi, Abd al-Karim Abu Umayya, Yahya ibn Said al-Ansari, and Hisham Ibn Urwa among others.

From him narrated: his son Hammad, Ibrahim ibn Tahman, Hamza ibn Habib al-Zayyat, Zafr ibn al-Hadhil, Abu Yusuf al-Qadi, Abu Yahya al-Hamani, Isa ibn Yunus, Waki (ibn al-Jarrah al-Kufi), Yazid ibn Zuray, Asad ibn Amr, al-Bajali, Hakkam ibn Yala ibn Salm al-Razi, Kharija ibn Musab, Abd al-Majid ibn Abi Rawad, Ali ibn Musshir, Muhammad ibn Bishr al-Abdi, Abd al-Razzaq [one of Bukhari's shaykhs], Muhammad ibn al-Hasan al-Shaybani, Musib ibn al-Miqdam, Yahya ibn Yaman, Abu Usma Nuh ibn Abi Maryam, Abu Abd al-Rahman al-Muqri, Abu Nuaym, Abu Asim, and others . . .[9]

[Remarks on Abu Hanifa's national origins and his father's profession.]

Muhammad ibn Sad al-Awfi said: I heard Ibn Main say, "Abu Hanifa was trustworthy (*thiqa*), and he did not narrate any hadith except what he had memorized, nor did he narrate what he had not memorized."

Salih ibn Muhammad al-Asadi said on the authority of Ibn Main, "Abu Hanifa was trustworthy (*thiqa*) in hadith."

Ibn Abd al-Barr relates in *al-Intiqa* (p. 127): Abd Allah ibn Ahmad al-Dawraqi said: Ibn Main was asked about Abu Hanifa as I was listening, so he said, "He is trustworthy (*thiqa*), I never heard that anyone had weakened him. No less than Shuba wrote to him (for narrations), and ordered him to narrate hadith." Ibn

---

9 Such as Abd Allah Ibn al-Mubarak and Dawud al-Tai: see al-Mizzi's *Tahdhib al-kamal* 12 and al-Dhahabi in *Manaqib Abi Hanifa* (p. 20). Al-Mizzi's list is about one hundred strong. Dhahabi relates in his *Tadhkirat al-huffaz* (1:306) in the biography of Waki that Yahya ibn Main said: "I have not seen better than Waki, he spends the night praying, fasts without interruption, and gives *fatwa* according to what Abu Hanifa said, and Yahya al-Qattan also used to give *fatwa* according to what Abu Hanifa said." *al-Hafiz* al-Qurashi in his *al-Jawahir al-mudiyya fi manaqib al-hanafiyya* (2:208-209) said: "Waki took the Science from Abu Hanifa and received a great deal from him."

Hajar said in Kharija ibn al-Salt's notice in *Tahdhib al-tahdhib* (3:75-76), "Ibn Abi Khaythama said: If al-Shubi narrates from someone and names him, that man is trustworthy (*thiqa*) and his narration is used as proof (*yuhtajju bi hadithihi*)."

Al-Haytami in *al-Khayrat al-hisan* (p. 74) and al-Qurashi in *al-Jawahir al-mudiyya* (1:29) relate that Imam Ali ibn al-Madini said, "From Abu Hanifa narrated: al-Thawri, Ibn al-Mubarak, Hammad ibn Zayd, Hisham, Waki (ibn al-Jarrah al-Kufi), Abbad ibn al-Awwam, and Jafar ibn Awn. He [Abu Hanifa] is trustworthy (*thiqa*) and reliable (*la basa bihi* = there is no harm in him). Shuba thought well of him." Ibn Main said, "Our colleagues are exaggerating concerning Abu Hanifa and his colleagues." He was asked, "Does he lie?" Ibn Main replied, "No! he is nobler than that."

Dhahabi in *Tadhkirat al-huffaz* (1:168) cites Ibn Main's statement about Abu Hanifa: *la basa bihi* (= there is no harm in him, i.e. he is reliable). Ibn Salah in his *Muqaddima* (p. 134) and Dhahabi in *Lisan al-mizan* (1:13) have shown that this expression by Ibn Main is the same as declaring someone as thiqa or trustworthy: "Ibn Abi Khaythama said: I said to Ibn Main: You say: "There is no harm in so-and-so" and "so-and-so is weak (*daif*)?" He replied, "If I say of someone that there is no harm in him, he is trustworthy (*fa thiqa*), and if I say *daif*, he is not trustworthy, do not write his hadith."" Abu Ghudda in his commentary to Lucknawi's *Raf* (p. 222 n. 3) has indicated that the equivalency of saying "There is no harm in him" with the grade of trustworthy (*thiqa*) is also the case for other early authorities of the third century such as Ibn al-Madini, Imam Ahmad, Duhaym, Abu Zura, Abu Hatim al-Razi, Yaqub ibn Sufyan al-Fasawi, and others. Note that like Abu Hanifa, Imam Shafii is declared trustworthy by the early authorities with the expression *la basa bihi* in Dhahabi's *Tadhkirat al-huffaz* (1:362).]

Abu Wahb Muhammad ibn Muzahim said: I heard Ibn al-Mubarak say, "The most knowledgeable of people in *fiqh* (*afqah al-nas*) is Abu Hanifa. I have never seen anyone like him in *fiqh*." Ibn al-Mubarak also said: "If Allah had not rescued me with Abu

Hanifa and Sufyan [al-Thawri] I would have been like the rest of the common people." [Dhahabi in *Manaqib Abi Hanifa* (p. 30) relates it as, "I would have been an innovator."]

Ibn Abi Khaythama said from Sulayman ibn Abi Shaykh, "Abu Hanifa was extremely scrupulous (*wari*) and generous (*sakhi*)."

Ibn Isa ibn al-Tabba said: I heard Rawh ibn Ubada say, "I was with Ibn Jurayj in the year 150 when the news of Abu Hanifa's death reached him. He winced and pain seized him; he said, "Verily, knowledge has departed (*ay ilmun dhahab*)." Ibn Jurayj died that same year."

Abu Nuaym said, "Abu Hanifa dived for the meanings of matters so that he reached the uttermost of them."

Ahmad ibn Ali ibn Said al-Qadi said: I heard Yahya ibn Main say: I heard Yahya ibn Said al-Qattan [Ahmad ibn Hanbal's greatest shaykh] say, "This is no lie on our part, by Allah! We have not heard better than Abu Hanifa's opinion, and we have followed most of his sayings." [This is also related by Dhahabi in *Manaqib Abi Hanifa* (p. 32).][10]

Al-Rabi and Harmala said: We heard al-Shafii say, "People are children before Abu Hanifa in *fiqh*."

It is narrated on the authority of Abu Yusuf that he said, "As I was walking with Abu Hanifa we heard a man saying to another: This is Abu Hanifa, he does not sleep at night. Abu Hanifa said: "He says something about me that I do not actually do." He would–after this– spend the greatest part of the night awake."

Ismail ibn Hammad ibn Abi Hanifa said that his father (Hammad) said: When my father died we asked

---

10 About Yahya al-Qattan, Imam Nawawi relates on the authority of Ishaq al-Shahidi: I would see Yahya al-Qattan–may Allah the Exalted have mercy on him – pray the midafternoon prayer, then sit with his back against the base of the minaret of his mosque. Then Ali ibn al-Madini, al-Shadhakuni, Amr ibn Ali, Ahmad ibn Hanbal, Yahya ibn Main, and others would stand before him and ask him questions about hadith standing on their feet until it was time for the sunset prayer. He would not say to a single one of them, "Sit" nor would they sit, out of awe and reverence.

Related in Nawawi's *al-Tarkhis fi al-ikram bi al-qiyam li dhawi al-fadl wa al-maziyya min ahl al-islam ala jihat al-birr wa al-tawqir wa al-ihtiram la ala jihat al-riya wa al-izam* (The Permissibility of Honoring, By Standing Up, Those Who Possess Excellence and Distinction Among the People of Islam: In the Spirit of Piousness, Reverence, and Respect, Not in the Spirit of Display and Aggrandizement) ed. Kilani Muhammad Khalifa (Beirut: Dar al-Bashair al-islamiyya, 1409/1988) p. 58].

al-Hasan ibn Amara to undertake his ritual washing. After he did he said, "May Allah have mercy on you and forgive you (O Abu Hanifa)! You did not eat except at night for thirty years, and your right side did not lay down at night for forty years. You have exhausted whoever comes after you (who tries to catch up with you). You have outshone all the readers of the Islamic sciences."

Ali ibn Mabad said on the authority of Ubayd Allah ibn Amr al-Raqi: Ibn Hubayra told Abu Hanifa to undertake the judgeship of Kufa and he refused, so he had him lashed 110 times, but still he refused. When he saw this he let him go.

Ibn Abi Dawud said on the authority of Nasr ibn Ali: I heard Ibn Dawud–al-Khuraybi – say, "Among the people concerning Abu Hanifa there are plenty of enviers and ignorant one's." . . .

Ahmad ibn Abda the Qadi of Ray said that his father said: We were with Ibn Aisha when he mentioned a saying of Abu Hanifa then he said, "Verily, if you had seen him you would have wanted him. Verily, his similitude and yours is as in the saying:

Censure them little or much: I will never heed your blame.

Try only to fill, if you can, the space that they filled.

Al-Saghani said on the authority of Ibn Main, "I heard Ubayd ibn Abi Qurra say: I heard Yahya ibn al-Daris say: I saw Sufyan [al-Thawri] being asked by a man, "What do you have against Abu Hanifa?" He said, "What is wrong with Abu Hanifa? I heard him say, I take from Allah's Book and if I don't find what I am looking for, I take from the *sunna* of Allah's Messenger, and if I don't find, then from any of the sayings that I like from the Companions, nor do I prefer someone elses saying over theirs, until the matter ends with Ibrahim (al-Nakhi), al-Shubi, Ibn Sirin, and Ata: these are a folk who exerted their reasoning (*ijtihad*) and I exert mine as they did theirs." [i.e. Sufyan criticized Abu Hanifa, a junior Tabii, for placing his own opinion at the same level as that of the senior *tabiin*] . . .

[Mentions of Abu Hanifa's date of death and of the

fact that Tirmidhi and Nasai narrated hadith from
him. End of Ibn Hajar's words.]

4.2. REFUTATION OF THE "SALAFIS" CLAIMS REGARDING IMAM ABU HANIFA'S RANKING IN HADITH

4.2.1. THE "SALAFIS" CLAIM THAT THE GRADING OF ABU HANIFA AS WEAK FOR HIS POOR MEMORIZATION "WAS THE POSITION OF DAARIQITMEE (AS-SUNAN P. 132)."

To this it is answered: Daraqutni did declare Abu Hanifa
weak in his *Sunan*,[11] and did not include him in his *Kitab al-
duafa*. However, his opinion of Abu Hanifa is rejected according
to the rules of narrator-criticism, since he is known to have fall-
en into extremism in his opinion of the Imam. . The hadith
master al-Badr al-Ayni, author of *Umdat al-qari*, a massive
commentary on *Sahih Bukhari*, said:[12]

> From where does he [Daraqutni] take the right to
> declare Abu Hanifa weak when he himself deserves to
> be declared weak! For he has narrated in his *Musnad*
> [i.e. his *Sunan*] narrations that are infirm, defective,
> denounced, strange, and forged.

This is a serious charge against Daraqutni as a narrator,
and many authorities have stated as much. Another hadith
master, al-Zaylai, said, "al-Daraqutni's *Sunan* is the compendium of defective narrations and the wellspring of strange narrations . . . It is filled with narrations that are weak, anom-
alous, defective, and how many of them are not found in other
books!"[13] Muhammad ibn Jafar al-Kattani said, "Daraqutni in
his *Sunan* . . . has multiplied the narrations of reports that are
weak and denounced, and indeed forged."[14]

Ibn Abd al-Hadi al-Hanbali wrote a large, still unpublished
volume on the merits of Abu Hanifa, entitled *Tanwir al-sahifa
bi manaqib al-imam Abi Hanifa*. In this book, he said, "Among

---

11 Daraqutni, *Sunan,* 1:132.
12 Al-Badr al-Ayni, in his commentary of al-Marghinani entitled *al-Binaya sharh
al-hidaya* (1:709).
13 Al-Zaylai, *Nasb al-raya* (1:356, 1:360).
14 Muhammad ibn afar al-Kattani, *al-Risala al-mustatrafa* (p. 31).

those who show fanaticism against Abu Hanifa is al-Daraqutni."[15] Abd al-Fattah Abu Ghudda also said, "al-Daraqutni's fanaticism against Abu Hanifa is well-known," and he gives several sources listing the scholars who held the same opinion.[16]

One of the reasons for Daraqutni's attitude is his extreme bias in favor of the school of Imam Shafii. This is demonstrated in Muhammad Abd al-Rashid al-Numani's commentary on the book *Dhabb dhubabat al-dirasat an al-madhahib al-arbaa al-mutanasibat.*[17] Al-Lucknawi also referred to this question:[18]

> It is related that when Daraqutni went to Egypt some of its people asked him to compile something on the pronunciation of the *basmala* whereupon he compiled a volume. A Maliki came to him and summoned him to declare on oath which were the sound narrations of this book. Daraqutni said, "Everything that was narrated from the Prophet (ﷺ) concerning the loud pronunciation of the *basmala* is unsound, and as for what is related from the Companions, some of it is sound and some of it weak."

4.2.2. THE "SALAFIS" CLAIM THAT THE GRADING OF ABU HANIFA AS WEAK FOR HIS POOR MEMORIZATION "WAS THE POSITION OF IBN ADEE (*AL-KAAMIL* 2/403)."

To this it is answered: Ibn Adi shows enmity to Abu Hanifa, as he reports nothing but criticism, and he relies on weak or inauthentic reports from his shaykh; some of them are the strangest ever related about Abu Hanifa.[19] His narrations are all problematic and none of them are reliable or sound. Imam Kawthari said:

---

15 It is quoted in Ibn Abidin's *Hashiyat radd al-muhtar* (1:37).

16 Abu Ghudda, in his commentary of Abu al-Hasanat al-Lucknawi's *al-Raf wa al-tadil* (p. 70 n.1).

17 Muhammad Abd al-Rashid al-Numani, commentary on *Dhabb dhubabat al-dirasat an al-madhahib al-arbaa al-mutanasibat.* (2:284-297) by the Indian scholar Abd al-Latif al-Sindi.

18 Al-Lucknawi, in his book *al-Ajwiba al-fadila ala al-asila al-ashra al-kamila* (p. 78).

19 Dar al-Fikr 1985 ed. 7:2472-2479.

> Among the defects of Ibn Adi's *Kamil* is his relent-
> less criticism of Abu Hanifa with reports that are all
> from the narration of Abba ibn Jafar al-Najirami, one
> of Ibn Adi's shaykhs, and the latter tries to stick what
> al-Najirami has directly to Abu Hanifa, and this is
> injustice and enmity, as is the rest of his criticism.
> The way to expose such cases is through the chain of
> transmission.[20]

The late Shaykh Abd al-Fattah Abu Ghudda, Kawthari's student, notes that Kawthari examined Ibn Adi's excesses against Abu Hanifa in three works: *Tanib al-khatib ala ma saqahu fi tarjimat abi hanifa min al-akadhib,*[21] *al-Imta bi sirat al-imamayn al-Hasan ibn Ziyad wa sahibihi Muhammad ibn Shuja,*[22] and the unpublished monograph *Ibda wujuh al-taaddi fi kamil ibn Adi.*[23]

Following are some examples of the strangeness of Ibn Adi's reports:

> Ibn Adi relates that Sufyan al-Thawri allegedly
> stated "he [Abu Hanifa] is neither trustworthy nor
> trusted"![24]

On the contrary, it is established that Sufyan narrated hadith from Abu Hanifa; so, he would be contradicting himself in saying that Abu Hanifa cannot be trusted, as he trusted him himself. Ali ibn al-Madini said, "Al-Thawri, Ibn Mubarak, Hammad ibn Zayd, Hisham, Waki, Abbad ibn al-Awwam, and Jafar ibn Awn narrated from Abu Hanifa."[25]

Furthermore, Sufyan praised Abu Hanifa in explicit terms when he said, "We were with Abu Hanifa like small birds in front of the falcon." When Abu Hanifa visited Sufyan after the death of the latter's brother, he stood up, went to greet him,

---

20 Kawthari, in the introduction to *Nasb al-raya* (p. 57) and in his *Fiqh ahl al-Iraq* (p. 83).

21 Kawthari, *Tanib al-khatib ala ma saqahu fi tarjimat abi hanifa min al-akadhib* p. 169.

22 Kawthari, *al-Imta bi sirat al-imamayn al-Hasan ibn Ziyad wa sahibihi Muhammad ibn Shuja* p. 59, 66, 69.

23 Abu Ghudda, in his annotation of Lucknawi's *Raf wa al-takmil* (p. 341).

24 Ibn Adi. *al-Kamil* 7:2472.

25 Narrated by al-Haytami in *al-Khayrat al-hisan* (p. 74) and al-Qurashi in *al-Jawahir al-mudiyya* (1:29).

embraced him, and bade him sit in his place, saying to those who questioned this act:

> This man holds a high rank in knowledge, and if I did not stand up for his science I would stand up for his age, and if not for his age then for his Godwariness (wara), and if not for his Godwariness then for his jurisprudence (fiqh).[26]

Sufyan's supposed criticism is qualified by what Ibn Adi himself narrates later in his section on Abu Hanifa; namely, Abd al-Samad ibn Hassan's statement that "There was something between Sufyan al-Thawri and Abu Hanifa, and Abu Hanifa was the one who restrained his own tongue more."

If there was any disagreement between Sufyan and Abu Hanifa, the nature of their disagreement was not so fundamental as to impel Sufyan to hold the exaggerated view related by Ibn Adi. Instead, their disagreement would only have pertained to issues of manners or competition. This can be gathered from Ibn Hajar's relation of Sufyan's disapproval of Abu Hanifa's saying, regarding the senior tabiis, "These are a folk who exerted their reasoning (ijtihad) and I exert mine as they did theirs." He used this statement to place himself, a junior tabii, at the same level of ijtihad as the senior tabiis, such as al-Nakhi, al-Shubi, Ibn Sirin, and Ata.[27]

The competition between Sufyan and Abu Hanifa was fostered by Sufyan's entourage, as shown by Ibn Adi's reports of the following:

> The dream of an unnamed man who saw the Prophet (ﷺ) telling him to take Sufyan's opinion rather than Abu Hanifa's.[28]

This report contains Ahmad ibn Hafs, who is *munkar al-hadith*—a narrator whose narrations are rejected.[29] It also con-

---

26 Both reports are narrated by Suyuti in *Tabyid al-sahifa* (p. 32) and al-Tahanawi in his book *Inja al-watan* (1:19-22).

27 Ibn Hajar, *Tahdhib al-tahdhib* (10:451).

28 Ibn Adi, *al-Kamil* 7:2473.

29 According to Ibn al-Jawzi in *al-Mawduat* (2:168, 3:94; see also *Tabsir al-mutan-abbih* 2:733, and *al-Mushtabah* p. 98, 359).

tains an unnamed narrator–the man who had the dream – and one whose reliability is not known (*majhul*), Abu Ghadir al-Filastini.

The contrived style of the narration of Sufyan al-Thawris story that "he [Abu Hanifa] is neither trustworthy nor trusted." Muammal said:

> I was with Sufyan al-Thawri in his room when a man came and asked him about something and he answered him, then the man said: But Abu Hanifa said such and such, whereupon Sufyan took his sandals and flung them exclaiming: he is neither trustworthy nor trusted!!

The narrator of this report from Sufyan, Muammal ibn Ismail, was denounced as making mistakes in his narrations by Ibn Hibban, al-Sajir, and Ibn Qani. Al-Saji said, "He is not a liar but he makes many mistakes, and he sometimes imagines things" (*saduq kathir al-khata wa lahu awham*).

All the above evidence is part of the reason why criticism of Abu Hanifa attributed to Sufyan al-Thawri is rejected, and why Ibn Adi's reliance on such criticism is not taken into account. Al-Taj al-Subki said, "No attention whatsoever is given to al-Thawri's criticism of Abu Hanifa or that of other than al-Thawri against him."[30] The same statement is found in Haytami's *al-Khayrat al-hisan*[31] and is echoed by Abd al-Hayy al-Lucknawi's warning, "Beware, beware of paying any attention to what supposedly took place (of enmity) between Abu Hanifa and Sufyan al-Thawri!"[32]

The story of Imam Malik's words related by Ibn Adi: "The consuming ailment is destruction in Religion, and Abu Hanifa is part of the consuming ailment" and "Is Abu Hanifa in your country? Then one ought not to live in your country."[33]

These are extreme statements attributed to Imam Malik by those of his companions who were of the so-called *Ahl al-*

---

30 Al-Subki, in *Qawaid fi ulum al-hadith* (p. 195) as well as his *Qaida fi al-jarh wa al-tadil* (p. 53-55).

31 Haytami, *al-Khayrat al-hisan* (p. 74).

32 Al-Lucknawi, in his *al-Raf wa al-takmil* (p. 425).

33 Ibn Adi, *al-Kamil* 7:2473.

hadith. As for the *fuqaha* among them, they reported no such statements from him. This is elaborated by the Maliki authority Ibn Abd al-Barr, who invalidates the evidence of Malikis against him.[34]

It is remarkable that Ibn Adi narrates Malik's statement "The consuming ailment . . ." from Ibn Abi Dawud, while it is established that Ibn Adi Dawud's own father, Abu Dawud, said, "*Rahimallah malikan kana imaman. rahimallah al-shafii kana imama. rahimallah aba hanifa kana imaman.* The last part means, "May Allah have mercy on Abu Hanifa, he was an *imam.*"[35] The strength of Abu Dawud's remark resides in the nature of his own specialty, which is hadith; it was in this function that he recognized Abu Hanifa's leadership among Muslims.

Ironically, Ibn Abi Dawud himself said, on the authority of Nasr ibn Ali:

> I heard Ibn Dawud – al-Khuraybi – say, "Among the people concerning Abu Hanifa there are plenty of enviers and ignorant one's."[36]

Ibn Adi's report of Yahyan ibn Main's alleged weakening of Abu Hanifa from Ibn Abi Maryam's saying: I asked Yahya ibn Main about Abu Hanifa and he said, "One must not write his narrations." (2473)

This is assuredly a false ascription to Ibn Main, since it is firmly established that Ibn Main considered Abu Hanifa a source of reliable and trustworthy narrations:

> Ibn Hajar relates from both Muhammad ibn Sad al-Awfi and Salih ibn Muhammad al-Asadi that Ibn Main said, "Abu Hanifa is trustworthy (*thiqa*) in hadith." He also relates from Ibn Mains own shaykh, Ibn al-Qattan, that he relied greatly on Abu Hanifa: Ahmad ibn Ali ibn Said al-Qadi said: I heard Yahya

---

34 Ibn Abd al-Barr, in his notice on Abu Hanifa in *al-Intiqa.*

35 It is narrated by Dhahabi in his *Tarikh al-Islam* (6:136) and, as noted by Muhammad Qasim Abduh al-Harithi in his book *Makanat al-Imam Abi Hanifa bayn al-muhaddithin* (p. 201).

36 Ibn Hajar relates it in his *Tahdhib* as we mentioned above, while Dhahabi relates it through Bishr al-Hafi in *Tarikh al-Islam* (6:142) and *Manaqib Abi Hanifa* (p. 32) with the wording: *ma yaqau fi abi hanifa illa hasid aw jahil* "None whatsoever inveighs against Abu Hanifa except an envier or an ignoramus."

ibn Main say: I heard Yahya ibn Said al-Qattan say,
"This is no lie on our part, by Allah! We have not
heard better than Abu Hanifa's opinion, and we have
followed most of his sayings."[37]

Dhahabi relates that Yahya ibn Main said, "I have
not seen better than Waki, he spends the night praying, fasts without interruption, and gives *fatwa*
according to what Abu Hanifa said, and Yahya al-
Qattan also used to give *fatwa* according to what Abu
Hanifa said."[38]

Ibn Abd al-Barr relates: Abd Allah ibn Ahmad al-Dawraqi
said: Ibn Main was asked about Abu Hanifa as I was listening,
so he said, "He is trustworthy (*thiqa*), I never heard that anyone had weakened him, and Shuba ibn al-Hajjaj wrote to him
and told him to narrate hadith. He ordered him to do so, and
Shuba is Shuba!"[39]

Ibn Adi's groundless conclusion, "Most of what he [Abu
Hanifa] narrates is wrong."[40]

This is applicable to Ibn Adi himself. As for Abu Hanifa, he
was just as Shuba and Ibn Main said: "He was, by Allah! good
in his memorization,"[41] and, "Indeed he was more than trustworthy (*naam thiqa thiqa*)."[42]

4.2.3. THE "SALAFIS" CLAIM THAT ABU HANIFA'S WEAK GRADING FOR HIS POOR MEMORIZATION "WAS THE POSITION OF MUSLIM (*AL-KUNAA WAL ASMAA*) [AND] NASAAEE (*AL-DUAFAA*)."

To this it is answered: It is correct that Nasai included Abu
Hanifa in his book, and that he said, "Numan ibn Thabit Abu
Hanifa, *laysa bi al-qawi fi al-hadith* (he is not strong in
hadith)."[43] Despite the fact that Nasai included Abu Hanifa in
his book, and apart from the validity of Nasai's saying "he is not
strong," such a remark does not constitute *tadif*; he did not say
"He is weak." His denying Abu Hanifa the rank of strength only

---

37 Ibn Hajar, *Tahdhib al-tahdhib* (10:450). This is also related by Dhahabi in
Manaqib Abi Hanifa (p. 32).

38 Dhahabi, in his *Tadhkirat al-huffaz* (1:306) in the biography of Waki.

39 Ibn Abd al-Barr, in *al-Intiqa* (p. 127).

40 Ibn Adi, *al-Kamil* (7:2479).

41 Ibn Abd al-Barr, *al-Intiqa'* p. 127.

42 Al-Khatib, *Tarikh Baghdad* 13:449.

43 Al-Nasai. *al-Duafa wa al-matrukin* (p. 233 #614).

means that Nasai found something objectionable in him, not that he considered him weak as a narrator. After all, one does not have to be strong in hadith in order to be a reliable narrator. Therefore, it cannot be claimed that "the grading of Abu Hanifa as weak was the position of Nasai in his *Sunan*," for this was not his position. If this were true, Nasai would have contradicted it himself, since, in his *Sunan*, he narrates hadith from Abu Hanifa.[44]

Equally false is the claim that Imam Muslim declared Abu Hanifa weak, since all he said is *sahib al-ray mudtarib al-hadith laysa lahu kabir hadith sahih*; "The scholar of the school of opinion, his narrations are not firm in their wording and he has not many sound ones."[45] Imam Muslim did not say that he was weak.

Furthermore, generally speaking, Muslim's judgment is biased due to the difference in methodology between himself and Abu Hanifa. This is evident in the fact that he calls Abu Hanifa *sahib al-ray*—a term loaded with criticism that the Hanafi's are labeled with by those who disagree with them. This methodological difference is the reason why neither Nasai's inclusion of Abu Hanifa in his book of weak narrators, nor Nasai and Muslim's remarks about Abu Hanifa are acceptable as a legitimate *jarh*, or criticism of the Imam. One of the fundamental rules of narrator-criticism is that if the critic is known to differ with the narrator in matters of doctrine and methodology, and it is widely known that the so-called "school of hadith" differed with the so-called "school of opinion" (*ray*), the critic must state the reason for his *jarh*. Both Nasai and Muslim omitted to state any reason for theirs. Therefore, their *jarh* is not retained until it is explained and can meet the criteria of the discipline.

Finally, it is a rule of *jarh wa al-tadil* that if the unexplained *jarh* (narrator-criticism) contradicts the explained *tadil* (narrator-authentication) by an authority of authentication who is fully aware of the *jarh*, the *tadil* takes precedence

---

44 As stated in Abu Hanifa's entries in al-Mizzi's *Tahdhib* (10:449), Dhahabi's *Tadhkirat al-huffaz* and his *al-Kashshasf fi marifati man lahu riwayatun fi al-kutub al-sitta* (p. 322 #5845), Ibn Hajar's *Taqrib* (2:248 #7179), and al-Khazraji's *Khulasat tadhhib tahdhib al-kamal* (3:95 #7526)!

45 Muslim, in his book *al-Kuna wa al-asma* (1:276 #963).

over the *jarh*. This is the case with Abu Hanifa's *jarh* by Nasai and Muslim not being retained by Abu Dawud or later authorities such as al-Mizzi, Dhahabi, Ibn Hajar, al-Khazraji, al-Suyuti, and others.

4.2.4 THE "SALAFIS" CLAIM THAT ABU HANIFA'S GRADING AS WEAK FOR HIS POOR MEMORIZATION "WAS THE POSITION OF . . . BUKHAREE (*AT-TAAREEKH AL-KABEER*)."

To this it is answered: Bukhari's negative opinion of Abu Hanifa, expressed in his *Sahih* and his *Tarikh*, is a rejected type of *jarh* and considered unreliable, since it is known that he had fundamental differences with Abu Hanifa on questions of principles, fiqh, and methodology, his *Sahih* is, in many parts, an unspoken attempt to refute Abu Hanifa and his school. The Indian scholar Zafar al-Tahanawi showed Bukhari's extremism against Abu Hanifa, and other scholars have highlighted the disagreement between them.[46] Among them is the Hanafi *faqih* and hadith master al-Zaylai, who said:[47]

> No student of the science adorned himself with a better garment than fairness and the relinquishment of fanaticism . . . Bukhari is very much pursuing an agenda in what he cites from the *sunna* against Abu Hanifa, for he will mention a hadith and then insinuate something about him, as follows: "Allah's Messenger said such and such, and some people said such and such." By "some people" he means Abu Hanifa, so he casts him in the ugliest light possible, as someone who dissents from the hadith of the Prophet (ﷺ)!
>
> Bukhari also says in the beginning of his book (*Sahih*), "Chapter whereby *Salat* is part of Belief," then he proceeds with the narrations of that chapter. His purpose in that is to refute Abu Hanifa's saying, "Deeds are not part of Belief," although many *fuqaha* do not realize this. And I swear by Allah, and again – by Allah! – that if Bukhari had found one hadith [sup-

---

46 Zafar al-Tahanawi, in the book edited by his student Abd al-Fattah Abu Ghudda under the title *Qawaid fi ulum al-hadith* (p. 380-384).
47 Al-Zaylai, in *Nasb al-raya* (1:355-356).

porting that *Salat* is part of Belief] that met his crite-
rion or came close to it, his book would certainly not
have been devoid of it, nor that of Muslim.

As mentioned above, among the kinds of rejected *jarh* are
those based on differences in school, *aqida*, or methodology. For
example, the fact that a narrator is Shia in *aqida* and shows
excessive love for Ali, or Nasibi in *aqida* and shows hatred of
Ali,[48] does not automatically mean that he is *majruh* (defective). An example of a Shii narrator retained by Bukhari is the
great *muhaddith* Abd al-Razzaq al-Sanani (d. 211), the author
of the *Musannaf* from whom Bukhari took a quantity of
hadiths. Two narrators retained by Bukhari and Muslim
although they were accused of being Nasibi are: Huswayn ibn
Numayr, from whom Bukhari narrates the hadiths "The
Communities were shown to me and I saw a great dark mass,"
and "The Communities were shown to me and there was a
Prophet (🖾) with only one follower, and a Prophet (🖾) with
only two followers;" and Ahmad ibn Abdah al-Dabbi, from
whom Muslim takes one of three chains of the hadith "I have
been ordered to fight people until they say *la ilaha ilallah* and
believe in me."

Another form of *jarh* that is rejected is the denouncement
of a scholar of the so-called "school of *ray*" [opinion] by a scholar of the so-called "school of hadith." For instance, the
denouncement of a Hanafi by a Hanbali. Therefore Ahmad's
denouncing of Mualla ibn Mansur al-Razi (d. 211) is rejected.[49]
Abu Dawud said, "Yahya ibn Main said that Mualla is trust-

---

48 Fayruzabadi in the *Qamus*, Ibn Manzhur in *Lisan al-Arab*, and al-Zabidi in *Taj
al-arus* define the *Nawasib* as those who made a point of opposing Ali ibn Abi Talib
They are part of the Khawarij, who are those Muslims (whether in past or recent
times) who oppose one whom the majority of Muslims have taken as their leader. Ibn
Abidin said in his *Radd al-muhtar ala al-durr al-mukhtar* (3:309), "*Bab al-bughat*"
[Chapter on Rebels]: "The name of *Khawarij* is applied to those who part ways with
Muslims and declare them disbelievers, as took place in our time with the followers of
Ibn Abd al-Wahhab who came out of Najd (in the Eastern Arabian peninsula) and
attacked the Two Noble Sanctuaries (Makka and Madina). They (Wahhabis) claimed to
follow the Hanbali school, but their belief was such that, in their view, they alone are
Muslims and everyone else is a *mushrik* (polytheist). Under this guise, they said that
killing *Ahl al-Sunna* and their scholars was permissible, until Allah the Exalted
destroyed them in the year 1233 (1818 CE) at the hands of the Muslim army."
49 As shown by Dhahabi in *al-Mughni* (2:270).

worthy while Ahmad ibn Hanbal would not narrate from him because he followed the methodology of *ray*."[50] Thus Abu Dawud rejects Ahmad's verdict and narrates from Mualla, as did Muslim, Tirmidhi, Ibn Majah, and others.

Bukhari's narration of reports that are ostensibly detrimental to Abu Hanifa, and of Yazid ibn Harun's labeling of Muhammad al-Shaybani, Abu Hanifa's student, as a Jahmi,[51] belongs to this category of rejected *jarh*.[52] Such reports are dismissed as mistakes for which Bukhari must be forgiven, as he is not faultless, *masum*.

The same is said of Ibn Hibban's outlandish declaration that Abu Hanifa is not to be relied upon because "he was a Murji and an innovator."[53] This judgment is discarded, as stated by al-Lucknawi, "Criticism of Abu Hanifa as a narrator on the claim of his *irja* is not accepted."[54] The so-called Murjia of the Hanafi Imams, such as Abu Hanifa, his shaykh Hammad ibn Abi Sulayman, and his two students Muhammad and Abu Yusuf, all belong to mainstream Islam, and are not to be called innovators. Al-Dhahabi said, "The disapproved Murjia are those who accepted Abu Bakr and Umar but withheld taking a position concerning Uthman and Ali."[55] It is obvious that such a definition does not apply to the Hanafi Imams. Imam Abu Hanifa said:[56]

> The best of mankind after the prophets (ﷺ), are Abu Bakr al-Siddiq, then Umar ibn al-Khattab, then Uthman ibn Affan dhu al-Nurayn, then Ali ibn Abi Talib al-Murtada, may Allah be well pleased with all of them—worshipping their Lord, steadfast upon truth and on the side of truth. We follow all of them (*natawallahum jamian*). Nor do we mention any of the Prophet's Companions except in good terms.

> A longer definition of the "Murjia" is given by Ibn Hajar.[57]

> *Irja* has the sense of "delaying" and carries two

50 Abu Dawud, in his *Sunan* (book of *Tahara*).
51 Yazid ibn Harun, in his *Khalq afal al-ibad* (1990 ed. p. 15).
52 Bukhari, in his *Tarikh al-saghir*.
53 Ibn Hibban, in his *Kitab al-majruhin* (3:63-64).
54 Al-Lucknawi, in *al-Raf wa al-takmil*.
55 Al-Dhahabi, in his *Tarikh al-islam* (3:358f).
56 Abu Hanifa. in his *Fiqh al-akbar* (as narrated by Ali al-Qari in his *Sharh*, 1984 ed. p. 96-101).
57 Ibn Hajar, in *Hadi al-sari* (2:179).

meanings among the scholars: some mean by it the delaying in declaring one's position in the case of the two warring factions after Uthman's time [i.e. neither following nor rejecting either one]; and some mean by it the delaying in declaring that whoever commits grave sins and abandons obligations enters the Fire, on the basis that in their view belief consists in assertion and conviction and that quitting deeds [i.e. ceasing from obeying commands and prohibitions] does not harm it."

The so-called Sunni "Murjia" belong to the second category, but with one important provision: they do not hold that quitting deeds does not harm belief. On the contrary, they hold that quitting deeds harms the quitter. As Ali al-Qari said, in the title of one of his chapters, "Acts of disobedience harm their author, contrary to the belief of certain factions."[58] Al-Mizzi relates a clarification overlooked by Ibn Hajar whereby the Sunni Murjia is so-called not because he believes that "quitting deeds does not harm belief," but because he professes hope (*yarju*) of salvation for great sinners.[59] They are different from the Khawarij, who declare sinners disbelievers, and the Mutazila, who do not believe in the Prophet's intercession for great sinners. In this sense, Abu Hanifa and the Maturidi school of doctrine support what all other schools of mainstream Islam hold. As for the Murjia who rely on faith exclusive of deeds, they belong to heretical sects, and the attribution of such belief to Abu Hanifa is *iftira* and fabrication.

The focus of Bukhari and Ibn Hibban's criticism is Abu Hanifa's view that *iman*, belief, represents one's Islam, and vice-versa, and therefore neither increases or decreases once acquired. It is a fundamental tenet of the Maturidi school with which Bukhari differed, as illustrated by his chapter-titles like "*Salat* is part of belief," and "Belief increases and decreases"

---

58 Ali al-Qari, in *Sharh al-fiqh al-akbar* (p. 67, 103).
59 Al-Mizzi, in his *Tahdhib al-kamal* from Abu al-Salt al-Harawi.

etc. The vast majority of Hanafis, and the entire Maturidi school of doctrine hold the opposite view, as illustrated by Ali al-Qari's naming two chapter-titles "Belief neither increases nor decreases,"[60], another "The believers are equal in belief but differ in deeds,"[61] and another "The grave sin [such as not performing *salat*] does not expel one from belief."[62]

All the above is also the sound doctrine of mainstream Islam, as opposed to that of present-day extremists, which holds that anyone who commits a major sin is a disbeliever who should repeat his *shahada* or be killed. Their view contradicts Imam Ahmad, who insisted that no Muslim should be called a disbeliever for any sin.[63]

After these preliminaries, it may now be shown why the scholars do not retain Bukhari's aspersion of Abu Hanifa, even though today's "Salafis" attempt to use them to justify Albani's position against the Imam.[64]

1st relation

Bukhari said in his *Tarikh al-saghir*:[65]

> I heard al-Humaydi say: Abu Hanifa said, "I came to Makka and took from the cupper three *sunna*s when I sat in front of him. He said to me to face the Kabah, he began with the right side of my head [shaving], and he reached the two bones." al-Humaydi said, "A man who does not have *sunna*s from the Prophet (ﷺ) nor from his Companions concerning the rituals of Pilgrimage or other things, how can he be imitated in questions of inheritance, obligations, charity, prayer, and the questions of Islam?!"

This relation is defective from several perspectives:

1 Abd al-Fattah Abu Ghudda said that his shaykh al-Tahanawi said:[66]

---

60 *Ibid*. p. 126, 202.
61 *Ibid*. p. 128.
62 Ali al-Qari, *Sharh al-fiqh al-akbar*. p. 102.
63 As shown by Ibn Abi Yala in *Tabaqat al-hanabila* (1:329).
64 C.f. Bukhari, in his *Tarikh al-saghir*.
65 Bukhari, *Tarikh al-saghir,* p. 158.
66 Abu Ghudda, in his annotations to al-Lucknawi's *Raf wa al-takmil* (p. 395-397).

Al-Humaydi wished to demean Abu Hanifa with his comments, but in fact he praised him without realizing. For Abu Hanifa was gracious and generous, and he would show gratefulness to whomever showed him kindness or taught him something, even a single letter. He was not one who kept hidden other peoples' goodness towards him, or their favors. When he obtained something related to matters of religion from a simple cupper, he told of the cupper's kindness and he showed him up as his teacher, fulfilling the right he held over him. And what a strange thing indeed to hear from al-Humaydi, when his own shaykh, al-Shafii, said: I carried from Muhammad ibn al-Hasan al-Shaybani knowledge equivalent to a full camel-load, and he would say: Allah has helped me with hadith through Ibn Uyayna, and He helped me with fiqh through Muhammad ibn al-Hasan. And it is well-known that the well-spring of Muhammad ibn al-Hasan's sciences are Abu Hanifa. Imam Shafii also said: Whoever seeks *fiqh*, let him frequent Abu Hanifa and his two companions; and he also said: Anyone that seeks *fiqh* is a dependent of Abu Hanifa. And yet, with all this, al-Humaydi does not show gratefulness for the Imam who is his Shaykh's Shaykh, nor for the favor he represents for him.[67]

2 Al-Tahanawi also mentioned that Abu Hanifa went to pilgrimage with his father as a young man, and that the incident may well have taken place at that time, since what is learnt in a young age is hardly ever forgotten.

3 Al-Tahanawi pointed out that, in the time of Abu Hanifa in Makka, knowledge was distributed everywhere among the people, and that it is not impossible that the humble cupper was one of the *tabiin* who had learned what he knew from the Companions themselves. He asks, "From where does Humaydi know that that cupper was not one of the knowledgeable Tabiis, and that he either narrated these three *sunna*s with their chain back to the Prophet (ﷺ), or suspended back to one of the great Companions?!"

Al-Tahanawi concluded:

---

67 Al-Tahanawi, in his book *Inja al-watan* (1:23), according to Abu Ghudda.

As for Humaydi's saying how can Abu Hanifa be imitated, we know that greater men than Humaydi did imitate him, such as Imam al-Shafii–whom al-Humaydi imitated–Yahya ibn Said al-Qattan, Malik ibn Anas, Sufyan al-Thawri, Ahmad ibn Hanbal (through Abu Hanifa's students the Qadi Abu Yusuf and Muhammad al-Shaybani), Waki ibn al-Jarrah, Abd Allah ibn al-Mubarak, Yahya ibn Main, and their likes. Then the kings, the sultans, the *khulafa*, the viziers imitated him, and the scholars of knowledge, the scholars of hadith, the saints, the jurists, and the commonality imitated him, until Allah was worshiped through the school of Abu Hanifa all over the world, and that was because of the good manners upon which Abu Hanifa was grounded, because he did not look down upon taking the highest knowledge from a cupper, and so Allah made him the Imam of the Umma, the greatest of the Imams, and the guide of humanity.[68]

5 Shaykh Abu Ghudda added:

In addition to the above it is noted that al-Humaydi said, "Abu Hanifa said without mentioning from whom he had heard it, and I have not found any proof that al-Humaydi (d. 219) ever met Abu Hanifa at all . . . It is clear to us that he was not born when Abu Hanifa died (d. 150) . . . The report is therefore weak due to the interruption in its chain of transmission, and that is enough."[69]

6 Shaykh Abu Ghudda concluded in saying that any criticism of Abu Hanifa attributed to Sufyan al-Thawri is rejected, out of hand, and there can be no reliance on such criticism to establish narrator-criticism.[70] This particular rule was enunciated by al-Taj al-Subki,[71] also Haytami,[72] al-Lucknawi,[73] and

---

68 Another illustration of Imam Abu Hanifa's great humility is the narration of Ishaq ibn al-Hasan al-Kufi related by Dhahabi in *Manaqib Abi Hanifa* (p. 38): A man came to the market and asked for the shop of Abu Hanifa, the *Faqih*. Abu Hanifa said to him: "He is not a *Faqih*. He is one who gives legal opinions according to his obligation."

69 Abu Ghudda, *al-Raf* p. 397-398.

70 As mentioned above in the section on Ibn Adi.

71 Al-Taj al-Subki, in *Qawaid fi ulum al-hadith* (p. 195) as well as his *Qaida fi al-jarh wa al-tadil* (p. 53-55).

72 Haytami, *al-Khayrat al-hisan* (p. 74).

73 Al-Lucknawi, *al-Raf wa al-takmil* (p. 425).

by Abu Ghudda in his marginalia on Subki's and al-Lucknawi's works.

2nd relation

Bukhari also said in his *Tarikh al-saghir*:[74]

> Nuaym ibn Hammad narrated to us and said: *al-Fazari* narrated to us and said: I was visiting with Sufyan al-Thawri and we received news of Abu Hanifa's death, so Sufyan said, *"al-hamdu lillah!* he was taking apart Islam branch by branch. No greater misfortune than him was ever born into Islam (*ma wulida fi al-islami ashamu minhu*)."

This relation is even more defective than the first for the following reasons:

1 Shaykh Abd al-Fattah Abu Ghudda said, "Our shaykh, the verifying scholar al-Kawthari, said in his book *Fiqh ahl al-Iraq wa hadithuhum* (p. 87), and in the introduction of *hafiz* al-Zaylai's book *Nasb al-raya* (p.58-59):

> There is a kind of criticism by which the critic destroys his credibility from the start through the fact that his words bear all the traits of rashness. If you see him saying, for example, "No greater misfortune than him was ever born into Islam," you will notice that there is no misfortune (*shum*) in Islam. Even if we should admit that there is–in the centuries other than the three mentioned in the hadith – still, without doubt, the gradations of misfortune vary. And to declare a certain person to be the worst of the worst without a statement to that effect from the Prophet (ﷺ) is to claim to know the unseen from which the people of Religion are clear. Such a statement, therefore, destroys the credibility of its speaker, if it is firmly established to come from him, before the credibility of the subject of the statement. In a very precarious position indeed is the one who records such an absurdity to the detriment of the leading Imams."[75]

---

74 Bukhari, *Tarikh al-Saghir*, p. 174.
75 Abu Ghudda, in his marginal notes to al-Lucknawi's *al-Raf wa al-takmil* (p. 393).

2 "And in his book *Tanib al-Khatib* (p. 48, 72, 111) Kawthari also said:

> If such a saying were ascertained from Sufyan al-Thawri, he would have fallen from credibility due to this word alone for its passionate tone and rashness. Suffice it to say in refutation of that narration that Nuaym ibn Hammad is in its chain of transmission, and the least that was said about him is that he conveyed rejected narrations and he has been accused of forging disgraceful stories against Abu Hanifa.

3 "And our shaykh, the verifying savant and hadith scholar Zafar Ahmad al-Tahanawi said in his book *Inja al-watan min al-izdira bi imam al-zaman* (Saving the Nation from the scorn displayed against the Imam of the Time) 1:22:

> "*It is a grievous saying that issues from their mouth. What they say is nothing but falsehood!*" (18:5).
> [Abu Ghudda continues] By Allah, there was not born into Islam, after the Prophet (ﷺ), greater fortune and assistance than al-Numan Abu Hanifa. The proof of this can be witnessed in the extinction of the schools of his attackers, while his increases in fame day and night. I do not blame al-Bukhari for it, since he only related what he heard. However, I blame for it his shaykh Nuaym ibn Hammad, even if the latter is a hadith master whom some have declared trustworthy [e.g. Ahmad, Ibn Main, and al-Ujli]. Nevertheless the hadith master Abu Bishr al-Dulabi said, "Nuaym narrates from Ibn al-Mubarak; al-Nasai said he is weak (*daif*), and others said: he used to forge narrations in defense of the *sunna*, and disgraceful stories against Abu Hanifa, all of them lies." Similarly Abu al-Fath al-Azdi said, "They said he used to forge hadiths in defense of the *sunna*, and fabricate disgraceful stories against Abu Hanifa, all of them lies." Similarly in *Tahdhib al-tahdhib* (10:460-463) and *Mizan al-itidal* (3:238, 4:268): "Al-Abbas ibn Musab said in his *Tarikh*: "Nuaym ibn Hammad composed books to refute the Hanafis" . . . [and in Hadi al-Sari

(2:168): "Nuaym ibn Hammad was violently against the People of Ray. Therefore neither his word nor his narration to the detriment of Abu Hanifa and Hanafis can ever be accepted . . .

It is, furthermore, established that Sufyan al-Thawri praised Abu Hanifa when he said, "We were in front of Abu Hanifa like small birds in front of the falcon." Sufyan stood up for him when Abu Hanifa visited him after his brother's death, and he said, "This man holds a high rank in knowledge, and if I did not stand up for his science I would stand up for his age, and if not for his age then for his God-wariness (*wara*), and if not for his God-wariness then for his jurisprudence (*fiqh*)."

Finally, Ibn al-Subki's instruction to hadith scholars, already quoted in the discussion of Ibn Adi: "Pay no attention to al-Thawri's criticism of Abu Hanifa," and Abd al-Hayy al-Lucknawi's warning, "Beware of paying any attention to what took place between Abu Hanifa and Sufyan al-Thawri . . ."

4.2.4 The "Salafis" claim that Abu Hanifa's grading as weak for his poor memorization "was the position of . . . al-Uqailee (*al-Duafaa* p.432) [and] ibn Hibban (*al-Majrooheen*)."

To this it is answered: It has already been mentioned that *jarh*, or narrator-criticism, is rejected if it is based on differences in methodology and school. Another category of *jarh* that is not accepted by the scholars is that declared by a scholar who is known for his fanatic or blind condemnation of others. This form of rejected *jarh* is exemplified by the fanaticism (*tanut*) of the following scholars against Hanafis and Imam Abu Hanifa: Daraqutni, Ibn Adi Ibn Hibban, and al-Uqayli, as will be shown presently.

Dhahabi said, in reference to Ibn Hibban's general method in narrator-criticism, "He vociferates, as is his habit;"[76] he calls him "Ibn Hibban the Shredder, the most reckless of the ill-natured ones" Ibn Hibban *al-khassaf al-mutahawwir fi arimin*.

---

76 Al-Dhahabi, *Mizan al-itidal* (2:185, 3:121).

Ibn Hajar said, "Ibn Hibban all-too-readily declares the trust-worthy to be weak, and acts as if he does not know what he is saying."[77] The editor of Ibn Hibban's book *al-Majruhin min al-muhaddithin wa al-duafa wa al-matrukin*, Mahmud Ibrahim Zayid, says the following in the margin of his notice on Abu Hanifa:[78]

> [Ibn Hibban] did not leave a single device of the devices of narrator-criticism except he used it [against Abu Hanifa], and in so doing he accepted the reports of narrators whom he himself does not trust for narration according to his own methodology. He discarded the reports of those who are considered trustworthy among the Imams of the Umma and he accepted the reports of the most extreme of those who have been criticized for weakness.
>
> Nor did he content himself with what he cited in the contents of his books in such attacks against the Imam, but he also composed two of his largest books exclusively as an attack against Abu Hanifa, and these books are: *Kitab ilal manaqib Abi Hanifa* (Book of the defects in Abu Hanifa's qualities), in ten parts, and *Kitab ilal ma istanada ilayhi Abu Hanifa* (Book of the defects of what Abu Hanifa relied upon), in ten parts!

As for the Hanbali scholar al-Uqayli, he is possibly the most fanatic and least reliable of narrator-criticism authorities. His notice on Abu Hanifa is, like that of Ibn Hibban on the Imam, a biased selection of very weak and fabricated reports.[79] As a result of this and other similar displays, he does not carry any weight with the hadith masters. To quote his opinion as evidence of Abu Hanifa's weakening is only proof of "Salafi" ignorance.

Uqayli attacked narrator after narrator relied upon by Bukhari and Muslim, as well as the Imams of *fiqh* and hadith, hacking down, in the process, the names of Ali ibn al-Madini, Bukhari, Abd al-Razzaq, Ibn Abi Shayba, Ibrahim ibn Sad,

---

77 Ibn Hajar, in *al-Qawl al-musaddad fi al-dhabb an musnad Ahmad* (p. 33).

78 Ibn Hibban, *al-Majruhim min al-muhaddithin wa al-duafa wa al-matrukin*, ed. Mahmud Ibrahim Zayid, 3:61.

79 Al-Uqayli, in his book entitled *Kitab al-duafa al-kabir* (4:268-285 #1876).

Affan, Aban al-Attar, Israil ibn Yunus, Azhar al-Saman, Bahz ibn Asad, Thabit al-Bunani, and Jarir ibn Abd al-Hamid. Dhahabi targets him:[80]

> Have you no mind, O Uqayli?! (*afama laka aqlun ya uqayli*) Do you know who you are talking about?! The only reason we mention what you say about them is in order to repel from them the statements made about them – as if you did not know that each one of those you target is several times more trustworthy than you?! Nay, more trustworthy than many trustworthy narrators whom you did not even cite once in your book . . . If the hadith of these narrators were to be abandoned, then shut the gates, cease all speech, let hadith transmission die, put the free-thinkers in office, and let the antichrists come out!

One of Uqayli's worse traits, in his *Kitab al-duafa*, is his attributing derogatory reports to the great Imams, such as the story that Imam Ahmad reportedly said that Abu Hanifa lies![81] If this were true, how would Imam Ahmad have allowed himself to narrate hadith from Abu Hanifa in his *Musnad*, as he did with his narration *al-dallu ala al-khayri ka failihi*, which he took from the Imam with a sound chain to the Prophet (ﷺ) from Burayda? The reason why Ahmad included it in the *Musnad* is that only Abu Hanifa narrated this hadith from Burayda. This is a proof against Uqayli's relation from Ahmad, since the Ahmad would not have related this hadith if he believed that Abu Hanifa lied.

A more explicit proof against this spurious attribution to Imam Ahmad is what is related by his close student, Abu Bakr al-Marrudhi (or al-Marwazi):

> I said to him [Ahmad ibn Hanbal], "*al-hamdu lil-lah*! He [Abu Hanifa] has a high rank in knowledge." He replied, "*Subhan Allah*! He occupies a station in knowledge, extreme fear of Allah, asceticism, and the quest for the Abode of the hereafter, where none whatsoever reaches him."[82]

---

80 Dhahabi, in *Mizan al-itidal* (2:230, 3:140).
81 Uqayli, *Kitab al-duafa* (4:284).
82 Dhahabi narrated it in *Manaqib Abi Hanifa* (p. 43).

Another proof against Uqayli's attribution is given by Ibn Main when he was asked, "Does Abu Hanifa lie?" He replied, "Woe to you! He is nobler than that."

Finally, it is established by Ibn Imad,[83] al-Dhahabi,[84] and al-Khatib,[85] that whenever Abu Hanifa was mentioned to Imam Ahmad he would speak kindly of him; and that when Ahmad, under the whip, was reminded that Abu Hanifa had suffered the same treatment for refusing a judgeship, he wept and said, "*Rahimahullah.*"[86]

4.2.6 THE "SALAFIS" CLAIM THAT ABU HANIFA'S GRADING AS WEAK FOR HIS POOR MEMORIZATION "WAS THE POSITION OF . . . IBN ABEE HAATIM (AL-JARH WAT TADIL)."

To this it is answered: Ibn Abi Hatims notice on Abu Hanifa is plagued with grave weaknesses in regard to reliability.[87] The reason is not that Ibn Abi Hatim is unreliable as an authenticator of narrations, but that he is intent on reporting what is damaging to Abu Hanifa at all costs, even if he must turn a blind eye to the inauthenticity of such reports. A flagrant sign of his bias is that he reports only a few derogatory stories and no positive reports about Abu Hanifa, against the rule of fairness imposed on all scholars of narrator-criticism and narrator-authentication. Those stories include:

Ibn al-Mubarak [d. 181], in his later period, quit narrating from Abu Hanifa. I heard my father [b. 195!] say that.[88]

If Ibn Abi Hatim were to see such a report, he would reject it and never adduce it as evidence for anything, because when Ibn al-Mubarak died, Ibn Abi Hatim's father was not even born. A report from Ibn Abi Hatim's father does not constitute reliable evidence about Ibn al-Mubarak, since the chain of transmission is cut off and misses one, two, or more narrators.

What puts a final seal on its inadmissibility is that the report contradicts the established position of the verifying

---

83 Ibn Imad, in his *Shadharat al-dhahab* (1:228).
84 Al-Dhahabi in *Tarikh al-islam* (6:141).
85 Al-Khatib, in *Tarikh Baghdad* (13:360).
86 See above, Ibn Hajar's notice on Abu Hanifa in *Tahdhib al-tahdhib*. The reader is also referred to Ibn Abd al-Barr's relevant section in his book *al-Intiqa*, where he systematically refutes al-Uqayli's narrations against Abu Hanifa.
87 Ibn Abi Hatim, in his book *al-Jarh wa al-tadil*.
88 *Ibid.*, (8:449).

scholars on Ibn al-Mubarak's transmission from Abu Hanifa, which is that he never stopped taking hadith from him whether in the early or later period.[89] This is confirmed by the following reports:

Ibn al-Mubarak praised Abu Hanifa and called him a sign of Allah.[90]

Ali ibn al-Madini said, "From Abu Hanifa narrated: al-Thawri, Ibn al-Mubarak, Hammad ibn Zayd, Hisham, Waki, Abbad ibn al-Awwam, and Jafar ibn Awn."[91]

Both Ibn al-Mubarak and Sufyan al-Thawri said, "Abu Hanifa was the most knowledgeable of all people on earth."[92]

Ibn Hajar also related that Ibn al-Mubarak said, "If Allah had not rescued me with Abu Hanifa and Sufyan [al-Thawri] I would have been like the rest of the common people."[93]

Abdan said that he heard Ibn al-Mubarak say, "If you hear them mention Abu Hanifa derogatively then they are mentioning me derogatively. In truth I fear for them Allah's displeasure."[94]

Hibban ibn Musa said: Ibn al-Mubarak was asked, "Who is more knowledgeable in *fiqh*, Malik or Abu Hanifa?" He replied, "Abu Hanifa."[95]

The last report echoes Imam Ahmad's statement that:

Nusayr ibn Yahya al-Balkhi said: I said to Ahmad ibn Hanbal, "Why do you reproach to this man [Abu Hanifa]?" He replied, *al-ray*="[Reliance on] opinion." I said, "Consider Malik, did he not speak on the basis of opinion?" He said, "Yes, but Abu Hanifa's opinion was immortalized in books." I said, "Malik's opinion was also immortalized in books." He said, "Abu Hanifa gave opinions more than him." I said, "Why then

---

89 This is stated by al-Mizzi in his notice on Abu Hanifa in *Tahdhib al-kamal* and al-Dhahabi in *Manaqib Abi Hanifa* (p. 20).

90 Al-Khatib reports it in *Tarikh Baghdad* (13:337) and al-Dhahabi in *Siyar alam al-nubala* (6:398).

91 Al-Haytami related it in *al-Khayrat al-hisan* (p. 74) and al-Qurashi in *al-Jawahir al-mudiyya* (1:29).

92 Ibn Hajar related it in his notice on Abu Hanifa in *Tahdhib al-tahdhib* and also Ibn Kathir in *al-Bidaya wa al-nihaya* (10:107).

93 Dhahabi in *Manaqib Abu Hanifa* (p. 30) relates it as: "I would have been an innovator."

94 Dhahabi related it in *Manaqib Abi Hanifa* (p. 36).

95 Dhahabi relates it in *Tarikh al-islam* (6:142) and *Manaqib Abi Hanifa* (p. 32).

will you not give this one his due and that one his due?!" He remained silent.[96]

Ibn Abi Hatim also claims:

> Ibrahim ibn Yaqub al-Jawzajani [d. 259] told me in writing, on the authority of Abd al-Rahman al-Muqri [d. 185] that the latter said: Abu Hanifa would talk to us, after which he would say, "All that you have heard is wind and null and void" (*hadha al-ladhi samitum kulluhu rih wa batil*).[97]

This is another report whose citation is against Ibn Abi Hatim, rather than to his credit, due to the uncertainty or absence of links in its chain of transmission.

As for the defect in the *matn*, or text, itself, it is so evident that it would be absurd to pretend that Ibn Abi Hatim missed it. Abu Hanifa was described as an Imam whose *fiqh* outweighed the intelligence of everyone on earth in his time by the following scholars: Abu Bakr ibn Ayyash, Ibn Jurayj, Yazid ibn Harun, Shaddad ibn Hakim, Sufyan ibn Uyayna, Makki ibn Ibrahim, Misar ibn Kidam, Ali ibn Asim, and Ahmad ibn Hanbal![98]

In fact, the reality of what Abu Hanifa said at the conclusion of his lessons is linked to his humility and great fear of Allah, as shown by the following reports:[99]

Muhammad ibn Shuja al-Thalji said: I heard Ismail ibn Hammad ibn Abi Hanifa say: Abu Hanifa said, "Our position here is only our opinion. We do not oblige anyone to follow it, nor do we say that it is required for anyone to accept it. Whoever has something better, let him produce it."

Al-Hasan ibn Ziyad al-Lului said: Abu Hanifa said, "Our science in this is only an opinion. It is the best that we have been able to reach. Whoever brings us better than this, we accept it from him."

The Imams clarifications of his method are a far cry from the words " All that you have heard is wind and null and void," which Ibn Abi Hatim wrongly attributes to him.

Ibn Abi Hatim claims on the written authority of the same

---

96 Related by Dhahabi in *Manaqib Abi Hanifa* (p. 41).
97 Ibn Abi Hatim, in *al-Jarh wa al-tadil* (8:450).
98 *Ibid.* p. 34.
99 Ibn Abi Hatim, in *al-Jarh wa al-tadil* (8:450).

Ibrahim ibn Yaqub al-Jawzajani that Ishaq ibn Rahawayh said: I heard Jarir say: Muhammad ibn Jabir al-Yamami said, "Abu Hanifa stole Hammad's books from me"![100]

Such an untruthful report is easily thrown out on the bases of its chain and text: Its chain is weak due to the inclusion of Muhammad ibn Jarir al-Yamani, whom Ibn Abi Hatim himself declared weak with the words *daif kathir al-wahm*, "He is weak and many times imagines things."[101] Others who declared this narrator weak are: Ibn Main,[102] al-Nasai,[103] Uqayli,[104] Ibn Hibban,[105] Ibn Adi,[106] al-Dhahabi,[107] among others.

The text of this report is absurd due to the fact that Abu Hanifa could easily have gotten Hammad ibn Abi Sulayman's books directly from him, since he was his student for more than twenty years. Furthermore, Abu Hanifa was extremely rich, and in no need of stealing what he could obtain through purchase. Finally, Abu Hanifa was reputed for his extreme fear of Allah (*wara*), which precludes him, in accordance with all those who testified to his character, from having committed such an act. Dhahabi related:[108]

> Ibn al-Mubarak said, "Abu Hanifa for a long time would pray all five prayers with a single *wudu*," and Hamid ibn Adam al-Marwazi said: I heard Ibn al-Mubarak say, "I never saw anyone more fearful of Allah than Abu Hanifa, even on trial under the whip and through money and property."

4.2.7. THE "SALAFIS" CLAIM THAT ABU HANIFA'S GRADING AS WEAK FOR HIS POOR MEMORIZATION "WAS THE POSITION OF . . . AL-HAAKIM (*MARIFA ULUM AL-HADEETH*)."

To this it is answered: It seems this is but another example

---

100 Ibid. (1:219).
101 Ibn Main, in his *Tarikh* (3:507).
103 Al-Nasai, in *al-Duafa wa al-matrukin* (p. 533).
104 Uqayli, in *al-Duafa* (4:41).
105 Ibn Hibban, in *al-Majruhin* (2:270).
106 Ibn Adi, in *al-Kamil fi al-duafa* (6:2158).
107 Al-Dhahabi, in *al-Mughni fi al-duafa* (#5349).
108 Al-Dhahabi, in *Manaqib Abi Hanifa* (p. 24).

of "Salafi" "fibbing," since al-Hakim mentions the Imam only among the "reputable trustworthy Imams."[109]

The forty-ninth kind [of the sciences of hadith]: Knowledge of the famous trustworthy Imams (*marifat al-aimma al-thiqat al-mashhurin*):

Among the people of Kufa: . . . Misar ibn Kidam al-Hilali, Abu Hanifa al-Numan ibn Thabit al-Taymi, Malik ibn Mighwal al-Bajali . . .[110]

4.2.8. THE "SALAFIS" CLAIM THAT ABU HANIFA'S GRADING AS WEAK FOR HIS POOR MEMORIZATION "WAS THE POSITION OF . . . IBN SAD (*TABAQAAT* 6/256)."

To this it is answered: Ibn Sad's denouncement of a narrator is questionable when it pertains to the scholars of Iraq, including Abu Hanifa. According to Ibn Hajar's words:[111]

Ibn Sad's *tadif* is questionable (*fihi nazar*), because he imitates al-Waqidi and relies on him, and al-Waqidi, according to the fashion of the scholars of Madina, is extremely adverse to the scholars of Iraq. Know this and you will be directed to what is right, with Allah's will.

4.2.9. THE "SALAFIS" CLAIM THAT ABU HANIFA'S GRADING AS WEAK FOR HIS POOR MEMORIZATION "WAS THE POSITION OF . . . AL-DHAHABEE (*AL-DUAFAA* Q. 215/1-2)."

To this it is answered: Dhahabi's authentic position on the reliability of Abu Hanifa is established in his notices on Abu Hanifa in *Tadhkirat al-huffaz* and *al-Kashif fi marifat man lahu riwaya fi al-kutub al-sitta*, in the monograph he wrote on him entitled *Manaqib Abi Hanifa*, and in his mention of him in his introduction to *Mizan al-itidal*. In none of the above texts does he mention any weakening of Abu Hanifa. Therefore, whatever contradicts these texts must be questioned and, if established as authentic, retained; if not, rejected as spurious and inauthentic.

Let us examine the text of a notice purportedly found in

---

109 Al-Hakim, in *Marifat ulum al-hadith*.
110 Excerpt taken from Said Muhammad al-Lahham's edition (Beirut: Dar al-hilal, 1409/1989).
111 Ibn Hajar, in his notice for Muharib ibn Dithar in *Hadi al-Sari* (2:164).

Dhahabi's *Diwan al-duafa wa al-matrukin*, according to Shaykh Khalil al-Mayss edition:[112]

Al-Numan: al-Imam, *rahimahullah*. Ibn Adi said, "Most of what he narrates is error (*ghalat*), corruption in the text (*tashif*), and additions (*ziyadat*), but he has good narrations." al-Nasai said, "He is not strong in hadith, he makes many errors although he has only a few narrations." Ibn Main said, "His narrations are not written."

This is a false attribution to Dhahabi and a clear case of interpolation into the text of his book. Dhahabi said, "Our shaykh Abu al-Hajjaj [al-Mizzi] did well when he did not cite anything whereby he [Abu Hanifa] should be deemed weak as a narrator."[113] He also said, "I do not mention [in my classifications of the weak narrators] any of the Companions, the Tabiin, or the Imams who are followed."[114] It is established that Abu Hanifa is a *tabii*, and foremost among the Imams who are followed. Moreover, in a book entirely devoted to Abu Hanifa, entitled *Manaqib al-imam Abu Hanifa*, Dhahabi mentions no such weakening, nor does he even allude to it. He does not even cite it in the chapter devoted to Abu Hanifa in *Tadhkirat al-huffaz*.

It is not consistent that he cite, in *al-Duafa*, Ibn Adi's and al-Nasai's biased opinions, which flatly contradict his other works and his method, without any explanation on his part. It is unthinkable that he relate, in the *Duafa*, that Ibn Main said, "His narrations are not written," while he relates in *Manaqib Abi Hanifa* and *Tadhkirat al-huffaz*, "Ibn Main said Abu Hanifa is trustworthy (*thiqa*)," and, Ibn Main said of Abu Hanifa: "*La basa bihi* (there is no harm in him)."[115]Note that in Ibn Main's terminology, *la basa bihi* is the same as *thiqa* (i.e. he is reliable).[116]

The reason for the discrepancy is clearly that the passage in Dhahabi's *Duafa* is a later addition by those who wanted to stamp Imam Abu Hanifa's weakening with Dhahabi's credibility, even at the cost of forgery.

---

112 Al-Dhahabi, *Diwan al-Duafa wa al-matrukin.* Ed. Shaykh Khalil al-Mays. (Beirut: Dar al-fikr, 1408/1988 2:404 #4389).

113 Dhahabi, in *Tadhhib al-tahdhib* (4:101).

114 Dhahabi, in the introduction of *Mizan al-itidal*, on which his *Duafa* is based.

115 Al-Dhahabi, *Manaqib Abi Hanifa* p. 45, and *Tadhkirat al-huffaz* 1:168.

116 As stated by Ibn Salah in his *Muqaddima* (p. 134) and Dhahabi himself in *Lisan al-mizan* (1:13).

A remarkable proof of this forgery is the near-identical notice on Abu Hanifa in Dhahabi's *Mizan al-itidal*, under the name of al-Numan ibn Thabit, Abu Hanifa. Dhahabi purportedly said, "Al-Nasai declared him weak from the perspective of his memorization, also Ibn Adi, and others."[117] This is an addition that was not made by the author, and which is found in the less reliable copies (*nusakh*) of the *Mizan* and not in the authentic manuscripts. There is a hint of this in the footnote by the editor, al-Bajawi, who says, "This notice [on Abu Hanifa] is missing from two of the manuscripts."

The proof that it is an interpolation is both internal and external, as is clear from Shaykh Abd al-Fattah Abu Ghudda's masterful demonstration:[118]

> Abd al-Fattah says: al-Lucknawi gave ample proofs for the tampering of the notice on Abu Hanifa in some of the manuscripts of the *Mizan* in his book *Ghayth al-ghamam ala hawashi imam al-kalam* (p. 146), where he mentions many factors for concluding that it does not authentically belong to the *Mizan*. I will mention only some of them and direct the reader to his book for the rest. He said, "There is no trace of this mention in some of the reliable manuscripts which I have seen, and the following confirms it:
>
> Al-Iraqi said in his *Sharh al-alfiyya* (3:260), "Ibn Adi mentioned in his book *al-Kamil* every narrator who was ever criticized even if he is considered trustworthy, and Dhahabi followed him in this in *al-Mizan*, except that he did not mention any of the Companions or the Imams that are followed."
>
> Al-Sakhawi said in his *Sharh al-alfiyya* (p. 477), "Although Dhahabi followed Ibn Adi in mentioning every narrator who was ever criticized even if he is considered trustworthy, yet he bound himself not to mention any of the Companions or the Imams that are followed."
>
> Al-Suyuti said in *Tadrib al-rawi sharh taqrib al-Nawawi* (p. 519), "Except that Dhahabi did not mention any of the Companions or the Imams that are followed."

---

117 Dhahabi, *Mizan al-itidal*. ed. Ali Muhammad al-Bajawi, Cairo: al-Halabi, 4:265 #9092.
118 Abu Ghudda, in his edition of al-Lucknawi's *al-Raf wa al-takmil* (p. 121-126).

Abd al-Fattah says: Dhahabi himself explicitly declares in the introduction of *al-Mizan* (1:3):

Similarly I did not mention in my book any of the Imams that are followed in the branches of the Law due to their immense standing in Islam and their greatness in the minds of people: such as Abu Hanifa, Shafii, and Bukhari. If I mention any of them, I do not do so except to render him his due (*ala al-insaf* i.e. to be very fair). This does not attack their standing before Allah and before men.

However, the edition of the *Mizan* published at Matbaat al-saada in Cairo in 1325 (3:237) contains a two-line notice on Abu Hanifa ["al-Nasai declared him weak from the perspective of his memorization, also Ibn Adi, and others"] that contains no defense of Abu Hanifa at all, and consists only in criticizing him and declaring him weak: and Dhahabi's words in the introduction preclude the existence of such a notice, since it is all faultfinding and renders him no justice
. . .

I looked up the third volume of *Mizan al-itidal* kept in the Zahiriyya library in Damascus under the number "368 New," a very valuable set indeed, which begins with the letter m and ends with the end of the book, all written in the hand of the savant and hadith master Sharaf al-Din Abd Allah ibn Muhammad al-Wani (d. 749) of Damascus, Dhahabi's student, who read this back to Dhahabi three times while comparing it to his original, as declared on the back of folios 109 and 159 of the volume, and elsewhere. I saw no mention of Imam Abu Hanifa in that volume under the letter n [for Numan] nor under the paternal names.

Similarly I saw no notice for Abu Hanifa in the manuscript kept at the Ahmadiyya library in Aleppo under the number 337, a good copy made in 1160 from an original made in 777 . . .

Nor in the manuscript of Dhahabi's own copy of *Mizan al-itidal* kept in the general storing-library in Rabat, Morocco under number 129Q which is signed by the hand of eight different students of his to the effect that they read it in his presence and were certified by him to have done so . . .

This is a tremendous and rare specimen in the world of manuscripts, and I did not find in it a mention of Abu Hanifa. Something such as this is a decisive proof for anyone that the notice found in some copies of the *Mizan* is not from the pen of al-Dhahabi, but was interpolated into the book by some of the adversaries of the Imam Abu Hanifa . . .

Dhahabi's *Mizan* has been tampered with by foreign hands in more than one place, and it is imperative that it be edited and published on the basis of a manuscript that has been read before the author himself, such as that in the Zahiriyya library of Damascus, or that in the library of Rabat . . .

Our friend the savant Shaykh Muhammad Abd al-Rashid al-Numani al-Hindi in his book *Ma tamassu ilayhi al-haja li man yutali sunan Ibn Majah* (p. 47) also showed another aspect of the tampering done with Abu Hanifa's notice in the *Mizan* and I refer the reader to it. The same proof was mentioned before him by Lucknawi's student, the brilliant verifying scholar Zahir Ahmad al-Nimawi in his book *al-Taliq al-hasan ala athar al-sunan* (1:88).

I also took notice of what was said by our shaykh the great savant Mawlana Zafar Ahmad al-Uthmani al-Tahanawi in his book *Qawaid fi ulum al-hadith* (p. 211) in commenting on Dhahabi's words–already quoted–from the introduction of his *Mizan*, whereupon Tahanawi said, "By this it is known that what is found in some copies of the *Mizan* concerning Abu Hanifa and his weakening due to poor memorization is an *ilhaq*–something added which was not there originally . . . And how could it be there when Dhahabi included Abu Hanifa in *Tadhkirat al-huffaz*, which he introduced with the words: "This is the memorial of the names of those who were declared the trustees among the carriers of the Science of the Prophet (ﷺ) and to whose *ijtihad* one refers concerning matters of narrator-certification (*tawthiq*), authentication (*tashih*), and falsification (*tazyif*)." End of our shaykhs words.

I also saw that the Emir al-Sanani said in *Tawdih*

al-afkar (2:277): "There is no notice for Abu Hanifa in *al-Mizan*.". . .

Nor is there any notice for Abu Hanifa in the manuscript of the *Mizan* that was copied by the meticulous hadith master and muhaddith of Aleppo in his time, Ibrahim ibn Muhammad Sibt Ibn al-Ajami who finished copying it in the year 789 from a copy that was certified in Dhahabi's handwriting.

It is therefore decisively ascertained that the notice on Abu Hanifa in the *Mizan* is an interpolation in some of its manuscripts in which Dhahabi had no part.

4.12. CONCLUSION

Imam Abu Hanifa's great merits are extremely numerous. Imam Dhahabi wrote one volume on the life of each of the other three great Imams, but he said, "The account of Abu Hanifa's *sira* requires two volumes."[119] Abu Hanifa's greatness was never attained by those who followed him, as predicted by his son Hammad when, over his father's body, he said, "You have exhausted whoever comes after you (who tries to catch up with you)."

He is the first to have recorded the topics of *fiqh* in a book, beginning with *tahara* and salat. Everyone who followed after him using that model, such as Malik, Shafii, Abu Dawud, Bukhari, Muslim, Tirmidhi, and others, are indebted to him. They give him a share of their reward because he was the first to open that road for them, according to the hadith of the Prophet (ﷺ) *man sanna fi al-islami sunnatan hasanatan*, "Whoever starts something good in Islam . . ." Al-Shafii referred to this when he said, *al-nasu iyalun ala abi hanifa fi al-fiqh* (people (scholars) are all the dependents of Abu Hanifa in *fiqh*)."[120] The *hafiz* al-Khatib al-Baghdadi narrated that the hafiz Abu Nuaym said:[121]

Muslims should make *dua* to Allah on behalf of Abu Hanifa in their prayers, because the *sunan* and the *fiqh* were preserved for them through him.

Like Imam Bukhari, Abu Hanifa used to make 60 *khatmas* (complete reading or recitation) of the Quran every Ramadan:

---

119 Dhahabi, in his *Siyar alam al-nubala* (6:403).
120 Al-Dhahabi relates it in *Tadhkirat al-huffaz* in the chapter on Abu Hanifa, and also Ibn Hajar in *Tahdhib al-tahdhib* (10:450).
121 Al-Khatib al-Baghdadi, in *Tarikh Baghdad* (13:344).

once in the day, once in the night, besides his teaching and other duties.[122] Al-Khatib,[123] Dhahabi,[124] and Suyuti[125] relate that Ibrahim ibn Rustum al-Marwazi said, "Four are the Imams that recited the entire Quran in a single *rakat*: Uthman ibn Affan, Tamim al-Dari, Said ibn Jubayr, and Abu Hanifa." Suyuti also relates that a certain visitor came to observe Abu Hanifa and saw him all day long in the mosque, teaching relentlessly, answering every question from both the scholars and the common people, not stopping except to pray, then standing at home in prayer when people were asleep, hardly ever eating or sleeping.[126] Yet he was the most handsome and gracious of people, always alert and never tired, day after day for a long time, so that in the end the visitor said, "I became convinced that this was not an ordinary matter, but wilaya (Friendship with Allah)."

It is proven without doubt that Abu Hanifa has been given the three highest gradings by the verifying authorities in hadith as he has been called *imam* by Abu Dawud, *hafiz* by al-Dhahabi, and *thiqa thiqa* by Ibn Main. More importantly, the claim that he was declared weak has itself been shown to be a weak claim no sooner made than proven wrong or worthless. Claims against him by present-day innovators were anticipated and rejected in advance by the hadith master Ibn Hajar al-Asqalani who said:[127]

> The Imam and his peers are of those who have reached the sky, and as a result nothing that anyone says against any of them can have any effect. They are in the highest level, where Allah raised them, through their being Imams that are followed and through whom one reaches guidance. Let this be clearly understood, and Allah is the Giver of success.[128]

---

122 Al-Subki relates it of Bukhari in *Tabaqat al-shafiiyya*, while Dhahabi and al-Haytami relate it of Abu Hanifa respectively in *Manaqib Abi Hanifa* (p. 23) and *al-Khayrat al-hisan*.

123 Al-Khatib, in *Tarikh Baghdad* (13:356).

124 Dhahabi, in the *Manaqib* (p. 22).

125 Suyuti, in *Tabyid al-sahifa* (p. 94-95).

126 Suyuti, in *Tabyid al-sahifa*.

127 As related by his student the hadith master al-Sakhawi in his biography *al-Jawahir wa al-durar* (p. 227).

128 Shaykh Muhammad Awwama mentioned it in his book *Athar al-hadith al-sharif* (p. 116).

With this is ended the last volume in this presentation of Encyclopedia of Islamic Doctrine. May Allah place us also in the company of His Friends here and hereafter, and accept from Muhammad Hisham Kabbani, his servant in need, the effort of this work to address certain urgent questions despite its mistakes and shortcomings. May He forgive us and all those who preceded us in faith, and guide all those who ask for the true knowledge of mainstream Islam, and protect them against the confusions of the seventy-two stray paths and their invitations to perdition. Success is from Allah. O Allah! Send abundant blessings and peace on Your Prophet (ﷺ), his Family and his Companions. The last of our speech is, Praise belongs to Allah, Lord of the Worlds.

APPENDIX 1: *FATWA* OF THE MINISTRY OF AWQAF OF THE EGYPTIAN REPUBLIC ACCORDING TO SHAYKH SALAH AL-DIN MAHMOUD NASSAR ON MEN SHAKING HANDS WITH WOMEN

Al-hamdulillah, wa salaat wa salaam ala Rasulillah.

First of all, on the subject of men and women shaking hands, it can not be definitely determined if it is permitted (*halal*) or forbidden (*haram*). Asking for Allah's support, we say: Some scholars think that non-*mahram* men and women shaking hands is absolutely forbidden. They cite the hadith of Aisha as narrated by Bukhari when she said: "No, by Allah, the Prophet's hands never touched a woman's hand when she was giving allegiance to him (*baya*). He never said more than: "I accept your allegiance (*baya*), on that (matter)."

However, this hadith is not considered adequate evidence that handshaking is forbidden because the Prophet's refraining from doing something does not prove that it is forbidden. He might refrain from doing something because it is forbidden (*haram*), or because it is disagreeable (*makruh*), or because it contradicts what is best. Moreover, his refraining from shaking hands with women is not agreed upon by all scholars. There is a narration by Umm Attiya al-Ansariya, may Allah be pleased with her, that indicates that a handshake did take place during the women's pledge of allegiance to the Prophet (ﷺ). She said: "And he stretched his hand forward from outside the house, while we stretched our hands from inside the house. Then he said: 'O Allah, bear witness.'"

This hadith is also narrated by Bukhari. Al-Hafiz said: "There is a possibility that the pledge of allegiance to the Prophet (ﷺ) took place more than once and that is why Bukhari mentioned the hadith of Aisha under the title: "When there come to you believing women refugees," while the hadith of Umm Attiya comes under: "When believing women come to thee to take the oath."

Therefore, those who say that handshaking is absolutely forbidden (*haram*) have no proof, because when there is a doubt in the evidence, it is rejected.

After this brief presentation, here is a summary of what we are inclined to believe: Handshaking is permissible in the absence of (sexual) desire, and bad intentions, but if there is concern about such a desire, or temptations on either side, then it is forbidden (*haram*). However, in order not to create any misunderstanding, not to raise suspicions, and to be on the safe side one should not overdo it. What is best for a Muslim, man or woman, is not to initiate. In other words, only if a hand has been offered to him or her, then he or she may shake hands. Allah knows best.

GLOSSARY

ahkam: legal rulings.

ahl al-bida wa al-ahwa: the People of Unwarranted Innovations and Idle Desires.

ahl al-sunna wa al-jamaa: the Sunnis; the People of the Way of the Prophet and the Congregation of Muslims.[1]

aqida pl. *aqa'id*: doctrine.

azaim: strict applications of the law. These are the modes of conduct signifying scrupulous determination to please one's Lord according to the model of the Prophet (ﷺ).

bida: blameworthy innovation.

faqih, pl. *fuqaha*: scholar of *fiqh* or jurisprudence; generally, "person of knowledge."

faqir, pl. *fuqara'* Sufi, lit. "poor one."

fatwa, pl. *fatawa*: legal opinion.

fiqh: jurisprudence.

fitna: dissension, confusion.

hadith: saying(s) of the Prophet, and the sciences thereof.

hafiz: hadith master, the highest rank of scholarship in hadith.

haqiqi: literal.

hashwiyya: uneducated anthropomorphists.

hijri: adjective from *hijra* applying to dates in the Muslim calendar.

hukm, pl. *ahkam*: legal ruling.

ibadat: worship, acts of worship.

ihsan: perfection of belief and practice.

ijtihad: personal effort of qualified legal reasoning.

isnad: chain of transmission in a hadith or report.

istinbat: derivation (of legal rulings).

jahmi: a follower of Jahm ibn Safwan (d. 128), who said: "Allah is the wind and everything else."[2]

jihad: struggle against disbelief by hand, tongue, and heart.

kalam: theology.

khalaf: "Followers," general name for all Muslims who lived after the first three centuries.

khawarij: "Outsiders," a sect who considered all Muslims who did not follow them, disbelievers. The Prophet said about them as related by Bukhari: "They will transfer the Quranic verses meant to refer to disbelievers and make them refer to believers." Ibn Abidin applied the name of khawarij to the Wahhabi movement.[3]

madhhab, pl. *madhahib*: a legal method or school of law in Islam. The major schools of law include the Hanafi, Maliki, Shafii, and Hanbali and Jafari.

majazi: figurative.

manhaj, minhaj: Way, or doctrinal and juridical method.

muamalat (pl.): plural name embracing all affairs between human beings as opposed to acts of worship *(ibadat)*.

muattila: those who commit *tatil*, i.e. divesting Allah of His attributes.

muhaddith: hadith scholar.

muhkamat: texts conveying firm and unequivocal meaning.

1 See the section entitled "Apostasies and Heresies" in our *Doctrine of Ahl al-Sunna Versus the "Salafi" Movement* p. 60-64.

2 See Bukhari, *Khalq afal al-ibad*, first chapter; Ibn Hajar, *Fath al-bari, Tawhid*, first chapter; and al-Baghdadi, *al-Farq bayn al-firaq*, chapter on the Jahmiyya.

3 al-Sayyid Muhammad Amin Ibn Abidin al-Hanafi, *Radd al-muhtar ala al-durr al-mukhtar, Kitab al-iman, Bab al-bughat* [Answer to the Perplexed: A Commentary on "The Chosen Pearl," Book of Belief, Chapter on Rebels] (Cairo: Dar al-Tibaa al-Misriyya, 1272/1856) 3:309.

mujahid, pl. *mujahidin*: one who wages *jihad*.

mujassima (pl.): those who commit *tajsim*, attributing a body to Allah.

mujtahid: one who practices *ijtihad* or personal effort of qualified legal reasoning.

munafiq: a dissimulator of his disbelief.

mushabbiha (pl.): those who commit *tashbih*, likening Allah to creation.

mushrik, pl. *mushrikun*: one who associate partners to Allah.

mutakallim, pl. *mutakallimun*: expert in *kalam*.

mutashabihat (pl.): texts which admit of some uncertainty with regard to their interpretation.

mutazila: rationalist heresy of the third century.

sahih: sound (applied to the chain of transmission of a hadith).

salaf: the Predecessors, i.e. Muslims of the first three centuries.

salafi: what pertains to the "Salafi" movement, a modern heresy that rejects the principles of mainstream Islam

shafaa: intercession.

sharia: name embracing the principles and application of Islamic law.

suluk: rule of conduct, personal ethics.

tawil: figurative interpretation.

tafwid: committing the meaning to Allah.

tajsim: attributing a body to Allah

tajwid: Quran reading.

takyif: attributing modality to Allah's attributes.

tamthil: giving an example for Allah.

taqlid: following qualified legal reasoning.

tariqa: path, specifically the Sufi path.

tasawwuf: collective name for the schools and sciences of purification of the self.

tashbih: likening Allah to His Creation.

tatil: divesting Allah from His attributes.

tawassul: seeking a means.

tawhid: Islamic doctrine of monotheism.

tazkiyat al-nafs: purification of the self.

usul: principles.

wasila: means.

BIBLIOGRAPHY

Abidin, Ibn, *Hashiyat radd al-muhtar.*

Abidin, Ibn, *Radd al-muhtar ala al-durr al-mukhtar*, 5 vols. (Bulaq 1272/1855). Reprint. Beirut: Dar Ihya' al-Turath al-'Arabi, 1407/1987.

Adani, Ibn Abi Umar al-, *Musnad.*

Adi, Ibn, *al-Kamil fi al-duafa.*

Ahdal, Shaykh Muhammad al-, *Sunniyyat raf al-yadayn fi al-dua bad al-salawat al-maktuba.* Ed. Shaykh Abd al-Fattah Abu Ghudda.

Ahmad, *Kitab al-wara.*

Ahmad, *Musnad.*

Ahmad, *Rawdat al-nazir.*

Ajluni, *Kashf al-khafa.*

Ajurri, *Akhlaq ahl al-quran.* 2nd ed. Ed. Muh. Amr ibn Abd al-Latif (Beirut: dar al-kutub al-ilmiyya, 1407/1987).

Albani, *Daif al-adab al-mufrad.*

Albani, *Sahih al-adab al-mufrad.*

Albani, *Sahih al-Jami al-saghir.*

Albani, *Sahih al-targhib.*

Albani, *Silsila daifa.*

Albani, *Silsila sahiha.*

Allah, Shah Wali, *al-Qawl al-jamil.*

Alwani, Ta Ha Jabir al-, *The Ethics of Disagreement in Islam.*

Amidi, *al-Ihkam fi usul al-ahkam.* 2nd ed. (Beirut, 1401/1982).

Arabi, Ibn al-, *Tuhfat al-ahwadhi.*

Asakir, Ibn, *Tarikh.*

Asfahani, al-Raghib al-, *Mufradat alfaz al-quran.*

Asqalani, Ibn Hajar al-, *Fath al-bari bi sharh Sahih al-Bukhari*, 14 vols. (Cairo: al-Maktaba al-Salafiyya, 1390/1970).

Asqalani, Ibn Hajar, *Tahdhib al-tahdhib* (1993 ed.).

Ata, *Musannaf Ibn Abd al-Razzaq.*

Athir, Ibn al-, *al-Nihaya fi gharib al-hadith wa atharih.*

Athir, Ibn al-, *Jami al-usul fi ahadith al-rasul.*

Awwama, Shaykh Muhammad, *Athar al-hadith al-sharif.*

Ayni, Al-Badr al-, *al-Binaya sharh al-hidaya.*

Azimabadi, Shams al-Haqq, *Awn al-mabud bi sharh sunan abi dawud.*

Baghawi, *Musannaf Abd al-Razzaq.*

Baghawi, *Sharh al-sunna*, 16 vols. (Damascus: al-Maktab al-Islami,

1400/1980).
Baghdadi, *al-Farq bayn al-firaq*.
Baghdadi, *Taqyid al-ilm*.
Barr, Ibn Abd al-, *al-Intiqa*.
Barr, Ibn Abd al-, *al-Istidhkar*.
Barr, Ibn Abd al-, *Jami bayan al-ilm*, (Cairo: dar al-tibaa al-muniriyya).
Bayhaqi, *al-Madkhal*.
Bayhaqi, *Dalail al-nubuwwa*.
Bayhaqi, *Kitab al-adab*.
Bayhaqi, *Shuab al-iman*.
Bazzar, *Musnad*.
Bukhari, *Adab al-mufrad*.
Bukhari, *Khalq afal al-ibad*.
Bukhari, *Sahih al-Bukhari*, 3 vols. Reprint (Beirut: Dar al-Jil, n.d.).
Bukhari, *Sahih al-Bukhari*, 9 vols. (Cairo 1313/1895).
Bukhari, *Tarikh al-saghir*.
Daraqutni, *Sunan*.
Darimi, *Sunan*.
Dawud, Abu, *Manasik*.
Dhahabi, *al-Kabair*.
Dhahabi, *al-Kashshasf fi marifati man lahu riwayatun fi al-kutub al-sitta*.
Dhahabi, *al-Mughni fi al-duafa*.
Dhahabi, *Diwan al-Duafa wa al-matrukin*. Ed. Shaykh Khalil al-Mays. (Beirut: Dar al-fikr, 1408/1988).
Dhahabi, *Lisan al-mizan*.
Dhahabi, *Manaqib Abi Hanifa*.
Dhahabi, *Mizan al-itidal*. ed. Ali Muhammad al-Bajawi (Cairo: al-Halabi).
Dhahabi, *Mujam al-shuyukh al-kabir*.
Dhahabi, *Siyar alam al-nubala*.
Dhahabi, *Tadhhib al-tahdhib* 1st ed. (Hyderabad: Da'irat al-maarif al-nizamiyya, 1327).
Dhahabi, *Tadhkirat al-huffaz*.
Dhahabi, *Tarikh al-Islam*.
Fayruzabadi, *Qamus*.
Ghazali, *Ihya ulum ad-din (Kitab al-adab)*.
Ghudda, Abd al-Fattah Abu, *Radd ala abatil wa iftiraat Nasir al-Albani wa sahibihi sabiqan Zuhayr al-Shawish wa muazirihima*.
Ghudda, Abu, *al-Raf*.
Guillaume, A. trans. *The Life of Muhammad: A Translation of*

Ishaq's Sirat Rasul Allah.

Hajar, Ibn *Fath al-bari* (1989 ed.).

Hajar, Ibn, *al-Isaba.*

Hajar, Ibn, *al-Qawl al-musaddad fi al-dhabb an musnad Ahmad.*

Hajar, Ibn, *Bulugh al-maram.*

Hajar, Ibn, *Fath al-bari bi sharh sahih al-Bukhari* (1989 ed.).

Hajar, Ibn, *Hadi al-Sari.*

Hajar, Ibn, *Nukat.*

Hajar, Ibn, *Tahdhib al-tahdhib.*

Hakim, *al-Tarikh.*

Hakim, *Marifat ulum al-hadith.*

Hakim, *Mustadrak.*

Hanafi, al-Sayyid Muhammad Amin Ibn Abidin al-, *Radd al-muhtar ala al-durr al-mukhtar, Kitab al-Iman, Bab al-bughat* (Cairo: Dar al-Tibaa al-Misriyya, 1272/1856).

Hanafi, Al-Zaylai al-, *Tabyin al-haqaiq: sharh Kanz al-daqaiq.*

Hanafi, Ibn Abidin al-, *Hashiyat radd al-muhtar ala al-durr al-mukhtar.*

Hanbali, *al-Mughni* (1994 ed.).

Hanbali, Ibn Qudama al-, *al-Aqaid.*

Hanifa, Abu, *al-Fiqh al-akbar.*

Harithi, Muhammad Qasim Abduh al-, *Makanat al-Imam Abi Hanifa bayn al-muhaddithin.*

Harun, Yazid ibn, *Khalq afal al-ibad* (1990 ed.).

Hasan, Ahmad, *The Doctrine of Ijma in Islam* (Islamabad: Islamic Research Institute, 1976).

Haskafi, *al-Durr al-mukhtar.*

Hatim, Ibn Abi, *al-Jarh wa al-tadil.*

Haytami, Ibn Hajar al-, *al-Khayrat al-hisan fi manaqib Abi Hanifa al-Numan.*

Haytami, *Majma al-zawaid.*

Hazm, Ibn, *al-Ihkam fi usul al-ahkam.*

Hazm, Ibn, *al-Muhalla.*

Hibban, Ibn, *al-Majruhim min al-muhaddithin wa al-duafa wa al-matrukin*, ed. Mahmud Ibrahim Zayid.

Hibban, Ibn, *Kitab al-majruhin.*

Humam, Ibn al-, *Fath al-qadir.*

Imad, Ibn, *Shadharat al-dhahab.*

Irabi, Ibn al-, *al-Qubal.*

Iraqi, *Mughni an haml al-asfar.*

Islahi, Muhammad Yusuf, *Everyday Fiqh.* Vol. I Trans. Abdul Aziz Kamal (Islamic Publications (Pvt.) Limited: Lahore, Pakistan, c.

1975 - 1993).

Iyad, Qadi, *al-Shifa*.

Jarrahi, *Kashf al-khafa*.

Jassas, *Ahkam al-quran*.

Jawzi, Ibn al-, *al-Mawduat*.

Jawzi, Ibn al-, *Manaqib ashab al-hadith*.

Jaziri, Abd al-Rahman al-, *al-Fiqh ala al-madhahib al-arbaa*.

Jaziri, *al-Fiqh ala al-madhahib al-arbaa*.

Jibali, Muhammad al-, ed. *The Night Prayer / Qiyam and Tarawih*.

Kabbani, Shaykh M. Hisham, trans. *The Doctrine of Ahl al-Sunna Versus the "Salafi" Movement* (As-Sunna Foundation of America, 1996).

Kamali, Mohammad Hashim, *Principles of Islamic Jurisprudence*.

Kasani, *Badai al-sanai*.

Kathir, Ibn, *al-Bidaya wa al-nihaya*.

Kattani, Muhammad ibn afar al-, *al-Risala al-mustatrafa*.

Kawthari, *al-Imta bi sirat al-imamayn al-Hasan ibn Ziyad wa sahibihi Muhammad ibn Shuja*.

Kawthari, *Fiqh ahl al-Iraq*.

Kawthari, *Nasb al-raya*.

Kawthari, *Tanib al-khatib ala ma saqahu fi tarjimat abi hanifa min al-akadhib*.

Khatib, *al-Faqih wa al-mutafaqqih*.

Khatib, *al-Kifaya*.

Khatib, *Tarikh Baghdad*.

Khattabi, *Gharib al-hadith*.

Khazraji, *Khulasat tadhhib tahdhib al-kamal*.

Lucknawi, Abd al-Hayy al-, *Umdat al-riaya fi hall sharh al-wiqaya*.

Lucknawi, *al-Ajwiba al-fadila ala al-asila al-ashra al-kamila*.

Lucknawi, *al-Raf wa al-takmil*.

Main, Ibn, *Tarikh*.

Malik, *Muwatta*.

Maliki, Ibn al-Arabi al-, *Aridat al-ahwadhi*.

Manzhur, Ibn, *Lisan al-Arab*.

Maqdisi, *al-Udda sharh al-umda*.

Marghinani, *al-Hidaya*.

Mawdudi, *Rasail-o-masail*.

Misri, *Umdat al-salik*.

Mizzi, *Tahdhib al-kamal*.

Muflih, Ibn, *al-Adab al-shariyya*.

Muhammad, Sayf al-Din Ahmad ibn, *al-Albani Unveiled*.

Mulaqqin, Ibn al-, *Tuhfat al-muhtaj ila adillat al-Minhaj*.

Munawi, *Sharh al-Jami al-saghir*.

Mundhir, Ibn al-, *al-Awsat*.

Mundhir, Ibn al-, *Kitab al-ijma* (Dar al-dawa in Doha: Qatar, 1401 H).

Mundhiri, *al-Targhib wa al-tarhib*.

Mundhiri, *Mukhtasar al-sunan*.

Muqri', Ibn al-, *al-Rukhsa fi taqbil al-yad* (Riyad ed. 1987).

Muslim, *al-Kuna wa al-asma*.

Muslim, *Kitab al-fadail*.

Muslim, *Sahih Muslim*, 5 vols. Cairo 1376/1956. Reprint. Beirut: Dar al-Fikr, 1403/1983, 1.222: 259.

Nas, Ibn Sayyid al-, *Sharh al-Tirmidhi*.

Nasai, *al-Duafa wa al-matrukin*.

Nasai, *Sunan*.

Nawawi, *al-Majmu*.

Nawawi, *al-Rukhsa bi al-qiyam*.

Nawawi, *al-Tarkhis fi al-ikram bi al-qiyam li dhawi al-fadl wa al-maziyya min ahl al-islam ala jihat al-birr wa al-tawqir wa al-ihtiram la ala jihat al-riya wa al-izam*. Ed. Kilani Muhammad Khalifa (Beirut: Dar al-Basha'ir al-islamiyya, 1409/1988).

Nawawi, *Fatawa*.

Nawawi, *Minhaj al-talibin*.

Nawawi, *Sahih Muslim bi Sharh al-Nawawi*, 18 vols (Cairo 1349/1930). Reprint (18 vols. in 9). Beirut: Dar al-Fikr, 1401/1981.

Nawawi, *Sharh al-muhadhdhab*.

Nawawi, *Sharh Sahih Muslim*.

Nawawi, *Sharh Sahih Muslim.Kitab al-Jihad* (al-Mays ed.).

Nuaym, Abu, *Hilyat al-awliya*.

Qalaji, Muhammad Rawwas, *Mawsuat fiqh Abd Allah ibn Umar* (Beirut: Dar al-nafais, 1986).

Qari, Ali al-, *Mutaqad Abi Hanifa al-Imam fi abaway al-rasul alayhi al-salat wa al-salam*.

Qari, Ali al-, *Sharh al-fiqh al-akbar* (1984 ed.).

Qasimi, Jamal al-Din al-, *Risalat al-jarh wa al-tadil*.

Qayrawani, Ibn Abi Zayd al-, *Jami fi al-sunan* (1982 ed.).

Qayyim, Ibn al-, *Zad al-maad*.

Qayyim, Ibn, *Alam al-muwaqqiin an rabb al-alamin*.

Qayyim, Ibn, *al-Hadi al-nabawi*.

Qayyim, Ibn, *Ilam al-muwaqqiin*.

Qudama, Ibn, *al-Mughni* (1994 ed.).

Qudama, Ibn, *al-Rawda fi usul al-fiqh*.

Qudama, Ibn, *Muqaddimat al-Mughni*.

Qudama, Ibn, *Rawdat an-Nazir*.

Qunfudh, Ibn, *Wasilat al-islam*.

Qurashi, *al-Jawahir al-mudiyya fi manaqib al-hanafiyya*.

Qurtubi, *Jami li ahkam al-quran* (Dar al-hadith ed.).

Qurtubi, *Tafsir*.

Rabi, *Kitab al-umm* (Azhar ed.).

Rushd, Ibn, *Bidayat al-mujtahid*.

Sabiq, Sayyid, *Fiqh al-sunna*.

Sad, Ibn, *Tabaqat*.

Sajzi, Abu al-Nasr al-, *al-Ibana*.

Sakhawi, *al-Jawahir wa al-durar fi tarjamat shaykh al-islam Ibn Hajar*, ed. Hamid Abd al-Majid and Taha al-Zayni (Cairo: wizarat al-awqaf, 1986).

Sakhawi, *al-Jawahir wa al-durar*.

Sakhawi, *al-Maqasid al-hasana*.

Sakhawi, *Fath al-mughith*.

Salah, Ibn, *Muqaddima*.

Sanani, *Raf al-astar li ibtali adillat al-qa'ilina bi fanai al-nar*. Ed. Albani (Beirut & Damascus: al-maktab al-islami, 1405/1984).

Sanani, *Subul al-salam*.

Saqqaf, Hasan Ali al-, *Qamus shata'im al-Albani*.

Saqqaf, Shaykh Hasan al-, *al-Lajif al-dhuaf li al-mutalaib bi ahkam al-itikaf*.

Saqqaf, Shaykh Hasan al-, *Qamus shataim al-Albani*.

Sarakhsi, *al-Mabsut*.

Sawi, Salah al-, *al-Thawabit wa al-mutaghayyirat* (Cairo: al-muntada al-Islami, 1414 /1994). Trans. Suhail I. Laher

Shafii, Ibrahim ibn Muhammad al-Bajuri al-, *Hashiyat al-bajuri ala sharh ibn al-qasim al-ghazzi ala matn abi shuja*.

Shafii, *Risala*.

Shatibi, *al-Muwafaqat*.

Shatibi, *Kitab al-itisam* (1995 Beirut ed.).

Shawkani, *Irshad al-fuhul*.

Shawkani, *Nayl al-awtar*.

Shayba, Ibn Abi, *Musannaf*.

Shurunbalali, *Nur al-idah wa najat al-qulub*. Trans. Muhammad Abu al-Qasim, *Salvation of the Soul and Islamic Devotions*. (London: Kegan Paul International, 1981).

Subki, Al-Taj al-, *Qaida fi al-jarh wa al-tadil*.

Subki, Al-Taj al-, *Qawaid fi ulum al-hadith*.

Subki, Ibn al-, *Tabaqat al-Shafiiyya*.

Subki, *Qaida fi al-jarh wa al-tadil*.

GENERAL INDEX

ENCYCLOPEDIA OF ISLAMIC DOCTRINE SERIES

VOLUME 1:
ISLAMIC BELIEFS (*AQIDA*)

VOLUME 2:
REMEMBRANCE OF ALLAH AND PRAISING THE PROPHET
(*DHIKR ALLAH, MADIH, NAAT, QASIDAT AL-BURDA*)

VOLUME 3:
THE PROPHET: COMMEMORATIONS, VISITATION AND HIS
KNOWLEDGE OF THE UNSEEN (*MAWLID, ZIYARA, ILM AL-GHAYB*)

VOLUME 4:
INTERCESSION (*SHAFAA, TAWASSUL, ISTIGHATHA*)

VOLUME 5:
SELF-PURIFICATION: STATE OF EXCELLENCE (*TAZKIYAT AL-NAFS / TASAWWUF, IHSAN*)

VOLUME 6:
FORGOTTEN ASPECTS OF ISLAMIC WORSHIP: PART ONE

VOLUME 7:
FORGOTTEN ASPECTS OF ISLAMIC WORSHIP: PART TWO

VOLUME 8:
INDICES